A PASSION FOR GOLF

A Passion for Golf

Celebrity Musings About the Game

ANN LIGUORI

Lynn -
Delighted to be
working with you!
All the best on &
off the course -
2000

TAYLOR PUBLISHING
Dallas, Texas

To my mom, whom I adore and respect with all my heart, who suggested I put this collection together—and I *always* listen to my mother.

Published by Taylor Publishing Company
1550 West Mockingbird Lane
Dallas, Texas 75235

Library of Congress Cataloging-in-Publication Data

Liguori, Ann.
A passion for golf : celebrity musings about the game / Ann Liguori.
p. cm.
ISBN 0-87833-972-8
1. Golf—Anecdotes. 2. Celebrities—United States—Interviews.
I. Title.
GV967.L446 1997
796.352—dc21 97-24658
CIP

Printed in the United States of America

10 9 8 7 6 5 4 3 2

This book has been printed on acid-free recycled paper.

Contents

BUSINESS, ART, AND POLITICS

Acknowledgments

Much appreciation to the special people who are the subjects of this collection of interviews. Their cooperation and fascinating personalities and achievements made these interviews possible. Special thanks to my husband Steve Geller, who edits both shows, *Conversations with Ann Liguori*, on The Golf Channel and *Sports Innerview with Ann Liguori* on SportsChannel/Fox Sports networks throughout the country. His knowledge and instincts helped immensely in editing the show transcripts. Many thanks to Dennis and Anne Watlington, who edited the introductions in the book and who have been friends for years, and to Lisa Edwards who helps organize my life. Thanks to researchers Brian Gibbons and Ryan Wickline.

Special thanks to The Golf Channel for enabling *Conversations with Ann Liguori* to become a reality. And many thanks to SportsChannel New York, Fox Sports West, and SportsChannel regionals throughout the country who air *Sports Innerview with Ann Liguori*.

Thanks to the following people who have been extremely helpful in the over-all project: Taylor Publishing, Mike Emmerich, Karen Gantz-Zahler, Andrea and John Stark, Bruce Parker, and Madison Skidgel.

The following people, organizations, resorts, and clubs helped make these interviews possible: The Jimmy V Foundation, Nicole Valvano, Joe Jemsek of the Cog Hill Golf and Country Club, The Don Drysdale Hall of Fame Golf Classic, Kelly Drysdale, Association of Tennis Professionals (ATP), Peter Alfano, Rudy Riska of the Downtown Athletic Club, Sal Schiliro, Jimmy Karvellas and the Celebrity Golf Association, The Starlight Foundation, Jill Madson, Jim McLean, Nannette Lopuszynski, Doral Golf Resort & Spa, The Nabisco/Dinah Shore Pro-Am and Tournament, Mission Hills Country Club, Murray and Nancy Olderman, Don Smith, The Lexus Challenge, KSL Recreation Corporation, Brad Quayle, Mike Shannon, Frank Sinatra Celebrity Golf Tournament, Scoop Marketing, Brener & Zwikel Associates, Ballymeade Country Club, Jody Shaw, Maggie Barrett, Toby Mamis, Deanna Hemby, Fred Scrutchfield, "The Vinny," The Golf Club of Tennessee, Peter Lopez, The Citrus Course at LaQuinta Resort & Club, PGA West, Marlene Palmer, Bally's Hotel & Casino, Sheraton Desert Inn Resort, Rick Fagan, Callaway Golf, Julie Davis, Jerry Woodward, Creative Associates, Inn at Spanish Bay, AT&T Pebble Beach National Pro-Am, ClubCorp International, Marcia Mayes, Robert Ravis, Wendy's Three-

Tour Challenge, Denny Lynch, The Mountain Course at LaQuinta Resort & Club, International Management Group (IMG), Charles Mechem, Jim Ritts, LPGA, PGA, and the Senior PGA.

The following have also been very supportive: Izod Club, Genuin Golf & Dress of America, Mirco Richardson, The Sharp Electronics Corporation, WFAN, PMK, Paul Wiebel, Mitchell Shuldiner, Lenny Simone, Tribeca Transportation Group, Carlos Pena, Bill Liederman, Mickey Mantle's Restaurant, Chin Chin, Nick Niles, Janice Platt, Jeff Freedman, David Garvey, Terese Flaherty, Duane Sevelin, Jason Smith, John Richo, Steve Martin, On-Line Design, Ed Gelband, Dan Liguori, Joel Drucker, Irene Geller, Jean and Steve Skidgel, Christian Skidgel, Margo Verkruzen, and last but not least, Max.

Introduction

My earliest memory of television was a midday talk show hosted by Ruth Lyons on WLW-TV in Cincinnati, Ohio. I loved to watch this elegant, white-haired woman as she interviewed the city's most fascinating people. I was three years old, and aside from my mother and father, she was my first role model. That's what I would do, I decided. My family moved from Cincinnati to Cleveland, and Ruth Lyons faded from my view, but the first threads of a plan for my future had begun to form.

Throughout my childhood, I was an athlete. My brother Jim and I spent our youth playing baseball, basketball, tennis, and football. Our backyard was the center of activities for all the kids in the neighborhood who liked to play ball. It was always satisfying to be one of the first to be picked when the boys were choosing teams. My competitive spirit was developed during these early days. I learned how to be a team player, how to win, how to deal with defeat, and how to compete with the guys.

In preteen years, summers were spent attending sports camp at Towson State College (now TSU) in Maryland. A dear friend of the family, Margo Verkruzen, who was the women's athletic director there, invited Jim and me to attend these camps, where we learned every sport from archery to lacrosse. Margo, with no family of her own, generously devoted her time and energies to exposing us to sports, photography, appreciation of nature and history. She became my first mentor.

In high school, my life was consumed with whatever sport was in season—volleyball, basketball, track and field, and tennis. Even though Title IX was passed my freshman year, our school did not have a tennis team for girls, so I competed on the guys' team and played number one singles. After a tennis match, I'd often join the girls' track team to run the 100-yard dash, relays, and compete in the long jump. I loved the challenge of participating in two sports at the same time and earned sixteen letters in high school. I was a jock, intensely driven by my competitive instinct and my passion for sports.

At the University of South Florida, I started to seriously pursue a career in radio and television, starting with internships at various radio and television stations in the Tampa market. One of the highlights was putting together a cable show that aired on a local channel when cable was in its infancy.

My curiosity about people must have been inherited from my father.

He had the knack for asking the right questions at the right time and could find out everything there was to know about a person in five minutes. My dad, as a college professor, was a very dynamic communicator in and out of the classroom. His talent for connecting with people fascinated me and heightened my desire to ask questions. Initially, the people I was most curious about were athletes.

After graduation, I earned a fellowship offered by the International Radio and Television Society (IRTS). Each year IRTS selects the top broadcasting students throughout the country to spend a summer in New York City, meeting and learning from leaders in the industry. I decided to remain in Manhattan after the program ended, and eventually landed a job at CBS Sports, working as an assistant on the *NFL Today* show. It was here that a cold stark reality descended upon me: if a woman wanted a career in sports broadcasting, the glass ceiling stopped at secretary. I decided to fight for my dream. I left the corporate environment in my early twenties and started free-lancing. I thought that if I were independent, I could get a variety of experiences by working for a number of companies and not get held back on any project or at any one job because of my gender.

Free-lancing was tough at first. Somehow I managed to earn enough to pay the rent. I became a producer and reporter for ABC Radio Sports while contributing sports stories to *USA Today*. With these jobs, I covered every team in New York and attended every press conference that was scheduled in the New York metropolitan area. I lived at Madison Square Garden covering the Knicks, Rangers, tennis, Millrose games, etc. Along with getting audio bits from players after games, I was writing for various publications, including a cover story on John McEnroe for *Inside Sports*, which attracted the attention of the industry.

Intrigued by the financial rewards and the programming flexibility that evolved with “owning” the rights to my own work, I then sold a weekly sports commentary titled *Ann Liguori in the Line-up!* to Miller Lite and got it distributed to radio stations throughout New England. An entrepreneur was born!

At the time, WFAN in New York was about to launch. The original programmers of the first radio station in the country to format twenty-four hours of sports, heard my commentaries. In 1987, the year WFAN went on the air, I was offered a show on the weekends. For the past ten years, that has been the base from which I have built a television career. In 1989, I put together and acquired the sponsorship for a half-hour show featuring top sports personalities. *Sports Innerview with Ann Liguori* is now seen on SportsChannel and Fox Sports regionals throughout the country and has been airing fifty-two weeks a year for the past eight years. The program has become the longest-running interview show on television hosted and owned by a woman. The Sharp Electronics Corporation has title-sponsored the show for eight years.

In 1994, The Golf Channel, programming their new venture, asked me if I would be interested in putting together an interview show. Golf was not one of the sports I played when I was a kid, but in my mid-twenties, I caught the golf bug and was intrigued by an offer to develop *Conversations with Ann Liguori*, a half-hour show in which I would interview and play golf with an eclectic group of personalities from the worlds of Hollywood, music, business, politics, and sports. The common denominator shared by all is a deep passion for golf, but the interviews go way beyond that, as we discuss careers, life-styles, and opinions on all kinds of issues.

My participation in the venture brings us to the point of this book, which is an edited collection of some of the best interviews from the first forty-six shows that aired on *Conversations with Ann Liguori* on The Golf Channel and *Sports Innerview with Ann Liguori*. These golf interviews are extra special to me. Those who are as passionate about golf, as I am, love to talk about the sport. The game has given me great access to celebrities who normally would not make themselves available for interviews. But things are different on a golf course. People tend to relax and speak more freely on the fairway. This atmosphere can seduce even the most guarded personalities into expressing themselves. Put a golf club in the hands of someone like Joe Pesci and watch the tough-guy actor retreat from the high-pressured world in which he excels to the often humbling but always stimulating challenge the game offers. The public relations cocoon disintegrates as a relaxed conversation on the golf course allows one's true personality to surface. The game is truly a window to the soul.

Listening to how some of the most successful people in the world articulate their joy and frustration with this most challenging sport was fascinating. Amateur golfers throughout the world can relate to these stories of triumph, disaster, humiliation, and ecstasy.

There is a certain fraternal element in the world of golf that bonds a diverse group of people. This makes the links one of the more interesting environments in the sports galaxy. One can have an image as far-out as rock star Alice Cooper, yet every time he takes his five-handicap game to the course, he fits right in with the bankers and the doctors.

The participants in this book discuss a variety of issues, from discrimination in the game to the difficulties of playing with spouses. Charles Barkley explains his views on the death penalty while lining up a putt, and former Vice President Dan Quayle shares his opinion on President Clinton while he is practicing on the range. Sylvester Stallone compares golf to marriage and somehow makes it all sound completely logical. The interviewees are as varied as the courses played.

Golf has taken me all over the world—from the beauty of Pebble Beach to the links at Ballybunion in Ireland to the plush, immaculate fairways of The Quarry in LaQuinta, California. Combining the excitement of playing extraordinary courses with the challenge of interviewing this group of exceptional people has been one of the most gratifying episodes of my career. I hope that golfers and non-golfers alike enjoy these interviews as much as I enjoyed doing them.

Sports

Charles Barkley

In August of 1996, I was invited to the Jimmy Valvano Celebrity Golf Classic at the Prestonwood Country Club in Cary, North Carolina. The event brings together people from the local community with prominent figures in the basketball world. In Carolina, a torrid enclave of round ball, this was the place to be. The "V" Foundation sponsors this annual tournament to raise money and awareness for the ever raging battle to fight cancer.

I lost my father to cancer and my brother Jim to leukemia and will go anywhere to help those who are trying to find a cure, so this was an easy call for me. The "V" Foundation members did a great job organizing a tremendous weekend of golf, tennis, dinners, and entertainment, highlighted by a Hootie and the Blowfish concert. Mike Krzyzewski, Duke University's basketball baron, was one of the board members who helped bring in big names like P. J. Carlisimo, Dean Smith, Dick Vitale, and Rebecca Lobo. Even Kevin Costner showed up. But the person who intrigued me the most on this occasion was the ever opinionated, forceful, charismatic, and controversial figure in the current basketball galaxy, Charles Barkley.

The word on Charles from the tournament host was that he basically does what he wants to, when he wants to do it. "Sir" Charles has a master's degree in individuality, with a minor in unpredictability. He has an opinion on just about anything, an interviewer's delight, if you can get to him. He does not use an agent or publicist to book interviews, so it's almost impossible to pin him down in advance.

On Saturday morning, before the Sunday tournament, the news was not good. It was announced that Charles was not going to do any interviews the entire weekend. My camera crew was already set up on the balcony of the clubhouse. We were hoping to interview Barkley, Meat Loaf, and other personalities who were friends of Jimmy Valvano. We spotted Charles on the course playing his practice round. Despite the embarrassing possibility of being turned down, I decided to approach him.

As my cart drew closer, Charles got bigger. Professional athletes over six foot, five inches, make a golf course seem smaller. I introduced myself, and before I was able to deliver my pitch, he said, "I see your show on The Golf Channel all the time." I was surprised and delighted when he agreed to do the interview right then and there. Instead of the typical sit-down interview, we would meet at the twelfth hole.

AP/WIDE WORLD PHOTOS

Interviews on the golf course are unlike any other. With the atmosphere so placid, yet the game such a challenge, the different aspects of one's personality force their way out into the open. It's the most revealing locale in the world. Given the magnitude of Charles' personality, I awaited the interview. He was sweet, flirtatious, irritable, arrogant, sensitive, aggressive, temperamental, and refreshingly, politically incorrect. What interviewer wouldn't love a subject who was able to give a different side of their character per fairway? With a golf club in hand, wearing a wireless microphone, Charles Barkley gets in your face.

He's controversial because he's brutally honest, and he's honest because he can afford to be. Born poor and Black in the deep South, he became a multimillionaire before reaching his thirtieth birthday. He's beaten some of the toughest odds our country has to offer. This Black Republican, the bizarro image of Colin Powell, walks the golf course with the same confidence he shows on a basketball court. Unlike Colin Powell, whom he deeply admires, Charles Barkley will not turn the other cheek in a barroom brawl. I witnessed his temper after his tee shot landed on a slope on the fourteenth hole, setting him up for a tricky second shot. He put aside his grandiosity for a moment to fill the air with expletives, bemoaning his predicament.

Charles says he plays golf every chance he gets and is a twelve handicap. He has driven the ball three-hundred-plus yards on occasion despite a terrible hitch he's developed in the middle of his swing that makes his swing look like a lawn chair snapping shut. As he takes his club back, he stops his swing completely, takes it back a little further, shuffles his feet, and then unleashes a mighty swing. It is the most unusual swing I've ever seen. And yet, though mechanically challenged, his athleticism and pride enable him to be a reasonably good golfer.

Barkley has angered a lot of people through the years with his attitude and actions, but I respect his courage and sincerity. I don't always agree with his approach. I wanted to slap him the time he spit on the little girl at a game. He claims it was a mistake and apologized to the unfortunate target, but not for the action. This complicated behemoth guards his individuality with the same ferociousness that he uses to attack the backboards. He repudiates extreme agitators, Black and White. Though he flirts with the idea of running for governor of Alabama, he doesn't particularly like politicians. No amount of money can motivate Charles to revoke his right to speak out against what he perceives to be racial stereotyping.

Charles Barkley fits nicely upon a mantle with others like Jim Brown, Bill Russell, and Muhammad Ali, prideful Black athletes who risk the public's wrath in order to speak their minds. The golf course that day provided him an unusual pulpit.

LIGUORI: Here I am with Charles Barkley out on the golf course.

BARKLEY: That would be me.

LIGUORI: Ten-time All-star [at the time].

BARKLEY: Is it ten? Man, I'm getting old. I'm getting real old.

LIGUORI: And quite the golfer. The passionate golfer.

BARKLEY: Quite the crappy golfer. Very passionate, though. Very passionate.

LIGUORI: You are very passionate and that's what's important.

BARKLEY: That is important. You have to love doing whatever you're doing.

LIGUORI: Why do you love this sport so much?

BARKLEY: Peace and quiet. Normally, you're not out there.

LIGUORI: Don't blame me for those bad shots out there.

BARKLEY: Just one swing of the clubs, we hit them bad.

LIGUORI: If you weren't playing in the NBA, what would you do for a living?

BARKLEY: I don't know the answer to that question, so I never answer that question, 'cause it's an unrealistic answer for me. I try not to ever lie. My friends say I'm brutally honest.

LIGUORI: Well, you are. That's good though. I admire that.

BARKLEY: Yeah, but it gets you in trouble.

LIGUORI: You've been in trouble a couple of times.

BARKLEY: You're right. Trouble is good. It makes you stronger. I love adversity.

LIGUORI: You were talking earlier about you in bar situations and in social situations, and how "proud' you are. You got in trouble for punching out a guy in a Cleveland bar. What happened?

BARKLEY: That guy was just a drunk prick. That's what he was. It's happened four times in my life. I don't want to fight. I'm not going to sit in the house. I like to go out and I like to have a good time. There's been four or five different occasions where some guy had too much to drink. Just some drunk redneck. But that doesn't bother me. That stuff is going to happen.

LIGUORI: Does that make you avoid going into bars?

BARKLEY: No, I want to go out and have a good time with my friends, and I've probably been out a thousand times. I'm not going to let five bad incidents affect me. I've probably been out fifteen hundred times in twelve years. A hundred times a year. Five incidents aren't going to make a difference. Some fans are bad. Let's just get that out there. All of them aren't good people. Some of them aren't good people. That's plain and simple. Ninety-five percent of them are great people.

LIGUORI: I remember reading where you once said that because you're so outspoken and because you're so brutally honest, you've lost maybe twenty million dollars in endorsement opportunities.

BARKLEY: Yeah, they want you to be one of them Uncle Tom brothers, but I ain't ever going to be like that. They want you to say the right thing all the time, even if it's bull. They don't want you to say anything significant, but I'm going to say what I want to say, and if I don't get any money for it, that's cool. It ain't no big deal to me. You can't put a price on my pride. I ain't ever going to be one of them Uncle Toms. That's what they want.

LIGUORI: Who are "they"?

BARKLEY: The people who run sports. They want you to make them a lot of money and do what they tell you to do. I don't think like that. I'm going to do my own thing because I made them a lot of money. I like guys like Dennis Rodman [Chicago Bulls], outspoken guys, because you know it is a corrupt system. I've had so many guys come up to me and say, "Thank you for standing up to the system." And that's all it was about. I don't care about who wins and who loses. I think it's just a matter of pride. That's why I had to get out of Phoenix. You've got to stand up. It's sort of like they want you to do everything they say. You're making them a lot of money. They pay you a lot, but they're making a lot more and they want you to do everything they tell you. I'm never going to be like that. If I'm good enough to make their money, I'm good enough to voice my opinion and say what I want to say. I'm definitely going to be my own man.

LIGUORI: So you admire Dennis Rodman for that?

BARKLEY: Well, I admire Dennis for being an individual. I think he's going overboard trying to promote himself, but I can't begrudge him for that. I wish he would just—he's a very good basketball player, but all the stuff he does with dresses, I understand he's trying to make money to promote himself, but he needs to get back doing what he does best and that's play basketball.

LIGUORI: Who do you think is the best rebounder in the game? You?

BARKLEY: I could be. Anybody's good when they play with Michael and Scottie [Michael Jordan and Scottie Pippen, Chicago Bulls]. But if somebody said I didn't have to do anything but get rebounds, I could get as many rebounds as Dennis. And Dennis is a good player. Really good.

LIGUORI: Tell me what you love about golf. You play all the time.

BARKLEY: There's nobody here bugging me, asking for autographs and stuff. Most of the people at these country clubs are stuck up so they leave me alone. I have a good time. You've got to talk trash out here. That's the best thing about golf. Getting away from people, getting some good friends, and playing.

LIGUORI: They probably love the fact that you're playing here.

BARKLEY: There's a lot of uppity people at these clubs, so they really don't bug me. I come out here to get peace and quiet. I love it out here, away from everybody with some good friends. It's great.

LIGUORI: Are you a member of a country club?

BARKLEY: A couple of memberships. One in Pennsylvania and one in Alabama.

LIGUORI: Are you "uppity"?

BARKLEY: No. I just play. I don't ask people for their autographs when they're playing golf. I think you should wait until they finish playing.

LIGUORI: No matter how good you are in basketball, this sport just has a tendency to humble you.

BARKLEY: I never believe that. I think people, number one, they really do get in the habit to get away from everybody. I think signing autographs all the time is tough, and this is the only sport you probably can do that, go out here and be left alone. I don't get humbled. I don't expect to be great at golf. I just enjoy playing it. If I shoot 100, I feel fine. If I shoot 80, I feel great.

LIGUORI: That's a good attitude to have.

BARKLEY: Remember, all the good guys, they play on TV on the weekend. The rest of us are hacks. That's it. I know a lot of you guys sitting at home think that you all can play, but if you could play, you'd be playing on the weekend on CBS or NBC.

LIGUORI: What's the best part of your game?

BARKLEY: Putting. My short game.

LIGUORI: I can see that. Normally, the short game is where amateurs lose the most strokes.

BARKLEY: No, putting is the best part of my game.

LIGUORI: Do you get out and practice a lot?

BARKLEY: No. That's one of my problems. I'd rather play. I'm not concerned with practicing. I just want to win money when I play. I don't care what I shoot. I just have to get enough strokes. [Barkley walks up to the tee and proceeds to smack his drive approximately 280 yards.]

LIGUORI: You have a nasty hitch in your swing.

BARKLEY: The problem is, I've got a hesitation in my swing now.

LIGUORI: Yeah, is that the way you always have done it?

BARKLEY: No, I've got a mental block right now, and I can't do what I want to do and release the club.

LIGUORI: What do you think that's from?

BARKLEY: I'm not sure what it's from. Like I said, I have a mental block. It's frustrating right now. I've got a hitch in the top of my swing when I take it back there. [Charles takes a practice swing.] When I take it back, I get hung back there.

LIGUORI: Have you taken any lessons?

BARKLEY: No, not lately. That's what I need to do.

LIGUORI: But you still get a lot of distance on the ball.

BARKLEY: Well, that's just power. When you don't hit it solid, it goes all over the place. But I can't worry about it.

LIGUORI: You have the right attitude about it. At least you're having fun with it.

BARKLEY: I didn't say that, now. I get mad a lot.

LIGUORI: Not you, Charles.

BARKLEY: You've got to realize I push myself hard. I don't want to be like the rest of these losers who accept failure. Anytime I mess up, I get furious. Once the shot is over, I get mad, but once it's over, it's over. I might curse and scream, but you've got to block it out of your mind. I don't ever want to settle. If I don't do something well, you should get frustrated. You don't want to be like the rest of these people who say, "It's all right to screw up." It's not all right to screw up. You've got to push yourself. You've got to want to be the best you can be.

LIGUORI: Yet you can be a fabulous athlete in basketball as you are, but the skills don't transfer over to golf. It's all mental, don't you think?

BARKLEY: Me personally? I still expect to do well. No matter what I'm doing, I want to do it really well. I don't care what it is.

LIGUORI: How did you acquire that attitude?

BARKLEY: I think it was something I learned, that I wanted to be the best. I think in the beginning when I was younger, I skated a little bit. When I say skated, I mean [I was] just content to get by. I wish I had done better in school. I would just do enough just to get by. And I knew I could do it, because I felt like the stuff was easy, but I was like, "This stuff is really not challenging me." But I really wasn't challenging myself. And then once I got older, you learn, you get mature. You realize you have to push yourself all the time to be the best.

LIGUORI: So you look back on your high school years and think, "I could have done better?"

BARKLEY: I could have done better in school. I think I was pretty good in high school as a player. Wasn't great or anything, but I was still pretty good, and I wanted to do better in school. If I had known what I know now, I would have been better, but that's okay though because as always, everything's better when you look back at it in hindsight. But I'm glad the way everything has turned out, and I have no complaints.

LIGUORI: How has your life changed being a dad? You have one child.

BARKLEY: That I know of. Just kidding, y'all!

LIGUORI: I know you're very close to your family.

BARKLEY: Well, my daughter is obviously by far the most important thing in my life, and I think it's important for me to take care of her, emotionally, physically, financially, whatever. My father was not there all the time and I had a tough life growing up and it's just important for me to make sure that my daughter is taken care of.

LIGUORI: How old is she now?

BARKLEY: Seven.

LIGUORI: Does she play any golf?

BARKLEY: No, I try to steer her away from sports right now. Sports are tough, and I don't want her getting caught up in all the hype and everything. The most important thing for her is to get her grades.

LIGUORI: But it's so important for girls to become athletes and participate. It teaches you so many skills, don't you think?

BARKLEY: It depends. I don't care about that right now. She's got talent. The system will separate the people who play from people who can't play. Right now, her priorities should be getting a good base of education because that's the foundation for the future. One of the problems is kids don't get an opportunity in the beginning to build a strong base. By the time they become teenagers, they're already whacked out and obviously society can't control them. There'll be time in her teen years when she can play sports. They're not going anywhere.

LIGUORI: Well, you want her to become coordinated.

BARKLEY: She's going to be coordinated. She's got some designer genes like her daddy.

LIGUORI: Athletics teach skills for a lifetime.

BARKLEY: It does to a certain extent. Academics gives you all of that, but athletics can be more of a negative than a positive. The problem is, everybody's not that good. If you've got the wrong people around you and you push kids into sports and they don't do well, they lose their self-esteem.

LIGUORI: So you're saying she may feel the pressure because of her father?

BARKLEY: There's no question. If you talk to any professional athlete, their kids have been under stress. You've got to realize the public doesn't understand what it's like. They don't understand the pressures of their siblings. People just assume because they're your kids, they got talent. And I think if you look around, most professional athletes' kids aren't that good, and if you get that peer pressure coming in, it puts them at a disadvantage. But if you say, "I can't play a lick of basketball but I make straight A's," that's all I'm concerned about. If my daughter don't ever play any professional sport or any college sport and she makes straight A's, that's going to be better for her because women are always going to be discriminated against. They can only go so far unless they are very special. I mean, it is very hard [to be] a professional athlete if you're a female. It's just that simple.

[Ann continues to walk with Barkley from hole to hole as he golfs.]

LIGUORI: You are surrounded by kids on every hole!

BARKLEY: I love kids. It's adults that are a pain in the ass.

LIGUORI: But you say you don't think you should be a role model?

BARKLEY: Oh no, no, no. You didn't listen to the commercial [laughing].

LIGUORI: You say role models for young people should be their parents.

BARKLEY: There's no question. For them to think they're going to be professional athletes, that's wrong and that's unfair. I think that the parents got to do a better job, and number one, I look at things from a Black perspective. I think the Black people have, because of racism, a low self-esteem. They've been beat down for so long. Now the kids think the only way they can be successful is through athletics and entertainment. I try to tell them they've got a better chance of being a doctor and a lawyer than they do becoming a professional athlete. And that's the method I try to get across to the kids. I wish everybody could be a professional athlete, but that's unrealistic.

LIGUORI: You're also saying that they have too much adoration for star athletes.

BARKLEY: You've got to give them more realistic goals. To think that they are going to make it to a professional sport, that's unrealistic. I mean, that's only like 1 percent of the people in the world who are blessed enough to play a professional sport. That's the message I try to get across to the kids. Everybody gave me a hard time. Not everybody. Actually, I got more positive letters about that commercial than I did negative. And more parents come up to me and say that because they understand.

LIGUORI: You also influenced other athletes to say the same thing.

BARKLEY: Most of them ain't got the balls to say it. They're chickenhearted. Most of these guys are so scared they don't know what to do. They're worried about what people say about them. Well, I try to tell them these people don't care about you anyway unless you're playing with them.

LIGUORI: You say in golf you love to play for money.

BARKLEY: Yes, I do. My goal in life is to spend all my money because I don't want my family to fight over it when I die.

LIGUORI: How much do you have to spend, then? What do you have? A couple million? Twenty million? Thirty million? Forty million?

BARKLEY: Somewhere in that neighborhood.

LIGUORI: How are you going to spend all of that money?

BARKLEY: If I don't improve my golf game, by the time I get ready to play the Senior Tour, I will be broke, and I'll need that money. So that's the thing. I've got to keep improving the golf, or I'm never going to have any money.

LIGUORI: How are you going to go through all that money?

BARKLEY: You all keep electing a Democratic president, I'll pay half of it in taxes, so don't worry about it.

LIGUORI: [Joking] When you turn fifty, you'll be good enough for the Senior Tour?

BARKLEY: No, I'll never be good enough. But I just want to have a good time and play with my friends. If I'm never good at golf, that's cool. I've been blessed. I know I'm good at one thing and I've had a great life and a great career, and if it ended tomorrow, I have no regrets. I have lived every person's dream. The majority of the people in the world, I have lived their dream.

LIGUORI: How's your mom doing?

BARKLEY: She's doing good. She's a pain. She and my grandmother are serious pains.

LIGUORI: Pains? Why are they such a pain?

BARKLEY: People from Alabama are pains.

LIGUORI: Do they play golf?

BARKLEY: Are you crazy? I play golf to get away from them.

LIGUORI: Get out of here.

BARKLEY: I do! In Alabama, if you don't play golf, you have to sit around the house and talk to your mother and your grandmother. They drive you nuts.

LIGUORI: You adore them both. I know you.

[Barkley hits a bad shot, then looks at Ann, shakes his head, and points.]

LIGUORI: Don't blame me [for your bad playing]. It's very easy to blame me and the camera crew.

BARKLEY: I'm going to do it the American way. I'm always going to blame somebody else. I never take responsibility. Every time somebody could do something wrong, they say it was television's fault. [They say,] "I saw it on television." They blame television or somebody else instead of taking responsibility for their own action. I just had a crappy day. My handicap went up.

LIGUORI: Michael Jordan plays in some of the Celebrity Golf Association events. Do you ever play in those?

BARKLEY: I play in the one in Tahoe. That's fun. I don't play well in front of people. I guess you could say I choke like a dog in front of all the people.

LIGUORI: So you love this game because it takes you away from all the madness?

BARKLEY: It's fun. It's a challenge. There's usually nobody out here. Obviously in a tournament like this, there are going to be a lot of people. But most other times, it's just me and three other guys. Betting a lot of money, I might add.

LIGUORI: Is there one foursome you enjoy playing with more than any other?

BARKLEY: Well probably when I play with Dan Majerle, Joe Kleine [former NBA teammates], and Roy Green [former NFL player]. We play teams. Me and Roy against Joe Kleine and Dan Majerle. The White guys against the Black guys. You know the brothers will be kicking some butt, I want you to know that.

LIGUORI: And you play in Phoenix normally?

BARKLEY: Well, during the summer I'm usually in Philly. I have some friends I play with up there. But I play with the same group of guys all the time because I don't like being around people I don't know.

LIGUORI: You feel more comfortable with them.

BARKLEY: Yeah. They might write a book about my gambling and stuff. [Barkley is waiting to putt.]

LIGUORI: What would you do if you were president?

BARKLEY: I'd make—number one, I'd improve the public school system 'cause if you don't have education you can't have pride and self-esteem. I'd put the National Guard and all the people in the army out on the street to help stop crime. The death penalty would be enforced regularly. You wouldn't be on death row that long.

LIGUORI: And you would improve the public education system?

BARKLEY: You've got to improve the public school system because if people aren't educated, they have no pride. They have no self-esteem, and they're going to do bad things.

LIGUORI: Alabama still needs so much improvement in that area.

BARKLEY: Alabama needs a lot. That's why I'm going there to help them. That state really needs a lot.

LIGUORI: Will you run for governor, do you think, after you retire from the NBA?

BARKLEY: I'd really like to be governor one day. Or, not necessarily to win, but I'd like to get on TV everyday and tell people the only way they can be successful is through education. People got to learn to get along and make the world a better place. Not all this crap they see on TV where they make you choose between being a Democrat and a Republican, or liberal and conservative or moderate, or rich and poor, or Black and White. All that stuff's irrelevant. We all want the same things in life. You've got to stop looking at television and reading the crap they put out there. [Charles looks at my blue sapphire diamond ring and teases.]

BARKLEY: Oh man, cubic zirconia. It's amazing what they can do with that now.

LIGUORI: This is real, baby.

BARKLEY: Did you get some Ginzu knives with that? I'm just curious. What's your husband do for a living?

LIGUORI: He's a producer.

BARKLEY: He produces what?

LIGUORI: This show.

BARKLEY: You sleeping with the boss?

LIGUORI: No, he's sleeping with the boss.

BARKLEY: Hey, that's good. I like that.

LIGUORI: Now tell me you've had fun today.

BARKLEY: I have had fun. You're all right. I don't care what everybody said about you. I like you. I watch your show all the time. I watch The Golf Channel a lot. They've got a lot of great foreign events on. I think you should do more of those. You know Arnie's [Arnold Palmer] got the money. The King's got the money.

Evel Knievel

Interviewing Evel Knievel requires the intestinal fortitude of a daredevil. His hectic schedule tests the limits of one's flexibility, but I was ready to deal with the robust pace of his worldwind retirement. Long after his days as the planet's most popular public exhibitionist since Houdini, Knievel has become a high stakes golfer who gambles his way across the better courses in America. His great passion for the game keeps him on the road constantly.

I first met Evel twelve years ago during one of my early interviews when I worked for ABC Radio Sports. When I called and asked if he was interested in doing another interview, I was surprised that he not only recalled our first meeting but also remembered the place, the time of day, and what I wore. He quickly agreed.

After our buoyant reunion, pinning him down to a time and place was another matter. Every time we would settle on a location, Evel would call from God knows where on the road and suggest a new one. We decided on Las Vegas, bowing to his natural affinity with the city. He was an important performer in that town, helping stake Caesar's Palace to its early fame with his highly publicized attempt to jump the fountains in front of the hotel. It nearly killed him. Evel spent twenty-nine days in a coma for that stunt. Vegas held special memories.

Evel told me he would be driving from Tampa to Vegas, and he gave me his car phone number. It would take a week. With plans in place, I was heading for the desert. A few days later when I called him on his car phone, he issued a change, "Meet me in Chicago." I gracefully slipped that punch and quickly agreed. I was scheduled to do an interview with Dan Quayle in Chicago, so it worked for me. After a few more anxious moments, we finally nailed down the interview a day before it was to happen.

When I arrived to meet Evel at the Cog Hill Golf Club outside of Chicago, Joe Jemsek, the legendary owner of one of the best public courses in the world, was standing in front of the clubhouse waiting for me and my crew. The eighty-year-old Jemsek, at Evel's request, had the room ready for us and every little detail taken care of. Jemsek has been friends with Evel for over twenty years. As we walked to the clubhouse, the statuesque Jemsek, wearing a hat and a wise grin, looked like he had more Evel stories in his memory than he cared to share. He had a striking resemblance to Henry

Fonda. Obviously, Evel had used his good standing with the club to arrange for us to tape on the closed golf course while the club prepared for the upcoming Western Open. This made the shoot much easier.

ANN LIGUORI PRODUCTIONS

After the crew was set up and everything was in place, Evel Knievel seemed to appear out of nowhere. His country, Elvis-like, lady-killer charm was arresting. I've always been intrigued by this rugged individualist. He has a sense of self-righteous danger about him that commands attention. Golf for high stakes is relaxing to a man who has jumped over thirteen buses on a motorcycle in front of a hundred thousand screaming fans. He considers the golf course his sanctuary. As we walked along the fairway, he was at peace with himself. The gambling provides a taste of fire for his belly, taking the edge off of his addiction.

Evel is a man who challenged the grim reaper several times a year for much of his adult life. Oddly enough, his lifelong passion for golf has run neck and neck with his flirtation with destruction. At this point in his life, after his many thrills and spills, the golf has won out. Why an intelligent and savvy businessman put himself at risk so often during his career, only another daredevil could know for sure. Getting some satisfactory answers was the challenge.

Five years ago, Evel was searching for a female companion who played a good round of golf. He found her at a national junior tournament. Krystal Kennedy was twenty-one when they met. Evel bragged, "She hits the ball a ton from the blue tees." Since coming together, the couple has been playing for money all over the world.

Evel's stint as America's Valvoline Cowboy has attracted a trail of characters, including Jemsek. I was impressed with the fondness they had for each other. Knievel once lived in a trailer home in his club's parking lot. Jemsek's compassion kept him there even when all of Evel's money and luck had run out. Jemsek has seen a lot of golf and respects Evel's love for the game. I think he understands that only the expansiveness of the golf course can contain the width of Evel's wild spirit.

LIGUORI: Evel, you're a twelve handicap. You love this sport.

KNIEVEL: Yes. Played it all my life. And I wanted to retire to just travel the world and play golf. That's what I love to do. And I do that. I took a twenty-year vacation in 1980, and I think I'm gonna extend that a little bit.

LIGUORI: What a life, huh? Going from one club to the next.

KNIEVEL: Yes, it is. I played in Clearwater, Florida, at Feather Sound and Countryside three or four days ago, and I played in Atlanta at Rivermont Country Club in the Atlanta National the day before yesterday, and here we are at Joe Jemsek's great Cog Hill Golf Club in Chicago where they host the Western Open.

LIGUORI: It's beautiful here, and it's a public facility with four courses.

KNIEVEL: It is the best public facility in the entire world. It's beautiful.

LIGUORI: And Joe Jemsek is known throughout the golf world.

KNIEVEL: Yeah, he sure is. He's the grandpa of them all. He's quite a guy.

LIGUORI: Now he told me that years ago, you came here with your...

KNIEVEL: I had a motor home, and I used to play here and gamble with my buddies here in Chicago. He put in a 220 hook up right down on the driving range for me so that I could sleep here at the golf course in the motor home. I had a seventy-foot motor home. And I'd get up and hit practice balls and play everyday. We played here seven days a week.

LIGUORI: Evel, how are you able to drive the ball 250 yards; because you've been in so many crashes and you've had so many surgeries, how does that affect your swing?

KNIEVEL: It doesn't. You see, I've got plates in each arm. I've got bionic arms. I did a motion picture with Lindsay Wagner [who played the Bionic Woman in the television series]. I found out the name of her doctor. I went and had her doctor operate on me. I've got steel plates in both of my arms. That's why I can hit it better [laughs].

LIGUORI: And so that means you're the bionic golfer?

KNIEVEL: Yes. And my left leg is a little shorter than my right leg. You can see the heel is a little bigger on my shoe here.

LIGUORI: But it doesn't effect your motion at all?

KNIEVEL: Yeah, it helps me get through the left side better. It helps me clear my left.

LIGUORI: Ah, so it helps you?

KNIEVEL: Yeah, it helps me. That's the way I think about it.

LIGUORI: That's a good way to look at it. How did you get into doing such dangerous stunts? The daredevil thing?

KNIEVEL: Well, I rode a motorcycle when I was very young. My dad got me my first motorcycle. A little Harley Davidson. And I rode a lot when I was very, very young. I started about the age of thirteen or fourteen. I thought that the motorcycle fraternity itself would support a daredevil show so I had a whole two-hour show I put together in California. But when I would get hurt, since my jump was the finale, then the whole show would have to stop and all the people would be out of work. And I had about thirty people working on it. But as time went on, as I jumped and performed and I kept getting back up after I was hurt, the jump in the performance got so much notoriety that pretty soon I didn't need the rest of the show. I could just go to a racetrack anywhere in the United States at that time, and it became anywhere in the world, and say, "Look, I'm here. I'll jump on Sunday. I'll help you with your publicity, and I want half of your gate."

LIGUORI: Three hundred jumps later, or almost three hundred, and you're still here to talk about it.

KNIEVEL: I don't remember. I've paid quite a price for the so-called success that I've achieved. I broke about thirty-five or thirty-six bones. I was operated on fourteen times, as to what they call a major open-reduction operation. I spent three and a half years, total, in hospitals. I broke my back four times. I was rendered unconscious many times.

LIGUORI: A lot of people don't realize you're a golf hustler as well.

KNIEVEL: No, I don't hustle golf.

LIGUORI: Come on.

KNIEVEL: I don't.

LIGUORI: You don't?

KNIEVEL: I've been accused of it, but I just go to different towns throughout the United States and Canada and play, and then Australia, England. Everybody knows that I play, and they know I like to gamble. And my handicap is twelve. I tell 'em it should be fourteen because I jumped fourteen buses in Cincinnati at Kings Island. But I play in a league in Florida in the wintertime at six or seven different golf courses, and the best golf courses are there. At Countryside, my quota is twenty-four. I'm a twelve handicap. At Feather Sound, my quota is twenty-four; I'm a twelve handicap. So they know I'm a twelve handicap and that's what it is, and if they want to play against me, I investigate their handicap because *they* are the hustlers. They would just love to beat me.

LIGUORI: *They're* the hustlers?

KNIEVEL: I'm there to be shot at. I come into town at noon and play 'em for whatever the hell they want to play for. And they have to establish their handicap. They can't lie. They can't tell me they play with their wife on Saturday and Sunday and that's how they get their handicap down.

LIGUORI: How do you know if they're lying?

KNIEVEL: Because their friends tell me, and the pro tells me.

LIGUORI: You scout them out?

KNIEVEL: Sometimes I watch them for a week. At every town you go into, in the United States especially, there's always one club in town, being in a major city, where there are a group of guys who get together and gamble. And they don't gamble for hundreds of thousands of dollars, but they gamble for, say, each guy bets five hundred or a thousand a day. So if you play with eight or ten of them, you can win eight or ten thousand dollars a day.

LIGUORI: Who did you most enjoy gambling against?

KNIEVEL: I played Bobby Riggs [former tennis hustler] for a lot of money in California. I think I played Bobby for ten thousand one day.

LIGUORI: Who won?

KNIEVEL: He beat me one time in his whole life. I played him a hundred times. So he didn't beat me. In fact, he told me one day, "I don't need you." He said, "I got so many guys that want to play with me, I don't need you. We're done." So we parted company. I'll tell you what makes betting on a golf course tough. There are times when I've gone to the golf course where I never had ten-thousand in cash. There are times when I played for five thousand and I only had two thousand. Because of who I am, I didn't want to lose and have to say, "Look, I'll pay you tomorrow." That always bothered me. I found that put more pressure on me than anything. It made me lose. Put too much pressure on me.

LIGUORI: You mean, when you'd bet more money than you had on you?

KNIEVEL: Yes, when I'd go without the money and know that I had a fair game and that I had to win it to pay. It puts undo pressure on yourself, so I just decided several years ago that I'm never going to do that. I'm not going to go to where if I can't play and I can't pay, and [if] I can't just bet enough to have a smile on my face and have a good time, what's the use of going out there and just punishing yourself? There's more to life than that. You want to go out—if someone doesn't want to gamble, I don't think less of them. Gambling to some fellows makes them feel uncomfortable. They love to play golf, and if they play for anything over five dollars, they almost choke to death on the golf course. They just can't do it. It's the makeup of that person. So it doesn't make them a bad person because they don't want to go out and gamble against me. However, at the same time, I don't like to go out and play with guys who are with two or three of us who *are* gambling, and think that they are entitled to come along and play with me. And then go back to the clubhouse and tell somebody they beat me when they didn't bet a damn dime. I don't need them. Let them go and play in their own group where they belong. They belong in a different patch of flowers.

LIGUORI: Everyone wants to say they beat Evel Knievel.

KNIEVEL: Well, if they do, they're going to have to pay for it. If they beat me.

LIGUORI: What's the biggest single bet you've ever won?

KNIEVEL: One game? One hundred thousand. Actually, I only put up fifty of it. I went to Myrtle Beach and played a guy at Baytree [Golf Plantation] some years ago. His name was Tyson Leonard. A fine guy and a great gambler, and we had a heck of a match. I eagled the first hole and beat him one down for eighteen holes. It was a tough match, and I won one hundred thousand, but the mayor and the judge and another guy bet fifty thousand on me. Because Tyson had beat them out of fifty.

LIGUORI: You got the mayor involved?

KNIEVEL: Well, when we go to play in the different cities, we usually have quite a group that follows us and bets on one guy or the other.

LIGUORI: Talk about Marty Stanovich, one of the greatest gamblers of all.

KNIEVEL: Marty Stanovich. The Fat Man. He's deceased now, God bless him, but he was—he kind of taught me really how to play golf and how to hit different shots and how to make bets. He had a nickname, called the Fat Man and he was really—I admired him and respected him very much, and a lot of the fellas did. All the pros knew him. All the great pros knew Stanovich. He'd go to the first tee, and he wouldn't make any bones about how good he could play. He'd say, "Where's your best player? Bring him to the tee. I want to play him for ten thousand." He played for some big, big money in the old days. One hundred thousand a day was nothing to him.

LIGUORI: What are some of the secrets he taught you?

KNIEVEL: Well, there are a lot of things. You have to watch *cheats* when you go to play. I try not to associate with cheats. I hate anyone that *cheats* on the golf course. I *hate* them.

LIGUORI: What do you do when somebody's cheating?

KNIEVEL: I've never really had a killer instinct in me to beat a guy. If I play a guy that's got a wife and some kids, it's hard for me to beat him. I don't like that. I just don't have it. But if I play a guy I know is a drug dealer for instance or a thief, I just love to beat the hell out of them.

LIGUORI: Why would you associate yourself with those people?

KNIEVEL: Because it's the only game in town. That's just the way it is. You don't find the guy that's a minister out there wanting to bet you ten thousand on the golf course. You have to get in the middle of it and you have to find the hustlers and you have to find the guys that think they can play and you have to find the wiseguys.

LIGUORI: But they're such grungy characters.

KNIEVEL: Some of them. Some of them wear ties and suits and they're thieves. You catch them kicking their ball.

LIGUORI: What do you do when somebody kicks their ball?

KNIEVEL: Well, if you think you can beat them, you just let them do it anyway. But if you think you can't—you might be down—you say, "Hey pal, you forfeit the hole. It's over with." And I love to do that.

LIGUORI: What if they don't listen?

KNIEVEL: I've whacked a lot of guys in the ass end with a five-iron I caught cheating, and don't think I haven't. They have all kinds of little tricks they pull. Some of them will put Vaseline on their golf cart and rub it on the face of their golf clubs so that the ball won't hook or slice.

LIGUORI: What do you do in that case?

KNIEVEL: Just let 'em do it. Until you lose a hole or two to them, then tell 'em they're disqualified. You know, you can do anything you're big enough to do in this country. You just have to play it the way you think it should be played.

LIGUORI: But you must run into such shady characters. I mean, if they're cheating and there's a lot of money at stake . . .

KNIEVEL: Some, but you'd be surprised. I've played with guys who are lawyers. Lawyers especially. CPAs. Car salesmen. They're cheaters! I played with a guy out in Vegas that was one of the most respected men in town. He'd put his ball down and throw his penny ten or twelve feet closer to the hole. He was just a filthy cheat! Yet he was a CEO at one of the casinos. He didn't have the guts of nothing.

LIGUORI: Have you ever lost to somebody like that? A cheater?

KNIEVEL: Not and let them get away with it. No. I've played a lot of guys.

LIGUORI: How do you settle things after something like that?

KNIEVEL: Well, there was one group I took a .357 magnum after at a Las Vegas golf course one day. Sheriff Ralph Lamb came on the golf course with two cop cars and he said, "Evel, they are not worth shooting. Don't go to the penitentiary because you shot four filthy cheats." He said, "We know they're cheats."

LIGUORI: How much money did they take from you?

KNIEVEL: Oh, probably twenty or twenty-five thousand dollars.

LIGUORI: And you were going to kill them?

KNIEVEL: Well, I was mad enough to shoot them, I'll tell ya. In fact, I played just the other day with an assistant pro and some friends of mine. The pro didn't make a bet with anybody, yet on the greens he'd putt, and wherever he was, he'd putt in the line so that another guy that was playing me for some money that was a friend of his could see when he putted, where the line was. I finally got fed up with it. He did it once too often. I just went over and knocked his club out of his hand and knocked the ball away, and said, "Your putt's good. Just pick it up and get the hell out of here."

LIGUORI: What did he say?

KNIEVEL: He picked it up and got the hell out of there.

LIGUORI: You don't take baloney from anybody.

KNIEVEL: I don't think there's anybody in the world after what I've been taught in the last twenty-some years—especially by Stanovich and a guy named Jack Swank out in California, who's a very good gambler, very smart, intelligent. I don't think there's anybody that plays golf legitimately or is a hustler that can say or do anything on the golf course that I don't know about. No way.

LIGUORI: Evel, you've risked your life so many times as a daredevil. What possibly could give you such a high on the golf course as some of those jumps?

KNIEVEL: Well, they say we all have two sides to us as human beings. I think it's the serenity I find out here. I love it. There are many times I'll go to the golf course wherever I'm at and go in and ask the pro what time he's going to close the practice tee, and he'll say, "You can hit balls as long as you want." You can call half the golf courses I've played at and they'll say, "That guy stands out there and hits balls until midnight." I really have gone through quite a change of life since I quit performing. This has been a wonderful thing for me. I love golf. Sometimes when I look at these golf courses, especially like this one here in Chicago, Cog

Hill, I say to myself, I just wish I could live another thousand years so I can enjoy this. Life's too short.

LIGUORI: You're also a writer and in fact, on your web site on the Internet, you have a poem that is titled "Why." And one of the lines reads, "for I know that tomorrow in some other place . . ."

KNIEVEL: ". . . I'll have that fear again to face."

LIGUORI: What fear are you talking about?

KNIEVEL: That was when I was jumping.

LIGUORI: The fear of dying?

KNIEVEL: The fear of dying, yes.

LIGUORI: But why did you put yourself through that?

KNIEVEL: That's something that made me exist. I loved it. I just loved the challenge, that's all.

LIGUORI: The challenge. And when you wake up every morning, what do you think about?

KNIEVEL: Now, I just live a different way of life. Then, I loved the challenge, and I made millions and millions and millions of dollars. I just loved to spend it just as fast as I could get it. I bought race horses. I bought yachts, two at a time. Two at a time. I didn't care if they were a million or two million apiece. A ship that cost me three or four million. Lear jets, two at a time. Homes, one in Miami, one in Montana—two at a time. Because I thought I was going to die, and money to me meant nothing because I felt that my existence here on earth maybe wouldn't be too long. Because of the jumping. I was hurt so bad so many times and came so close so many times; I was not like your average guy who gets a kick out of saying, "I have ten million dollars in stock" or "I have ten million dollars in CDs." To me, they were fools. Now I still love to spend money that I earn, if I can save any after taxes, but I'm a little more conservative than I was then.

LIGUORI: I understand that somebody you know is buried under a putting green.

KNIEVEL: That's right. George Low. America's Guest.[1] They did a story on him in one of the golf magazines not too long ago, and it said he never paid for anything. And I knew him very well. He didn't, and he was a tough gambler, I'll tell ya. But he had a great reputation of going to country clubs and going to hotels and having breakfast and signing all the checks and leaving his hotel bill unpaid, and going to people's houses and mooching off of

[1] George Low, golf hustler and one of the finest putters ever, is buried under the practice green at Cog Hill.

them. You know, Joe Jemsek, who owns Cog Hill, is a wonderful guy, and he knew George. They buried him right here at Cog Hill on a putting green. I've made some wonderful friends while I've traveled, and I have put the ashes of three of them on different golf courses, public courses, country clubs, put their ashes on in the morning with their families. Every time I go by, I think of them.

LIGUORI: Would you rather be known as Evel Knievel the golfer or Evel Knievel the daredevil?

KNIEVEL: No, no, I'm very happy and very proud about what I've done. If I had to do all over again, there are some things I wouldn't do. I think we all have regrets. But I'm happy with my life. I know that I've made a difference in some people's lives. Sometimes, I get young kids that come up to me. They're the finest young gentlemen in the world. They say to me, "Evel, I was fifteen or sixteen when you jumped the Canyon, and I remember what you said about not taking narcotics and trying to take care of yourself. And I just want to tell you I think the world of you and you helped change my life, and I want to shake your hand and say hello and get an autograph from you." That's the most wonderful thing in the world that I can receive for what I did. They can't take away from you what you've done. Ever.

Johnny Bench

The Cincinnati Reds' Hall of Fame catcher Johnny Bench is consumed with golf. Sport fans remember Bench as the captain of the "Big Red Machine" that dominated the National League in the 1970s, winning six division titles, four pennants, and two World Series. Bench's individual achievements include ten straight Gold Glove awards, two MVP awards (1970 and 1972), as well as the 1968 National League Rookie of the Year award.

Bench's greatness on the ball field obscures the fact that he is an accomplished golfer who hopes to play on the Senior Tour one day. He is a regular at celebrity golf events, and he plays five to six rounds of golf a week. I caught up with Bench at the Don Drysdale Hall of Fame Golf Classic in Indian Wells, California. The event brings Hall of Fame legends in all sports together for a weekend of golf, dinners, and storytelling. The proceeds benefit the Boys and Girls Club of Coachella Valley. If you're a contemporary sports historian, then this event is your Mount Rushmore. In attendance were Willie Mays, Brooks Robinson, Julius Erving, Bob Cousy, and the great basketball player Ann Meyers, the widow of Don Drysdale. It was here that I taped Hall of Fame tennis player Pancho Gonzales's last interview months before he succumbed to cancer.

After the Gonzales interview, Johnny Bench came strolling into our interview suite in the Hyatt Grand Champions Hotel. He is a happy, energetic bolt of electricity. His passion for golf bolsters an ever present smile when he is on the course. Our sit-down interview was interesting and thought-provoking, but it was on the course that Bench made his strongest impression on me.

The next day, with my camera person, I ran into Bench during his practice round at the Desert Falls Country Club in Palm Desert, California. It was late in the afternoon, the sky had darkened, and it was getting windy. He invited me to walk a couple of holes with him. On the first hole, he got to the green in two and had to sink a twenty-foot putt for birdie. Now, Bench's success in baseball has given him confidence that carries over to the golf course. To say he has a healthy ego is an understatement! During the interview, I'd asked him to compare which was more difficult, hitting a ninety-mile-per-hour fastball or hitting a golf ball. His reply dripped in sarcasm, "*You* could hit a golf ball!" I understood that I could not hit a ninety-mile-per-hour fastball, but Bench's statement grated on my nerves.

PAUL LESTER

As he sized up his putt for birdie, he looked into the camera, winked, and asked me to read his putt, thinking I didn't have a clue. I calmly restrained myself and told him his putt would break left to right, less than an inch out. He smiled, got in position, stroked the putt straight towards the hole and it broke to the right of the cup. I said, "You should have listened to me! I told you it broke left to right!" I smelled a bit of a setup when he said, "Okay, you try it." I wasn't prepared to play. I didn't have my clubs, I was wearing jewelry, and the wind was blowing my hair all over. But nothing was going to stop me from attempting to bring Mr. Bench down a peg.

Off came the rings as I borrowed his putter and took my time lining up the shot. Bench tried to psyche me out when he joked to the cameraman, "Do you have enough tape in that camera?" I tried to settle down and concentrate, ignoring the fact that I had not picked up a putter in two months. I knew if I made it I'd have bragging rights over Mr. Gold Glove forever. I was going to deliver a victory for women players who are tired of male golfers putting them down.

The camera rolled as I hovered over the ball thinking, nice smooth stroke, keep the body still, remember the pendulum motion. I let it go and the ball found the bottom of the cup. Johnny couldn't believe it as he watched me splash about in ecstasy. He smiled and gave me a high five. My work for womankind was accomplished for the day. As for that ninety-mile-an-hour fastball, I was ready to bat leadoff for the Big Red Machine. Just another day at the office.

LIGUORI: Ten-time Gold Glove award winner, Hall of Famer. You're always in your golf clothes.

BENCH: This is Palm Springs. This is Palm Springs. You have to understand this is like, "Ho hum, another day in paradise."

LIGUORI: It's always gorgeous here.

BENCH: Last year I think in the three months, October, November, December, I think I was out of shorts one day. I mean, it's just the greatest place on earth.

LIGUORI: When did you start playing golf?

BENCH: Well, whenever you signed a bat contract with Louisville Slugger, you either got $500 or a set of clubs. And everybody took the set of clubs. They weren't worth $200, but you make them worth it, and the bag and everything—so you really got a good deal out of it. So everybody took the clubs rather than the $500. [We would think,] "Man, I can get a real set from Louisville Slugger." And so I started playing with the guys. Everybody in spring training really played, and they took me along. I was twenty years old, and I just got hooked on it.

LIGUORI: You brought the clubs with you on the road?

BENCH: No, no, no.

LIGUORI: Oh, you didn't?

BENCH: No, no, no. That's these days.

LIGUORI: Most baseball teams do now.

BENCH: That's pitchers these days [who] do that. No, Sparky Anderson caught me one day. [Sparky was manager of the Cincinnati Reds from 1970–1978.]

LIGUORI: What happened?

BENCH: Well, it was in Houston and I was with a good friend of mine, and he says, "Why don't you come out?" I said, "Well, all right. I mean, it's far enough away nobody will ever know about it." [Sparky] heard about it by the time we got to the airport, and he called me in. "John, that's not a good idea."

LIGUORI: You didn't get fined?

BENCH: No, not really. I mean, I never abused that. I never did it. I mean, that was just a rare occasion. He said, "Hey John, you can't catch and play golf during the daytime. Especially here in Houston to begin with." And he was right. I got three hits that night. I really forced myself to play hard that particular night.

LIGUORI: Thank God, or Sparky Anderson would have been a little upset.

BENCH: Oh yeah, but he was the greatest to play for, so you didn't really mind.

LIGUORI: Did Sparky play golf?

BENCH: Sparky plays golf now. He kind of looks like a caveman killing lunch. I mean, he beats it all over the world and he has the greatest of times. Can't hit it very far. Spring training, I caught him one time, and he said, "John, I'm working. My chipping is so good." I said, "Where are you doing this?" He says, "In my room! You know how thick those drapes are in the hotel? I can tee it off and I hit it into the drapes. It's perfect!" That's what he was doing the whole time. Sparky loves it, and I've played with him twice. And he's never satisfied because he says, "I didn't hit it good, did I? That was not—was that a good swing?" He was always analytical and everything else. But the last time I talked to him about a couple weeks ago was when he said, "Yeah, my golf game—it's never going to be any good. I accept it. I'm just going to go out and have fun."

LIGUORI: Well, it must be tough to play with you because you're a scratch golfer. These guys are probably a little intimidated.

BENCH: Well, I think there are certain people who are, but that's the greatest thing about golf and that's why I don't play tennis. 'Cause I can't play [tennis]—you can't always find somebody your level. And I don't want to pitter-patter with someone that can't play. So I'd rather play golf with you or with the guy out there or whoever is playing in the tournaments who have twenty handicaps. Because I can play with them. I mean, it doesn't matter where they hit it. They have to go find it and play it and everything else. You give some lessons, you try to work with them, you try to do something, but you try to just make sure they have a good time. Because the first time I ever played in a pro tournament, in a Pro-Am, I couldn't get the ball on the tee. I was with Arnold Palmer.

LIGUORI: Oh God. How embarrassing was that?

BENCH: Nineteen seventy-one in Bob Hope's tournament. I went around the world with Bob during his Christmas trip, his Christmas show. He invited me to the tournament in 1971. We played a par five, and they were five deep on both sides of the par five. They had bleachers going up by the tee. I'm playing with the King. Bob wanted me to come over with him while they teed off, which was a group ahead of us. That was Bob Hope and Spiro Agnew and Willie Mays. And Spiro teed off hitting that way and hit it right on the end of the club and hit a guy right there in the first row. And they said, "Give him a mulligan. Give him a mulligan." And he teed off and hit the guy next to him! Willie duck-hooked one down there, almost took somebody's head off. And that group goes down the fairway. Arnold tees off and he's walking down there, and he's hitching his pants up. I cannot get the ball on the tee, I am so nervous. So I understand what everybody feels like at certain occasions. I still get nervous. I guess you should when you're playing a tournament. Man, golf is just the greatest equalizer, I think, and socializer that there is.

LIGUORI: In baseball, you've played in front of thousands of people!

BENCH: How would you like to sing at the Met [Metropolitan Opera]? How would you like to walk out on stage at the Met? Now, you know what you can do here, but then you get out there and you're thinking, "Where does that first crackle come?" or "Where does that first note I've got to reach—where does that breathing come in?" Any time you get out of your element. And people expect so much of you. I think they automatically do that. "There's a pop-up. There's a double play. There's a ground rule double. There's a foul ball." I mean, you hear it all the time. So they are focused right on you. When you play the game of baseball, you didn't hear people. I mean, you heard some of the barbs when you went back to the dugout but not while you were doing it, that you paid any attention to, because I knew I could play baseball.

LIGUORI: Do you kind of wish the galleries would make more noise? Do you wish there would be a little more baseball atmosphere on these golf courses?

BENCH: It would be all right if it was constant. But any time you give a fan, which is short for fanatic—any time you give him a license to say something, they've either got to be the loudest or the most unique. They'll scream louder than anybody else just to make a fool out of themselves and to be noticed and maybe get on camera. If you could rely on the average fan who comes out to appreciate what the game is, then I think they would be very understanding and they would say things in constant order. But enough. Don't give fans too much. They've never been in the arena, so they don't understand. Besides that, they've had a tough day with the boss. They had a tough day with the wife. The wife had a bad day with the husband. Who can they holler at? They can't holler at the boss. So they can go pay their money and scream at that guy standing out in the middle of the field making millions of dollars.

LIGUORI: You're a scratch golfer and want to qualify for the Senior Tour in a couple of years.

BENCH: I'd like to be that good. John Brodie [former NFL quarterback] is probably one of our idols out here because he's done so well. He's won a golf tournament on the Senior Tour and made that transition from being a professional athlete in the world of sports as far as football, baseball, or basketball. And all of us, let's face it, we're all golf junkies. We're addicts. We love it. We want to improve. We want to get to a level. And the biggest thing we face is we go from a fifteen to about six handicap fairly quickly, if you've got any kind of skills. And now you think, well, I've got this made. But from six to three is like an eternity. From three to two is tough. From two to one and down to scratch is just hard to do. And then you've got to go beyond that. You've got to go to plus three, meaning you have to be able to shoot 69 on any golf course you walk out on to compete at that level. These guys fall out of bed and shoot 67. I mean, they are so good. So if I can get a shot better every year, and get to that plus three, I'll go out and try to qualify. But it also gives me a complete out. Everybody thinks I'm out there working to be on the Senior Tour when for three years I can have the greatest time of my life. I play golf, and everybody says, "He's really working." Where I could be having the greatest time in my world, and everybody would admire me for what I was doing, but all I was doing was goofing off.

LIGUORI: So either way, it's a win-win.

BENCH: I can't lose.

LIGUORI: In baseball, you took your talent to the ultimate level. With golf, obviously there's so much room for improvement no matter what handicap you are.

BENCH: Nick Price, he's always tinkering. Nick Faldo, always tinkering. They miss a cut or something, and that's an absolute disaster to these people. Why? Because the swing let them down? Well, where was the swing supposed to be? What you never understand is why some people can win on the West Coast and can't win on the East Coast. They can't play on that particular grass. Their lies are difficult. The ball does different things. The altitude does. The wind bothers them, or whatever. And you would think as talented and as skilled as they are, that they could go out there and shoot 69 every round. But yet they struggle. And what most people don't realize is that we get upset at shooting. Let's say the average golfer shoots 85 one day. Shoots 93 the next and he's an absolute basket case. He shot eight shots higher. And then you go out and watch a pro who shoots 64 one day and 74 the next. So their discrepancy is ten shots, so why in the world should we ever get angry shooting eight shots worse than we really are. [Some guys say,] "What did I shoot today? I shot 75,

76, and I played so bad." You know, somebody ought to come up and just slap you real good. Get your attention. You're only going to shoot 68 or 69 every now and then.

LIGUORI: How often do you play?

BENCH: In Palm Springs, you play no more than seven days a week. No less than five or six. It's just something about it. You can't do it. This weather is perfect.

LIGUORI: Well, there are a hundred golf courses within five miles.

BENCH: Yeah. Why would you not want to be outside with some friends? You can't let the day go by. And even if you don't play—I play about five rounds a week, and even if I don't play, I've got to get in the golf cart and drive it and hit some balls, chip some balls, try to help one of my friends' swing.

LIGUORI: The age old question, Johnny. What's harder? Hitting a ninety mile-per-hour fastball or a stationary golf ball?

BENCH: Well, *you* can play golf. But you *can't* play baseball.

LIGUORI: How do you know?

BENCH: Well, I've seen Pete Rose and the greatest hitters in all of baseball, and I've played it at the highest level through the first early part of the seventies before the lung surgery. And there were people I had trouble hitting. And if they threw fastballs and you knew what was coming all the time, yeah. But when they don't tell you what's coming and they throw ninety-five miles an hour and they throw at your head—I've never seen too many golf balls thrown at people's heads. To be able to measure—I've seen people who are nonathletic looking—I mean, you would never think that. They weigh 350 pounds. They're not lineman, but these are people that go out and can play golf. There are ladies that play; I mean, I was with Sandra Palmer this morning. A little mite of a lady. Five-foot-one and she can just play and win tournaments and do that. But you could never get to the level where you could play baseball. To hit a round ball with a round bat square and not know what's coming and to make an adjustment within like a tenth of a second or less, and make that adjustment in order to do it, is very, very difficult, I think.

LIGUORI: Now golf enthusiasts are going to say, "But you can foul off a couple of balls." In golf, you have one chance and one chance only.

BENCH: And it's *sitting* there. And it's sitting there. They say, "Give me three swings and I could do it." Yeah, they could because they can set the ball back on the tee or whatever. I mean, it's not a judgment. Baseball players love golfers and golfers love baseball players. We all want to play. I've never seen a hockey player or a golfer that wouldn't come to the park if you ask him to and take swings. That's what happened with Michael Jordan. Goes down to the park, takes some batting practice, and somebody says, "You've got a great swing. You probably could have played!" "Played? I could have played?" So he wants to go out and play.

LIGUORI: Davis Love III teased Michael, saying he should stick to baseball. He taught Michael how to golf at the University of North Carolina, by the way.

BENCH: Yeah, and Michael's a good golfer. Michael's one of those guys that got to six or seven handicap and then thought he could play. We all did that. And it's just irrational that it happens that quickly. You just can't do it.

LIGUORI: So what do you have to do to get to that Senior Tour level and be able to compete with those guys?

BENCH: Drive the ball a little straighter. I've got length, so that's not a problem. I've really need to work around the greens a lot more. You see the golfers that are playing, you see them hit. The best golfers on the PGA Tour average hitting about thirteen to fourteen greens a round. So they miss four to five greens per round and shot 68. So all those greens they were making the putts, which is where it counts, but they were getting the ball up and down. Seventy-five percent of all your time should be done on chipping and putting.

LIGUORI: Is the psychological game in golf the same as baseball in your mind? When you go out and play a round of golf, does anything from your baseball days transfer over?

BENCH: I don't take it as seriously, probably, as others. I hate to see it when they're really so involved and so absorbed that they get upset. They hit a drive that may be five feet off of where they want to hit, and they get so upset. And I say, "Man, I don't even want to be here sometimes." So my mind wanders sometimes. I don't want to get out and have to concentrate totally on golf for eighteen holes. I want to be psyched for it and everything else but there are other things. I played with a guy the other day, and from the first tee he just had me going. I thought, oh, it's going to be a long day. And you have to get away from that. Again, getting into the competition of how I have to get my game face on, or golf face on at that time in order to play eighteen holes and compete.

LIGUORI: Do you have as much fun on the course as you did playing ball?

BENCH: I have a lot more fun on the golf course. We had a lot of fun in baseball because we won all the time. You go out on the field and you have to catch that half inning, and when you come back to the dugout, you're puttering around, you get something to drink, you're taking equipment off—you're doing something that's not always totally involved so you can take away from it a little bit. When you're on the field as a catcher, I had to call every pitch and had to maneuver, move people around and get all that stuff. It was pretty easy to concentrate because I was expected to, and I love that role.

LIGUORI: Do you miss that camaraderie?

BENCH: Yeah. More than anything. That's the one thing that I think every athlete will say when they retire, if they were involved in a team. And that's what golfers don't get that much into. They have their friends and everything else, but the guys that you travel with for six, seven months—you're on the road, you're eating, you're going to movies, you're going out after the game, and it's always something that when you really get home, that's the thing that you miss the most. When spring training comes, you miss baseball, but you miss being in that locker room and smelling the sweat and smelling the guys, and listen to the ugly old things guys say and look at their ugly old butts walking by in the shower. I mean, it's just things that you miss because they become a part of you. They're more of a family probably than anything that's ever been because even though you had your brothers and everything else, you could never be that close, where you had to be sitting next to them on the bus. You get to the plane ,and you're riding together, you're playing cards, you're doing this, going to the movie you want to go to. So it's a respect and a love that you really miss. It's a void that's hard to fill.

Pete Sampras

Pete Sampras is one of the few gentlemen left in big-time sports. He has modeled his career and behavior after the legendary and classy Rod Laver, who is the only player to have won two Grand Slams in the same year.[1] Sampras is also setting his sights on equaling and surpassing Laver's eleven major-tournament wins.[2] With Pete Sampras, what you see on the court is what you get—guts, heart, and character. Those qualities transfer to the golf course. He is a pleasure to play golf and hang out with.

Despite verbal jabs by writers who labeled him and his style of play boring early in his professional career, Sampras had let his on-court performance do the talking, until several very emotional, come-from-behind victories changed the public's perception of him. In the 1995 Australian Open quarterfinals against Jim Courier, Sampras broke down during the match as he struggled with the fact that best friend and coach Tim Gullikson had been admitted to the hospital for what would later be diagnosed as brain cancer. Sampras rallied back from being down two sets to love to beat Courier in five. At the 1996 French Open, soon after Tim passed away, Sampras was able to pull out three dramatic five-set matches. And in one of the most compelling and memorable matches I've ever covered, Sampras overcame an upset stomach and a two-set-to-one deficit to beat Alex Coretja in a fifth set tiebreaker in the quarterfinals of the 1996 U.S. Open. Early in the tiebreaker, Sampras threw up on the court. At seven all, after surviving one match point, Sampras aced Coretja on his second serve to go up eight points to seven. Coretja then double-faulted to lose the match. The fact that Sampras hung in to win it was heroic.

I caught up with Sampras during the Champions Cup in Indian Wells, California, hosted by the Hyatt Grand Champions and conveniently situated near two golf courses amongst the ninety courses in the Palm Springs desert resorts area. Golf has become such a popular sport amongst tennis professionals that oftentimes, in between practice and tournament play, they'll hit the links for relaxation. When Sampras found out that the subject of our interview would be golf and tennis, he did what he could to maneuver

[1] Laver won the Australian Open, the French Open, Wimbledon, and the U.S. Open all in the same year. Rod Laver did this in 1962 and 1969.

[2] The all-time record for major singles titles is held by Roy Emerson, with 12.

EDDIE SANDERSON

his schedule so that he could accommodate me.

After our sit-down interview, Sampras and I went out to the range. He seemed eager to show off his driving prowess. In tennis, he's a power player with one of the biggest serves in the game. His serve has been clocked as fast as 132 miles per hour. When Sampras is in top form, his opponent's service return games consists of walking from the deuce to the ad court and back to the deuce court, while Sampras smokes one unreturnable serve after another.

He applies the same power to his golf swing. Nothing makes him happier than taking the driver out and belting one 300 yards. He comes out of his shoes to distance the ball that far, though the ball seldom goes straight and down the middle. But in the 1996 Isuzu Celebrity Golf Championships long-drive competition in Lake Tahoe, Nevada, Sampras outdrove football, baseball, basketball, and hockey players to win the competition with a blast of 332 yards. If he only had more time to practice, he would be dangerous.

LIGUORI: Pete, how does the number-one tennis player in the world find time for golf?

SAMPRAS: Well, when I'm on my time off from tennis is really the only time I can play golf. When I'm playing the Tour and whatever, I'm doing so many things and I don't really have any time. I have a home in Tampa on a golf course and I own a golf cart, so I hop on the golf cart and go out and play as much as I can.

LIGUORI: How did you get interested in golf?

SAMPRAS: I got interested in golf when I turned pro, at sixteen, seventeen. All the guys on the Tour played golf, and I just took it up. I enjoy it. It's a time when I can just escape, get away from the media, and tennis and business and all this stuff. It's really relaxing. There's no one to bother me there. You can go out with three of your good friends, have a good time, and have a lot of fun.

LIGUORI: I hear you're a fourteen handicap?

SAMPRAS: Yeah, fourteen.

LIGUORI: You have a pretty good temperament for golf, right? I mean, you control your emotions. You're pretty laid-back. Most good golfers know how to channel their anger, frustration, delight.

SAMPRAS: Yeah. I think my golf game is so erratic and I'm so inconsistent with my shots because I don't get to play enough. But you've got to admire someone who basically, for four rounds of golf, you hit two bad shots and you're going to lose a tournament. Where in tennis, you can hit many bad shots and still win. I've always respected that from golfers. The toughest thing I have is that the ball is not moving. It's staying there and it's the same swing—it can go anywhere. At least for me. You know, I don't get to practice enough. But I enjoy it and hopefully I can get a little bit better the more I play.

LIGUORI: Who have you played with in golf? Some of your more memorable foursomes.

SAMPRAS: I had a really fun game with Jerry West and Mitch Kupchak from the Lakers.

LIGUORI: Jerry's a good golfer. We interviewed Jerry years ago for my *Sports Innerview Show*. He's a perfectionist, Pete. In fact, he once told me he shot the lowest score at Bel Air Country Club and he would never play again because he couldn't shoot that well every time he went out.

SAMPRAS: I believe it.

LIGUORI: He's a perfectionist.

SAMPRAS: He's a very competitive guy. Just a funny story—I was playing with him and we were at about the fourteenth hole and I asked him about his clubs. He had some really old looking drivers, and I asked him if I could hit one of them. He's been hitting this driver for twenty-five years and loves it. So I took a big whack at it, because I always do that—I broke the club! I broke the club! The head fell off, and it came about a hundred yards into the fairway, and he was so pissed. I was with Mitch Kupchak on the ground laughing.

LIGUORI: And it was his favorite club?

SAMPRAS: Yes, but he got it fixed.

LIGUORI: But he must have been upset.

SAMPRAS: He took it pretty well, but I could tell he was pissed.

LIGUORI: That happened to me once on the driving range. I said, "Oh, by the way, when you pick up these balls, can you find the head of my driver and send it to me? It fell off." Is it competitive when you play with your tennis colleagues on the golf course?

SAMPRAS: You know, we take it serious to a certain point. I go out to play well, but I go out for the most part to have some fun and mess around and give each other a hard time like I always do. I play a lot of rounds with [fellow tennis pros] Todd Martin and Jim Courier.

LIGUORI: And your weakness is your short game?

SAMPRAS: I'd say I drive the ball pretty well, but when it comes to the short game, the chipping and putting, that's where I'm terrible.

LIGUORI: Well, you know, a lot of people say that. That means you spend too much time on the range trying to hit the hell out of your drives.

SAMPRAS: Just as long as I drive the ball 300 yards, I'll come back the next day.

LIGUORI: Do you drive 300 yards?

SAMPRAS: I have, yeah, but it goes straight, right into the woods. I do the John Daly workout. Bring out my driver and hit the ball as hard as I can. I go out on the first tee and . . .

LIGUORI: "Grip it and rip it" [from PGA player John Daly's instructional video].

SAMPRAS: My favorite video.

LIGUORI: You watch that video?

SAMPRAS: Yes. It's not too instructional, but it's good fun to watch. My tennis swings are pretty long and gangly, where golf you really need to shorten that up, 'cause my swing is so long. Kind of like John Daly in a way, but he can control it better than I can.

LIGUORI: [Tongue in cheek] Can you outdrive John Daly?

SAMPRAS: I don't think so. Maybe with a shotgun or something.

LIGUORI: Does golf hurt your tennis game, or vice versa? Because a lot of people say that you shouldn't mix both of those sports. In fact, some golfers have quit playing tennis. I remember Raymond Floyd once said that he stopped playing tennis because it was hurting his golf game.

SAMPRAS: Maybe for golfers to play tennis, that might affect them, but for tennis players to play golf, it has absolutely nothing to do with any stroke mechanic or anything that's negative about it. So I don't have any problem playing.

[On the range, Sampras drives one 250 yards straight and down the middle.]

LIGUORI: Let the club do the work.

SAMPRAS: What are you, my golf instructor?

[Sampras sets up another ball and hits it again, this time 275 yards and straight down the middle.]

LIGUORI: Oh, nice!

SAMPRAS: Not bad if you like it perfect.

LIGUORI: Is it nerve-racking for you to play golf in front of a lot of people watching? Because you're so used to it in tennis. But in golf for some reason, people say there is nothing more nerve-racking than placing that ball on the first tee.

SAMPRAS: Oh, it's definitely nerve-racking. I've only played in one pro-am in Tampa, the TPC course there. And I was playing with—who was I playing with? I was playing with Dale Douglas, and the first tee, about a hundred people were around the tee, and for the first time I was really nervous. I hit it pretty well, but when I'm out, that's why I play, to get away from people. To get away from everyone and just have some fun.

LIGUORI: Who do you follow on the PGA Tour?

SAMPRAS: Pretty regularly, I like watching Freddie Couples. It seems like our mentality is pretty similar. Me on the tennis court, him on the golf course. It seems like we're pretty laid-back guys. I enjoy watching him play. I watch Greg Norman, who hits the ball a ton. I follow it quite a bit. If it's on the weekend, I'll watch it all the time.

LIGUORI: Are you a couch potato?

SAMPRAS: Couch potato, yeah. I've got the RCA satellite dish.

LIGUORI: Would you watch golf over tennis?

SAMPRAS: Oh yeah, absolutely. When tennis is on TV, I get away from that sport as much as possible. So golf and NBA basketball, that's it.

LIGUORI: You're a basketball fan. Who's your favorite team?

SAMPRAS: The Lakers. I grew up in LA, and so I've always been a Lakers fan.

LIGUORI: If you weren't playing tennis, would you dream of becoming a golf professional?

SAMPRAS: I'd say that golfing is something that is played more or less in the States. A little bit in Europe, and the travel doesn't seem quite as bad as tennis travel. And you can play for thirty years. Tennis, basically, you're going to last for maybe ten or twelve years. Golfers, I mean, look at guys like Ray Floyd on the Senior Tour. He's still making good money. He's fifty-two years old. I mean, you don't see that in tennis obviously because the body gets a little pounding from all the running. So golf would be the sport I'd most like to play if I wasn't playing tennis.

LIGUORI: Why is golf so popular while tennis ratings and the overall popularity of the game is on the downside?

SAMPRAS: Well, everyone plays golf because it doesn't take a lot of effort. A lot of CEO's of big companies play golf, whereas tennis takes a lot more energy, and you need to be in shape. And golf is marketed really well.

LIGUORI: One of the most successful marketing tools for all the golf tours have been the pro-ams that are held early in the tournament week. Pros play with amateurs and mix with corporate sponsors and all kinds of people. Do you think tennis should do something like that in the beginning of the week, although you guys play matches all week long?

SAMPRAS: I've heard about it. I'd be willing to help as much as I can, but I think golfers are pretty accessible. They're older than tennis players. Most tennis players are in their early twenties, and golfers are in their thirties so they kind of understand the business aspect and you've got to give back a little bit. I think there are some tennis players who are pretty selfish, but you know, golfers try to help their sport. They do a lot of pro-ams, a lot of cocktail parties, do whatever they can for the PGA Tour, and they do a good job marketing it. Hopefully the ATP [Associated Tennis Professionals] can get to that level, but only time will tell.

LIGUORI: When your critics called you boring and your style of tennis boring, I've always defended you. You let your tennis do the talking. Plus, I've seen you on shows and in interviews—you can be funny!

SAMPRAS: Thank you. Everyone is different. I think the press and public were so used to seeing controversial guys like John McEnroe and Jimmy Connors, and guys that really showed a lot of personality and a lot of emotion. And I really don't. I'm pretty much to myself, and that's the best way I play my best tennis.

LIGUORI: Sure, you have to do what it takes to win and you have to be yourself.

SAMPRAS: And that's really the most important thing when I walk out on the court is to win and play good tennis. Through that, I hope I can entertain the public and people watching at home. And so I think maybe there's some reporters in Britain especially that really didn't have a lot to write about me, so they just called me boring. And at first, that was really the first place that I heard a negative criticism about me. I thought, I'm a good guy, I do the right things, try to say the right thing, and it kind of disappointed me a little bit. But you just can't worry about stuff like that. Just let it roll off your back.

LIGUORI: And you won't change.

SAMPRAS: I'm not going to change, and I can't change because that's just not my personality.

LIGUORI: What would be the ultimate for you? If you could say, "This is what I want to do in my tennis career," what would you say it is?

SAMPRAS: I'd say to win every major.

LIGUORI: To win the Grand Slam of tennis? Could you do that?

SAMPRAS: All in one year, I think in today's game it's something very tough to do. Realistically, I think the French Open is the one title that I've not won, and I'd love to win more of *any* title right now. It's really a huge challenge. It's not really my surface. I'm getting better on clay, but it's going to take some more time and maybe a couple more years. But that's, if I can answer that question right now, it would be the French Open. That's the one I don't have. And then I'll have all four, and then I can live with that for the rest of my life.

Yogi Berra

Yogi Berra is proof positive that a national treasure can be fun on the golf course. Watching Yogi play at Marsh Landing Country Club in Ponte Vedra, Florida, in a Heisman Trophy tournament sponsored by the Downtown Athletic Club, I was enthralled by his mannerisms on the course. His passion for the game enables him to maintain a good deal of the enthusiasm he brought to the ballpark as the catcher and feared slugger of the New York Yankees. Yogi's team crushed opponents for over a decade. Can this humble, unassuming, humorous man of advanced age hold most of the important batting statistics in World Series history? His records for games (75), at-bats (259), hits (71), and doubles (10) may never be broken. As the purported light touch to the glamorous Yankee teams of DiMaggio, Rizzuto, and the Mick, Yogi's penchant for reading comic books didn't obscure the fact that he caught just about every important pitch thrown in that era, when his team won ten World Championships in fourteen trips to the big show.

Yet the cute, easygoing man, with an ugly golf swing that resembles his batting stroke, short and choppy, makes solid contact every time. He's crafty around the greens and as skilled with chips and pitches as he was at "golfing" low pitches out of the ballpark. Yogi grunts, groans, cheers, talks to the ball, and puts a little body English into shots that need help. In fact, Yogi talks to the golf ball as much as he talked to opposing batters. On one hole, he reached the fringe of the green about 160 yards away with a seven-iron and yelled, "Get up." When the ball crept up a few more inches, he replied, "I'll take it!" Attempting a bump and run, Yogi yelled, "Stopppp! Stopppp!" And an overly aggressive putt forced a "whoa horsey" and an "Egads."

Yogi's passion on the golf course must reflect the simpler times of his playing days, when ballplayers were powerless, so their bond was a love for the game. The complaints were minimal, they didn't whine in public, and they had a blast. Nowadays, as Mickey Mantle once said to me, "The players bring briefcases to the ballpark." It's all business.

Of course, along with the mannerisms and the unabated enthusiasm, Yogi's colorful expressions add to the fun. Yogi transcends baseball; he's an internationally known celebrity whose "Yogisms" are part of the national discourse. At a tournament to benefit the Special Olympics at Wingfoot, many gathered to watch Yogi and other sports celebrities tee it up. While walking a few holes with the Hall of Famer, I asked some in the gallery to recite a Yogism. Almost everyone could. Here are a few we heard that day: "It ain't over till it's over." "A little ol' lady said to Yogi, 'You look cool today.' He said to her, 'You don't look so hot yourself.'" "Yogi went to a pizza parlor and ordered a pizza. When he was asked if he wanted the pie cut in eight slices or six slices, he said, 'Cut it in six slices, I'm not that hungry.'" My favorite was one told to me by the great golfer, Chi Chi Rodriguez. "Yogi's wife asked him, 'Yogi, we're from St. Louis, we live in New Jersey, and you play in the Bronx. I don't know whether to bury you in St. Louis, New Jersey, or New York.' Yogi replied, 'Well, why don't you surprise me.'"

PAUL LESTER

It's no wonder that Yogi will always be one of baseball's most popular figures. I wish I could have known him years ago, when he played for the Yankees, but playing with him at celebrity golf events, playing at his own charity tournament, and attending the same sports banquets, we've talked a lot. And his many stories provide me with a bridge to his past.

LIGUORI: Yogi, you look refreshed after that round of golf today.

BERRA: It was a little hot out there. I came back and took a nice shower.

LIGUORI: You played in fourteen World Series championships as a New York Yankee, winning ten of them. You also hold the record for most World Series games played (75) and hits in World Series games (71). You're considered one of the greatest clutch hitters of all time.

BERRA: I don't know about that. That was just lucky. I'm just fortunate I did.

LIGUORI: Why was it that you hit bad pitches? You just didn't think about it?

BERRA: No, I didn't think about it. I could see a high ball real good and I'd swing at it—there's times I wouldn't swing at it because I didn't see it that good. To me, if it looked like it was a strike, I swung at it. You know that I copied that from Joe Medwick, my idol in

St. Louis. He was my idol and he was a bad ball hitter. Maybe that's it. I always say, "If you see it, hit it."

LIGUORI: When you were growing up, your father didn't want you to play baseball, and he didn't let your older brothers play. But you wanted to play!

BERRA: Very bad, I wanted to play baseball, and my two brothers made me go out and play. They all had jobs. They said, "Let him go out and try it."

LIGUORI: Did you go to see games in St. Louis?

BERRA: We used to go every Saturday.

LIGUORI: And so you learned how to play watching some of these guys?

BERRA: Oh yeah. Actually I didn't like to watch games. I'd rather be playing games. We had a lot of sandlot ball when we were kids. We played a lot when we were kids up on the hill. We played softball in the morning and baseball in the afternoon.

LIGUORI: Sandlot baseball was a big part of your life, but I know that you were very athletic in other sports as well.

BERRA: We played a lot of soccer. Whatever was in season we played up on the hill. We played football. We had a lot of clubs up on the hill, and we played against each other, the clubs played against each other. We couldn't afford the uniforms, and we used to like to play the guys who had the uniforms, Ann. We beat 'em bad.

LIGUORI: They were the rich guys, those guys could afford the uniforms.

BERRA: We played with sneakers and they had their spiked shoes on.

LIGUORI: Ballplayers in your era had to have second and third jobs. You only made ten thousand to twenty thousand dollars a year when you first started playing.

BERRA: My first year was the five thousand minimum. I could tell you my whole salary going up the line.

LIGUORI: So you started at five thousand dollars.

BERRA: That was good money. We thought that was good. We could not have made five thousand dollars working.

LIGUORI: But you also had to have another job obviously in the off-season.

BERRA: In the off season, I worked at the American Shop with Phil Rizzuto in Newark [New Jersey] in a clothing store.

LIGUORI: You and Phil were salesmen?

BERRA: Gene Hermanski was there too. [Gene played for the Brooklyn Dodgers.]

LIGUORI: Did you sell a lot of suits?

BERRA: Yeah, we sold some.

LIGUORI: I'd buy a suit from you. So, could you bring your golf clubs on the road with you back then?

BERRA: No. At that time we couldn't play golf. None of us had an off-day, at home or something. We never brought them on the road.

LIGUORI: Now pitchers play golf all the time on the road. They bring their golf clubs all the time.

BERRA: Not only pitchers, everybody does. When I quit Houston in '89, I asked the clubhouse man, "How many sets of golf clubs you got on the trip?" He says, "Seventeen." "Seventeen?" They carry their own golf clubs now. That's great.

LIGUORI: Tell me about your life now, because you are one of the most popular players ever to play the game and you never get tired, it seems, of signing autographs and making special appearances and shaking hands with people.

BERRA: I do a little bit, Ann. I do it, if I got the time I do it. I like to play golf. I'm with a chocolate milk company now. I farm land out in New Jersey. You better buy some, too. It's a good drink: Yogi Berra's Chocolate Milk. They have it out.

LIGUORI: People who may not have followed your baseball career still know of you because of your Yogisms. Do you remember the first Yogism?

BERRA: I think the first one was in 1947. I was with Bobby Brown in St. Louis. They gave me a car, and I asked Bobby Brown to write out a speech for me. He wrote it down. I only had a one-liner and I fouled it up. He said, "Just tell them thank you for making this night possible." I got up there and said, "I wanna thank everybody for making this night necessary."

LIGUORI: That's classic. And what happened after that?

BERRA: That's it. They asked me, "Did you know what you said?" And I said, "No." They said, "That's what you said." "I didn't say 'possible'?" "No, you didn't."

LIGUORI: So the legend grew from that moment.

BERRA: My wife [Carmen] could tell a lot. She could write a book on it.

LIGUORI: She should. Why doesn't she?

BERRA: No, she doesn't want to.

LIGUORI: I also have some Yogisms written down here. Once in a restaurant you said, "Nobody goes here anymore, it's too crowded."

BERRA: I said that.

LIGUORI: Did you really say that? Because sometimes the legend of Yogisms expands in such a way that you think, well, maybe other people are making them up.

BERRA: Well, I got some. "You can't think and hit at the same time." They'd say, "What's the time?" I'd say, "Now?"

LIGUORI: "A nickel ain't worth a dime anymore."

BERRA: I said that.

LIGUORI: Yogi, you're a twenty-two handicap. You've been playing golf a long time. You played when you were playing baseball with the Yankees.

BERRA: Yes, I did. We never played though during the summer. We never played. We only got a chance to play during the winter, and we never had much of a winter. We used to get a lot of snow way back then, and if we had a month or two to play, we were lucky. I enjoy it, I really do. I have a lot of fun. You meet a lot of people. I play with the kids, all my boys play it, and we have a lot of fun.

LIGUORI: You've played with a lot of interesting celebrities—Bob Hope and Frank Sinatra, etcetera. If you could put any foursome together in the world, who would you want to play with more than everybody else?

BERRA: You play with all of them. They're all fun. We got some good players. I liked playing with Mickey [Mantle] when his legs were all right. Johnny Bench plays good golf. Graig Nettles is a good golfer. Gene Michael's a good golfer. George [Steinbrenner] don't let him out much to play though.

LIGUORI: He certainly won't. George is pretty tough on Gene.

BERRA: Bobby Murcer's a hell of a golfer.

LIGUORI: So if you could play with anybody, you'd play with baseball players?

BERRA: No, I'd play with everybody. You got some good guys. I play with the hockey players. I play with the pros. The most fun I ever had, I played with Babe Zaharias [the legendary golfer and track and field star]. When I first joined the Yankees in '47 she used to live in St. Petersburg. We used to go out and play golf.

LIGUORI: What was that like?

BERRA: It was great, and I didn't know how to hit a ball either.

LIGUORI: Did she teach you a little bit?

BERRA: Well, she was a fan. They owned a golf course out there. Her and her husband, George Zaharias. He was a wrestler. She married a wrestler.

LIGUORI: She was quite an athlete.

BERRA: Oh yeah, a good athlete.

LIGUORI: She hit the heck out of the ball, huh?

BERRA: Patty Berg I played with, Pat Bradley I played with, Judy Dickinson, Donna Andrews; I played with quite a few of 'em.

LIGUORI: Do you think you'll ever go back to Yankee Stadium? [Ever since being fired as manager by George Steinbrenner seventeen games into the 1985 season, Yogi has not gone back to Yankee Stadium—not for Old-Timers games, not as a guest at any function there.]

BERRA: George always gets me on the wrong days, Ann. I've always got a golf game.

LIGUORI: You're too busy playing golf. Is that your excuse?

BERRA: On weekends, oh yeah. I love it.

LIGUORI: They have not invited you back to an Old-Timers game?

BERRA: Oh, I've been invited, sure.

LIGUORI: You get invited? But you won't go?

BERRA: No.

LIGUORI: Why?

BERRA: I don't wanna.

LIGUORI: Why?

BERRA: I don't know.

LIGUORI: You just don't want to. Have you talked to George at all since he fired you?

BERRA: No, I don't talk to him much, no. I might see him at the Hall of Fame once in a while, and we say hello and that's it.

LIGUORI: You're so much a part of Yankee history that the fans would love to see you at the Old-Timers games!

BERRA: You get pros and cons on that. Some say they're glad you're not going out there; some say they wish you'd come out there.

LIGUORI: Who says they're glad you're not going?

BERRA: A few of 'em.

LIGUORI: If you hadn't played baseball, if you didn't have such a legendary career, do you think you would've wanted to play golf?

BERRA: No. I couldn't make a living in golf, no, because I'm no good at it.

LIGUORI: Say if you were good.

BERRA: No, I don't think I would. No kidding, Ann. I'd be working someplace else.

LIGUORI: If you didn't play baseball what would you do?

BERRA: I worked in a shoe factory. I worked with my brother at a shoe company in St. Louis. I was making pretty good money. I was making just as much—I got a working permit when I got out of school. I worked when I was fourteen making seventy dollars a week. That was good money for a kid at fourteen. I only made ninety dollars in a month for playing ball in the minor leagues.

LIGUORI: Did you almost say, "Forget baseball, I'm gonna stay in the shoe business"?

BERRA: I'll tell you one story. I used to call home for money. Actually, I had seventy-five dollars I needed for eating and everything. My mom said, "Don't let your father know or you'll come right home." I always would tease my dad [years later]. Both of 'em are dead now, but I used to tease him. I said, "Dad, you know if you had all your sons play ball, you would've been a millionaire." He said, "Blame your mother."

LIGUORI: What's your best score in golf?

BERRA: Seventy-eight.

LIGUORI: And where were you?

BERRA: Pinehurst, North Carolina.

LIGUORI: Good place to be.

BERRA: That's when I was young, Ann. I could hit the ball then.

LIGUORI: Oh, come on, you're a good player. You're seventy years old, Yogi!

BERRA: That's why I can't hit the ball.

LIGUORI: You looked good out on the course. You look like you're fifty.

BERRA: I work out in the morning. I do stretching exercises and then take a nice steam bath, shave in a steam room, and then weigh in and see what I lost.

Ivan Lendl

AP PHOTO/JAN TRESTIK

While covering tennis during my broadcasting career as a reporter for WFAN SportsRadio in New York (and earlier for ABC Radio Sports, and as a freelance journalist for *USA Today* and *Inside Sports* magazine), I witnessed many of Ivan Lendl's ninety-four career titles. For a stretch of eight years at the U.S. Open in Flushing Meadows, New York, it was expected that Lendl would play on the final Sunday, and he didn't disappoint the prognosticators. Lendl was at the top of tennis for a total of 270 weeks—he held the number-one ranking longer than any player in the Open era. His astounding success should have made him the toast of the sport, but in his seventeen-year career he never figured out that all-encompassing credo—image is everything.

Czech born and a step behind the Conners-McEnroe juggernaut, Lendl's stoic personality and regimented style of play led American writers to portray him as a charmless robot. This was bad casting. Lendl has a great sense of humor and is quite personable, but much like Bob Dole's candidacy, the public never found it. Perhaps this can be attributed to joining the professional tennis circuit at eighteen years of age and coming from a communist country. While his American counterparts were filled with flash, Lendl was dead serious and did not feel compelled to entertain the crowd with anything other than by drilling forehands past his opponents. The most compelling component in Lendl's career was his well-scrutinized difficulty on the grass courts of the all-England club where his quest for a Wimbledon title eluded his tightly disciplined grasp.

On the golf course, I found that Lendl's discipline and focus resembled his approach to tennis. After being forced to retire from professional tennis prematurely because of a degenerative back injury, golf provided Lendl with a tranquillity fix as well as a physical reprieve. When we had our sit-down interview at a Celebrity Golf Association tournament in Providence, Rhode Island, a childlike enthusiasm for golf dissolved his rigid posture as his appetite for the game revealed itself. The transition seemed painless. The sport fulfilled his competitive desire for challenge. The perfectionist who has won eight Grand Slam titles, including the three U.S. Opens, three French Opens, and two Australian Opens, needs this game.

The potholes on the golf course can humble the greatest of athletes. In golf, one can't blame the bad calls or one's whiny opponents. A blazing forehand motion will not aid Lendl's goal, nor do foot speed and power come into play. But as Lendl tries to master the sport, his tremendous work ethic will help him become an accomplished golfer. The well-honed precepts that made him a great tennis player will carry over to his new challenge on the links, and that is three-fourths of the battle. Finally, Ivan Lendl has found happiness on grass.

LIGUORI: Ivan, what a career you've had. You were actually ranked number one for more consecutive weeks than any other player in tennis history.

LENDL: Yeah, I think the number-one ranking week by week is overrated. I don't think it's nearly as important as winning some Grand Slam tournaments.

LIGUORI: And you won eight Grand Slams.

LENDL: That's how you become number one, by winning the Grand Slam tournaments.

LIGUORI: You had a real interesting childhood, which I think has molded you obviously into who you are, who you were on the tennis court and also who you are on the golf course. Senior golfer John Brodie [former pro quarterback] was telling me that of all the guys out on the CGA, he thinks that you have more potential than all the other players at getting very good, really improving your game.

LENDL: Well, I don't know about it. I just know I enjoy the game, and I would like to get better.

LIGUORI: I was reading about your childhood, and your mom was very tough on you. Very strict. Your parents were both pretty good tennis players.

LENDL: Yes, they were both good tennis players, and that's the way they were brought up and that's the way they brought me up. Strict rules, a lot of love, but also strict rules, and as long as I followed the rules, everything was fine.

LIGUORI: Do you resent that looking back now? Do you think they were too strict?

LENDL: No, I didn't think they were way too tough. I thought, sometimes I didn't like the rules, but it was too bad. I thought it was good, actually. It doesn't really matter how tough the rules are as long as they are consistent.

LIGUORI: So do you apply the same kind of discipline to your own children, or are you a different kind of dad than your parents were to you, do you think?

LENDL: It's hard to tell. It was so long ago, and you don't really remember. You're looking at it from a different view. I'm sure if I looked at it from the point of view my kids look at it, maybe they would think I'm too tough or something like that.

LIGUORI: Really?

LENDL: And I don't think I'm nearly as strict as my parents were, and sometimes I'm saying to myself, well, maybe I should be a little stricter.

LIGUORI: When I look at what makes a person great as an athlete, one of the areas I study is their childhood. And you played a lot of tennis. Your mom took you out there, and you hit balls at a very early age, and she didn't show too much emotion. Even when you were playing tournaments, she didn't want you to look at them, as far as getting any kind of reaction from them. I mean, it was a real serious kind of thing.

LENDL: First of all, I didn't want to look at them because they take it too seriously. Every time I would miss a shot, if I would look over, I would see them going, "Oh no." You don't want that. My mother was still working, and I would go to kindergarten or to school, and she would work half-day. We would meet at home; she would cook lunch. She would go and practice, and she would take me along. I would just run around the tennis club, there was nothing else to do, and I would be a ball boy for somebody or play with other kids or just hit balls against the wall. I really enjoyed it, and I think if you want to find a common thread for all athletes who have achieved something, I think it's a love of the sport and nothing else.

LIGUORI: Yes, you really have to have that passion. They didn't push you too much, obviously.

LENDL: No, as a matter of fact, if I had a bad grade in school or misbehaved, the punishment was I wasn't allowed to go to the club.

LIGUORI: Well, it obviously worked.

LENDL: It worked.

LIGUORI: What was the feeling when you finally beat your mother in tennis? Because for a long time, she was a very good player herself.

LENDL: Yeah, she played very well, and it took me a while to beat her. But I beat her once, and then I couldn't beat her for a while again. I didn't like that.

LIGUORI: Did you and your parents play golf when you were young?

LENDL: No, they didn't know anything about golf.

LIGUORI: Really? I guess golf was not a popular sport in Czechoslovakia?

LENDL: No, I believe they had at that time two or three golf courses, not even eighteen holes.

LIGUORI: So when did you get exposed to golf?

LENDL: I got exposed to golf in the early eighties, in Boca West, Florida. I was their touring pro, and they had some outing out there for charity, and they asked me to participate in it. I said, "Come on, I can't play golf." And they said, "Oh, just show up on the first tee. It doesn't matter what you wear." I just came off the tennis court, changed my T-shirt, and went out with tennis shoes and all that. It was after the rain. It was quite an experience.

LIGUORI: You went out there never having swung a club and played?

LENDL: Unfortunately.

LIGUORI: What was it like?

LENDL: It was a little tough. I remember slipping, falling face down a few times with tennis shoes.

LIGUORI: You swung the heck out of the club.

LENDL: Well, I figured it's sitting there. How much easier it has to be than a tennis ball. Don't have to chase it.

LIGUORI: That's right. So how long after that initial experience did it take before you went back?

LENDL: The next day.

LIGUORI: Oh yeah, you loved it?

LENDL: I didn't like the fact that I didn't hit it well.

LIGUORI: Did you wear golf shoes the next day?

LENDL: I don't remember. Probably. Or it was dry. I don't know.

LIGUORI: Put on those cleats to help you out a little bit!

LENDL: I don't like wearing cleats, actually. I prefer the soft spikes, and I wear them all the time whenever I go. Either in the tournaments or in the rain, I wear soft spikes.

LIGUORI: So you were exposed to it just out of the clear blue. Liked it so much . . .

LENDL: I liked it, and I saw a potential in it for relaxation at tennis tournaments. I really enjoyed it because if you're at a tennis tournament, you play your match and you have, let's say, four hours on your hands after it. You don't want to do something where you get tired, and you don't want to sit in your room either. You can get a headache just doing that. So I started playing golf more, and I really enjoyed it. Just go out there and ride around in the cart for a couple of hours. And go back and get ready for the next match the next day.

LIGUORI: You're playing on the Celebrity Golf Association, and you've got your handicap down to what?

LENDL: I don't know. I don't turn cards in.

LIGUORI: You don't?

LENDL: I don't believe in handicaps.

LIGUORI: You don't?

LENDL: I don't believe that you should give me strokes only because you're better and you worked at it harder than I did. I don't believe that if I want to play somebody I can beat, and you're better than me, I shouldn't play with you. If I play with you, I learn and I shouldn't take strokes.

LIGUORI: So you never use handicaps?

LENDL: I would much rather they spot me the tees or I spot them the tees than strokes.

LIGUORI: Do you still follow the men's professional tennis Tour? Do you keep up with who's winning and who's doing well?

LENDL: I keep up with the results, and I watch if I have a chance and there is an interesting match going on.

LIGUORI: Do you enjoy it?

LENDL: I do. I really enjoy watching Pete Sampras and Andre Agassi play each other. That's the match I would make time for if I can.

LIGUORI: What do you think of Pete Sampras? I had him on my show, and he told me he was a fourteen handicap.

LENDL: I guess he has to work on his golf game. He's playing too much tennis.

LIGUORI: He says that when he's at home, in the few days when he's in Tampa, he watches golf. Either NBA or golf. When you're at home, do you watch more golf than tennis?

LENDL: Absolutely. I watch more ice hockey, actually. I really like ice hockey, and that's what I watch most.

LIGUORI: Did you play hockey when you were growing up?

LENDL: No, I didn't. I played a lot of street hockey with the boys in the winter in front of the apartment building we lived in. I enjoyed it. I always went to the hockey games since I was five, and it stayed with me.

LIGUORI: Hockey players take to golf very easily because it's a similar swing, on a lower plane. The tennis swing, though, is a totally different motion.

LENDL: Not if you play left-handed. It's like a backhand, a lot. A lot like backhands. A lot of tennis players who play double-handed backhand, they play golf that way.

LIGUORI: So was it, do you think, a little easier for you to pick up golf because of your tennis?

LENDL: I don't know. I really don't. You're getting too technical here for me.

LIGUORI: Now you've almost entirely focused on golf. Golf seems to be, aside from your businesses, your main focus in life.

LENDL: Oh, it's my hobby. I really enjoy the time outside, and playing and trying to learn a little more about the game. It has been a lot of fun so far.

LIGUORI: And you play left-handed.

LENDL: That's correct.

LIGUORI: And you putt left-handed.

LENDL: That too.

LIGUORI: In tennis, Ivan, grass was not your surface. You never won a Wimbledon title, and I read that you had said you were allergic to grass.

LENDL: It's true that you read it. It's not true that I said it.

LIGUORI: Is that right?

LENDL: I did say it, but they took it the way they wanted to instead of the way it was. They asked me what—obviously they noticed that I have allergies, hay fever. And they asked me what I'm allergic to, and I said I am allergic to grass. Obviously, it was very handy and convenient to say I don't play Wimbledon because I'm allergic to grass.

LIGUORI: I see.

LENDL: I said I don't play Wimbledon. I said I'm allergic to grass. And they put the two together even though it was never said in the same sentence. But that's typical media, so I don't worry about it.

LIGUORI: Now how about your back, because I know obviously your long tennis career came to a halt because of chronic back problems, and in golf, some of the top pros who play on the Tour have back problems, but you don't suffer any back ailments at all?

LENDL: No, my back [problems] come from the pressure of running up and down. I could play tennis if I didn't have to run. If I could stay in one spot, I could play tennis no problem. I can rotate. I just can't run, and in golf, obviously you don't run, and when you walk, you walk on soft grass. And that's one of the reasons I don't wear spikes most of the time. I just wear soft spikes because you can walk on the cart parts and anywhere. Plus, I'm lazy, so whenever I get into the car, I don't have to change shoes.

LIGUORI: And where did I read you once said, "In golf, you don't have any bad calls"?

LENDL: That's right. That's one thing I like about golf and I, maybe hate is a little strong word, but very much dislike about other sports. And that's that sports are being judged by people, whether it's figure skating, gymnastics . . .

LIGUORI: Very subjective.

LENDL: Diving, tennis—there are matches decided on bad calls. I really enjoy the sports where there is no human element. Swimming, track and field, golf—even though you can have some rulings in golf which can be questionable, but it's very rare from my experience so far.

LIGUORI: Do you get upset on the golf course when you're out there?

LENDL: I get mad at myself, but you don't necessarily see it. That's one thing good from tennis I learned is that you can miss a shot. And you have to forget it right away, and it really helps because in golf, I find if you get upset and you keep thinking about it, it only gets worse. It doesn't get better.

LIGUORI: I guess in golf, the experienced, wise golfer knows that you have to maintain your composure and you can't let your opponent see that you're getting upset. It really affects your game.

LENDL: Show me a sport where it helps.

LIGUORI: Well, that's a good point, but the rap on you when you were playing tennis was that you didn't show your emotions enough. People wanted to feel with you. They wanted to see the number-one player in the world really enjoy the wins and grieve the losses.

LENDL: Do you have to show on your face that you're happy and that's the only time you can be happy? Or can you be happy and you don't have to show it?

LIGUORI: Well, I think fans want to see "personality" on the court. Fans didn't see that humor and they wanted the number-one player in the world to show more emotion. I mean, it's the same criticism that Pete Sampras initially suffered from. People complain about his lack of personality on the court.

LENDL: I think that's really sad, actually, what Pete Sampras is going through. I mean, you have a guy who is probably good-looking. I'm not a woman to judge that, but . . .

LIGUORI: He's very good-looking.

LENDL: Okay, "very good looking." That's your quote. He dresses well. He behaves very nicely.

LIGUORI: Classy guy.

LENDL: He plays a great game. He is intelligent and so on, and he has to defend himself against the press and public for his behavior, and I think that's very sad. I think he should really be commended for his behavior. He should be the role model for the kids.

LIGUORI: Absolutely. I can't agree with you more. I think he's one of the nicest and classiest athletes, and really here you have a role model in a society where there are so few.

LENDL: He's not rebounding from [an] alcohol problem. He's not rebounding from [a] drug program. Why couldn't he be a role model like somebody who is overcoming a problem is a role model? I don't understand it and I never will.

LIGUORI: It's unfortunate that society often rewards negative behavior—it's an upside-down mentality.

LENDL: It's definitely upside-down in that case.

LIGUORI: When you look back on your career, do you ever feel like you should have not been as robotic on the court; to show more personality?

LENDL: I could have been any way I wanted on the court. I could have been killing the umpires if I wanted to. I could have been smiling all the way. But my job was not to do that. My job was to win the tennis matches, and that was the only objective I had, and I didn't really care much about anything else. If you win, it doesn't matter whether you smile or not. I don't think it does.

Sugar Ray Leonard

February 9, 1991, Madison Square Garden. The great Sugar Ray Leonard wanted to be a champion again. So he shed a few pounds to fight Terry Norris for the super welterweight title. Though I was a bit reluctant, I had to be there. We thought it was his last fight and he'd been such a great champion, but it was also one of those assignments that make you wince. Was Ray going back to the well once too often? Would the young and strong Norris bury a legend? I'd covered many of Leonard's fights when he was bigger than the sun. He was the first genuine made-for-television fighter, a real talent who had Howard Cosell and ABC-TV recording every significant moment of his career. In the annals of boxing, between Ali and Tyson, there was Leonard. But on this cold February night, Ray Leonard's magic would run out, and he would receive a whipping you'd think he'd never forget.

Five years later, we met in Seattle, Washington, at the Kenny G Golf Tournament to benefit the Starlight Foundation. I hadn't seen Ray since the night of his last fight, and I wondered how he was dealing with being out of the mega-spotlight. He looked great, still maintaining his fighter's physique. He seemed to be doing well, enjoying a successful marriage, living in a multimillion dollar mansion in Pacific Palisades, California. With his fighting days behind him, Ray had become a golf fanatic.

These days, when Leonard is not thinking of boxing comebacks, he's fighting with a little white ball. He continually hones his skills, but never gets the results he realized when training for a fight. Ray has to sense the irony of this stationary ball being harder to hit than Roberto Duran. Golf is the only sport that can humble championship athletes. In other sports, a champion's superior athleticism enables them to fake it, but golf is its own brand of truth serum, the ultimate challenge. Ray Leonard, a man noted for his ability to put blinding combinations together, is now trapped in a world of one shot good, two shots bad, athletic mediocrity—golf's own rabbit punch.

Despite the challenges and fun that golf provided for Ray and his buddies, his eyes during our sit-down interview couldn't hide the fact that golf was not the answer to the competitive peace he was looking for. There had been rumors in 1995 that he was interested in another comeback, a rematch

JAMIE SQUIRE/ALLSPORT

with Marvin Hagler, whom he barely beat in a controversial split decision in 1987. That fight was his first after a two-and-a-half-year layoff. He took this last great triumph and retired again the following day.

I guess great champions only remember the victories. Five years after the Norris whipping, Sugar Ray Leonard and I were talking golf. Ray smiled when I mentioned the possibility of another comeback, but he did not deny it. His intentions were as clear as the smile on his face. With a body still young enough to lie, Ray wanted back in.

A year after our interview, when I heard that Ray was making his fourth comeback, it was my turn to smile. I felt differently about Ray's most recent comeback. In the past I was bothered by athletes who attempted comebacks after their best days were behind them. I thought it was ego, money, or boredom. (How dare they get bored.) They missed the spotlight. (Who wouldn't!) The athletes who attempt comebacks will tell you it's simply because it's what they do best. Ray Leonard is a fighter, pure and simple. The same champion heart that helped the half-blinded Leonard save his career by knocking out Tommy Hearns in the late rounds of their first fight continues to beat. If he can get a fight he believes he can win, then why not? That sense of invincibility that great champions feel is still there. It is why he must try again.

I believe that golf helped drive Ray back to the ring. He's a decent golfer, but for legendary athletes, not being able to conquer the sport of golf leaves you thinking of other options. Beware of that little white ball. It can beat you up.

LIGUORI: Ray, you've only been playing for three years. That's not long.

SUGAR RAY: Three years. Well, considering. I love the game so much; for me, it's therapy. You challenge yourself, and there's always room for improvement. There's always room to learn something new. And I'm just having a great time. I wish I had found this sport years ago. My life would have probably been a lot easier, too.

LIGUORI: Really? Why do you say that?

SUGAR RAY: Because I find that you're dealing with nature. You have an opportunity to get out there, experiencing some of the most beautiful golf courses in the world, and it's just you against that little ball.

LIGUORI: Very tranquil.

SUGAR RAY: Very much so.

LIGUORI: You play regularly in Los Angeles, I would assume.

SUGAR RAY: Yes, I do. I play at the Riviera a lot, and I play Spanish Bay [on the Monterey Peninsula] with a friend of mine, Johnny—Johnny Gill. I play Detroit. I have a friend there, Walter Bridgeport, who I beat recently. He's a better golfer than I am, but I beat him big-time.

LIGUORI: Got to put that one in. A little jab, no pun intended.

SUGAR RAY: It's just a wonderful, wonderful game.

LIGUORI: Who do you play with at Riviera? There are so many big names who are members there.

SUGAR RAY: I play at least three times a week, maybe four times a week, and I go out there and hit fifty to one hundred balls. I play with Kenny G, Johnny Gill, and just my friends.

LIGUORI: Do you take a lot of lessons?

SUGAR RAY: I take a lot of lessons; now I do, which I think is vital. I think you try not to accumulate too many bad habits because it's tough changing a certain swing if you've been using that swing for so long. I've been given good advice, and I watch. I tend to emulate people who are pretty good golfers.

LIGUORI: You study some of the guys on the Tour?

SUGAR RAY: I do. I love Corey Pavin.

LIGUORI: U.S. Open Champ in 1995. Won the big one.

SUGAR RAY: Yes, he won the big one. I watch those guys, and I love the Senior Tour. I like Lee Trevino, Jim Dent. I like those guys. I just watch them. And Tiger Woods is a young man who is giving me inspiration because I watch this guy, this young kid actually. . . .

LIGUORI: Amazing. He's capable of outdriving pros on the Tour by fifty yards.

SUGAR RAY: I used to think my upper body strength would give me distance, which is actually a no-no. It's almost just the opposite. It's all rhythm and finessing the ball.

LIGUORI: It's all tempo.

SUGAR RAY: Tempo.

LIGUORI: It must have been difficult when you realized that hitting a golf ball doesn't have much to do with upper-body strength.

SUGAR RAY: Yeah, it was kind of a transitional period I was going through, and I'm still facing that problem sometimes because I really try to muscle the ball. I try to show that I can knock my ball further than the other guy. Take for example Cory Pavin. He's not big, but he has that nice delivery. And I try to out-muscle the ball. In fact, the ball out-muscles me, so that's a lesson.

LIGUORI: True. In boxing, your opponent reacts, trying to counterpunch. In golf, the ball is just sitting there. It's just you against you, basically.

SUGAR RAY: Right, and the thing about it is there should be no head movement. That ball is there. It's a stationary target. All you have to do is swing and hit the ball.

LIGUORI: So what could be so tough about that? Come on, Sugar!

SUGAR RAY: If I knew?

LIGUORI: Is golf tougher to get good at than boxing? I mean boxing, the guy's moving constantly. You're moving constantly. You have to deliver powerful blows against a moving target. In golf, it's a stationary ball. You only get one chance, though.

SUGAR RAY: One chance, yeah. Let's put it this way. There is such a major difference because in golf you can make a mistake, but in boxing, you make a mistake and it's somewhat disastrous. So there is a different mind-set. If you're playing with a couple of buddies, you get a mulligan, so it's okay. You can drop a ball, but in boxing, all you do is drop your opponent. You don't get mulligans or a second chance.

LIGUORI: Does the showman you were in boxing show up on the golf course?

SUGAR RAY: It showed up a week or so ago. I was in Las Vegas at the TPC. Fourteenth hole, par three. I was playing 128 [yards out] but with the wind, it was like 110 [yards]. I hit a pitching wedge. I made a hole in one.

LIGUORI: Congratulations.

SUGAR RAY: Thank you. It's a great feeling. It's like your child being delivered. It's a wonderful, wonderful experience.

LIGUORI: Was that your first one?

SUGAR RAY: First ever in three years.

LIGUORI: Not that everybody makes more than one, or even one. How did you react?

SUGAR RAY: Other than scream? I shook everybody's hand. Just gave them high fives. They actually gave me a plaque [that said,] "Hole in one," "TPC," and "Sugar Ray Leonard, June 17th, 12:30."

LIGUORI: That's fabulous.

SUGAR RAY: Time and everything. But it was great. It was a wonderful, wonderful experience.

LIGUORI: Can that compare to any of your biggest wins in boxing? That feeling?

SUGAR RAY: The hole in one? I think there's to a large degree that jubilant factor. You know, that excitement, that adrenaline, that euphoria—well, I don't know if euphoric is the word I want to use, but it's a great feeling. And the big fights that I won, it was just great. It's like, *Yes! Yes!*

LIGUORI: Similar, kind of?

SUGAR RAY: Yes, so it is similar I would say, yeah. But I get true satisfaction from playing golf.

LIGUORI: You play a lot, obviously.

SUGAR RAY: I play as much as I can, and wherever I can. I carry my clubs with me. Before I bring my luggage, I have my bag, my sticks as they call them.

LIGUORI: Your sticks. You travel with your sticks everywhere?

SUGAR RAY: Always. Everywhere.

LIGUORI: Are there any skills in boxing that help your golf swing? Anything physical or mental that you bring over from the sport of boxing?

SUGAR RAY: I think one of the key points and attributes is balance. To transfer the weight from right to left. Balance is a key. I think that has helped me out tremendously. But again, without allowing my upper body to take over.

LIGUORI: Do you think like a boxer on the course?

SUGAR RAY: Well, you know what happens. I get there, and when I'm over the ball, I really just relax. And that, too, has contributed to me playing a little better than I had played in the past. I'm relaxing. Just hit that little ball.

LIGUORI: You wouldn't consider coming out of retirement again? Look at some of these guys. George Foreman. You're nowhere near George Foreman's age, but look at the comeback he's made.

SUGAR RAY: But for me, it's always been mental. When I beat Hagler, it was tough for me to come back and fight anyone else. And they did ask me. Someone mentioned the fact that Marvin Hagler stated on some sports show that he wanted to fight me again. And I would definitely entertain the thought with him. Only him. No one else.[1] I don't need a career. I've had a career. I had a quite

[1] Sugar Ray Leonard came out of retirement yet again to fight Hector Camacho in 1997, and Camacho won in a fifth-round TKO.

successful career, and it would be just a one time only.

LIGUORI: But why Marvin Hagler? You've beat him already.

SUGAR RAY: Well, because he doesn't personally feel that I beat him, because he felt it was somewhat controversial because it was a split decision. And for whatever it's worth, he would be the only guy.

LIGUORI: So you're leaving it open?

SUGAR RAY: Well, there's a window of opportunity, and it's there.

LIGUORI: Do you miss boxing?

SUGAR RAY: No, not really. My career was great. And that's why I manage fighters. My career was wonderful.

LIGUORI: But why come back and fight Hagler?

SUGAR RAY: You know, it's difficult for you to understand that, as an athlete, we do what we've done for years and this is our nature. This is what we do. And it's not just boxing. It's basketball, it's football. If the guys could come back and get a contract, the football players who retired, they would come back. But it's not the same thing, because my sport is an individual sport. We can come back when we want to come back. Football, because of the franchise, they say, "No, you're too old." That's what's so great about boxing. You're pretty much your own man. Well, I was. I am.

LIGUORI: Your last fight with Marvin Hagler was in '87. Boxing experts say it was one of the biggest upsets ever. And you think because he wasn't happy with the split decision, you would go out and satisfy the skeptics out there. I mean, this happened years ago.

SUGAR RAY: There are no skeptics. It's not about skeptics. It's a personal matter. It's a man thing. I'm not a chauvinist, but it's a male thing. Guys understand.

LIGUORI: Is he saying you're chicken?

SUGAR RAY: Oh, no. I mean, that wouldn't work anyway. Guy's understand there's one guy on the street and the other guy on the street. One guy's from this neighborhood, that guy's from that neighborhood. And they may have tussled one time or another, and then five, eight, ten years later they sit in a bar and [one says,] "I beat you." [The other says,] "No, you didn't" They try it again. It's a male thing.

Jim Brown

One of the greatest athletes in history admits that golf is his favorite sport. Jim Brown, in New York City preparing to meet with the New York Theological Society to discuss their potential involvement in his Amer-I-Can program, was resting comfortably in his hotel room. Jim, Steve Geller, Lisa Edwards (our assistant), Ryan Wickline (our intern) and I had just returned from the Ernie Davis Heisman Memorial Dinner and Golf Tournament in Elmira, New York, an annual fund-raiser for the Ernie Davis community center. More than twenty-five sports personalities are flown up each year on the Corning private plane to help raise funds to support the young people who use the center.

I was happy to see Jim again. We have had a long history of intense discussions on both my radio show on WFAN and my *Sports Innerview* cable show. The last time we spoke, Jim was on my late night sports radio call-in show. It was early during the O.J. Simpson trial and the discussion became very heated. The sparks always fly when Jim is my guest. One of the things I admire about Jim is that he is never afraid to voice his opinion no matter how controversial it is. His convictions and wisdom flow from his mouth as fearlessly and effortlessly as when he plowed through defensive linemen during his legendary career with the Cleveland Browns. That evening we discussed, among other things, our mutual feeling that O.J. was guilty. It was still very early in the trial and few people were voicing their opinions publicly. The show rocked with callers and diverse opinions all night long.

Back in 1991, Street & Smith (sports publications) presented Jim with the all-time, all-pro award at their annual "Legends of the Game" Exemplary Player Dinner at the Downtown Athletic Club (DAC) in Manhattan. Judge Ken Molloy, a long-time father figure to Jim during his boyhood days in Manhasset, New York, was to present this prestigious award to Brown but to my surprise, when he was unavailable, Rudy Riska, of the DAC, asked me to give the tribute. I was honored, to say the least. I was a toddler in the early sixties when Brown set rushing records and racked up Most Valuable Player Awards and All-NFL honors. I had gotten to know Jim Brown, the individual, years after his playing days. I had sat in the early Amer-I-can meetings that were held in his house in the Hollywood hills—meetings where gang members from the Crips and the Bloods gathered to

JIM GILL/*THE LEADER*

talk about their differences and settle their disputes peacefully. Before entering Jim's house, everyone had to walk through a metal detector and check their weapons at the door. These were some meetings! At first, I wondered if I should enter the front door as several three-hundred pound guards secured the entrance. I looked at Steve, with eyes and mouth wide open and at the same time we uttered, "Should we go through with this?"

There were no signs of Jim's football career inside his living room as his focus was upon members of two of the most violent gangs in South Central Los Angeles. Yet Jim had them in the palms of his hands as he was preaching the gospel of the Amer-I-can program—that with proper life management skills and self-esteem, they can turn their lives around. I remember feeling part of something very special and realized at that moment that my friendship with Jim would last for a long time, even though our worlds often clashed.

The strength of Jim's convictions are undeniable. Although Jim has had scrapes with the law himself, he has turned his life around and embraces the challenge of sharing his time and experience with young people who need it most. His greatness on the football field fades a little every autumn as new gridiron heroes erase another of his accomplishments from the record book. But if he can make a positive contribution in the plight of young urban African-Americans, his great feats on the football field will be reduced to a mere footnote.

LIGUORI: Jim, I've seen you at a lot of these tournaments and you've been playing golf for as long as I've known you. Talk a little bit about your passion for golf.

BROWN: Golf is my favorite sport. Period. I was one of those people that, when I first won some clubs, I didn't play golf. I thought it was a silly game. I didn't understand why people loved it. I used to laugh at it until a friend of mine who golfed saw my clubs and said let's try it. That summer I started practicing and playing and I played everyday. And fell in love with it.

LIGUORI: And how long ago was that?

BROWN: It was when I was with the Cleveland Browns about thirty years ago. I used to practice until my hands would bleed. That first summer I shot a 77, my best score. So on and off all these years I've played golf. I loved to compete and play for money. They're lovely courses; I like the ambiance, I love the oceans, the trees, the grass. It's great companionship—you play with people you like. It's great competition on many levels, because on the first level, you compete against yourself, and the course. You want to do better. You then can set up a game and have handicaps, which is great. I don't like to take any strokes, I don't like to give strokes. I like to play with people better than me and beat them and mentally try to take their minds.

LIGUORI: What do you mean by mentally taking their minds?

BROWN: In golf, magic happens. Even if you are not the greatest golfer, and you have the confidence, and under pressure you can maintain your stroke and maintain your swing. And the anxiety and the stiffness and the fear don't come in, you can beat people. And there are money limits that people have, some people play good for five dollars, some play good for a hundred dollars. A lot of people can't play good for larger sums of money. But the key is to do things at times when your opponent doesn't think you should. And to maintain a certain calm and a certain confidence when the pressure is there and if you do that three or four times, it starts getting around. So, under certain circumstances, if you do it enough the fear sets in and then the word of mouth gets around. After a while they won't play for the same amount of money anymore.

LIGUORI: Do you have to gamble and bet to enjoy this game?

BROWN: Golf is a gambler's sport. But it isn't for the money. It's like backgammon. When you don't play backgammon for money it's a different sport. If you don't play for money, you don't know if you can play in golf. That money puts the pressure on. The one thing you hate to do is to have to go into your pocket after you play somebody and pay them. It's the embarrassment and humiliation of going in your pocket because when you go in your pocket and pay, there's nothing else to talk about. You just shut up and wait until the next time you get a chance to play the guy. I love that stimulus of playing for money.

LIGUORI: What's the most you ever won?

BROWN: In Cleveland, over the course of one summer, I won thirty thousand dollars.

LIGUORI: Doesn't everyone want to say that "I beat Jim Brown at something?"

BROWN: Of course, Joe Louis (boxing great) is the typical golf story. Joe Louis was a golfer and everybody across the country said they beat Joe Louis. And what I say, "This is no Joe Louis guys. You guys can go around and say you beat Joe but you can't say that you beat me."

LIGUORI: Tell me about the time you sneaked into The Masters.

BROWN: One of my great heroines was a woman named Maggie Hathaway who had integrated a golf course in Los Angeles, and who was a freedom fighter. She was a correspondent and she got some credentials to cover The Masters when Lee Elder became the first black to play in The Masters. I flew down with her and she couldn't get me in. So we decided that I would put on a chauffeur's cap and drive her in. And that's how I saw my first Masters.

And I'll tell you something about The Masters. The Masters is a tournament where the white players love it because it's like the good ole' boys club, with a lot of good rules and a great manicured golf course and all of those traditions. A part of that tradition was that Caucasian clause. And then you had the black caddies with the white coveralls on. Then you have the tournament name *Masters*. So you got this name *Masters*. So to me, it is like the tradition of the South, not based on segregation but based on the life that white Southerners love, exclusive, these high standards for the white folks, lovely course and this whole tradition. And I've never seen anyone really spell that out. So a lot of the players that loved it didn't even realize that they were loving it because it had that *kind* of tradition. I'm not saying they were racists. So if you look at The Masters and you look at the praise that it gets, it's almost a slap in the face to a black American because it's like the film *Gone with the Wind*. It's a classic for you and a tragic kind of a film for me because my image from it is Butterfly McQueen screaming and acting simple. And Big John or whoever it is that's trailing that chariot saying, "I'm a comin' Miss Scarlett, I'm a comin'." I don't like *Gone with the Wind* but I can understand you liking it because Scarlett O'Hara was a tough chick. She was a bad bitch that ate up Rhett Butler, tore him to pieces. So if I were a white female, I would love *Gone with the Wind*. If I was a strong white man I might not like Rhett Butler because the only thing he could say in the end was, "I don't give a damn," or something like that, as he was walking out.

LIGUORI: Yes, I really enjoyed *Gone with the Wind*. It's a rarity to see such an independent and strong woman on screen—especially back then. Tell me what your thoughts were seeing Tiger Woods win The Masters by an unprecedented 12 strokes.

BROWN: I have admired that family so much because of the father. He's special to me. And the mother in her own way was special and the way they dealt with their son and the way he carried himself. I've been aware of Tiger for many years. We saw the talent before The Masters. I saw a couple guys choke with Tiger, the effect his game had on everybody, so when he got in The Masters that first day I didn't know what was going to happen. But, when he came back with a thirty on the back nine, I knew it was on.

My favorite moment in The Masters was after he made that putt to set the record, he went off and hugged his father. That had tremendous significance for me because that's who he hugged. It wasn't Phil Knight of Nike or Donald Trump, it was his father. It was one of the greatest moments for me emotionally. I thought it was a very great moment in the history of sports.

LIGUORI: You have told me that you admire the way Earl Woods has handled Tiger, particularly the way Earl and Tiger make their own decisions, independent of Phil Knight and IMG. [International Management Group represents Tiger Woods.]

BROWN: Most of the black athletes today should take note of that relationship and understand the difference between them and Earl Woods and Tiger Woods. Earl is his own man and Tiger is his own man and they have opinions, they have intelligence, they have goals and they have purpose. They come alive so unlike the average black athlete today who is basically a puppet, trying to say the right things, or dancing around to make more money. Tiger himself has an honesty about him. He says, "Hey, I come to a tournament to win, why else would I come?" That's not braggadocio, that's real. He's articulate, and he's extremely bright and he's been schooled and trained and he has worked hard and his purpose so right on. He is a biological reality. He is bright enough to understand that, to have coined a phrase on that. To publicly speak that regardless of what African-Americans want him to claim. To give his mother's culture credit. To give his father's culture credit like nobody does. When he came down recognizing that he is perceived as an African-American breaking something down, he credited Teddy Rhodes and Lee Elder and Charlie Sifford with the things they did which allowed him to be able to do this. He gave respect to them.

LIGUORI: What kind of impact do you think Tiger Woods will ultimately have on not only sports but society as well?

BROWN: Greatness is not playing golf. Greatness is for each and every human being to live a life based on character, morality and treating people as you'd have them treat you. I choose my high school coach over everybody else, but most people don't even know who he is. To me Paul Robeson is the greatest man in modern history because of his sacrifice, his activism, the Peekskill Riots and his cause for freedom, equality and justice.[1] If you deal with Harriet Tubman, if you deal with Branch Rickey, now you're talking about the kind of greatness that is great. Because greatness is tied into human development.

The greatness of a Tiger Woods and Earl Woods is the character that I'm talking about, having their point of view. Recognizing the truth of his racial mixture. Giving that respect. Having a great game, working hard all their lives, developing a plan. Why are they so great this year? Because they won The Masters? And because the ratings go up? And they attract people? It will be in their longevity and if they can change the crime and the drugs and the prison system and make life better for all Americans, that's when they will truly be great. That is a lot of work! They may have a good start in that direction. But it's a journey.

LIGUORI: How do you feel other players on the Tour relate to Tiger?

BROWN: The resentment is a negative take on this [issue]. The positive is, I've heard Jack Nicklaus, who does not give praise easily, and is considered the best golfer who ever lived, gave Tiger the utmost praise. I think Jack was wonderful and honest. I don't think there is an ounce of resentment there.

LIGUORI: What goes through your mind when you are standing over a golf ball, about to hit? What do you think about?

BROWN: I think about my take away. I don't have a good shoulder turn and so I don't really keep my left arm as stiff as I should to get

[1] Paul Robeson was the first black football All-American. He graduated with honors from law school. He became one of the highest-paid, most respected black performers in the first half of the twentieth century and sacrificed fame and fortune for his principles on civil rights.

that particular movement where all your power and accuracy come from. I have to think of not just picking the club up and cutting across it. I have to think of the shoulder and the turn and waiting, not rushing, not swinging from the top.

LIGUORI: Do you visualize your swing prior to hitting?

BROWN: No, I don't use visualization with my swing. I use my mind saying turn and don't rush and use the left side.

LIGUORI: Have you taken any lessons?

BROWN: No. I read the Ben Hogan book and I go and practice. I never wanted to take lessons because I never wanted to be that great a golfer. If I wanted to mechanically play the game, I could go take instruction and do all of that. But the fun for me in golf is to read and to listen. I don't want to go through the process of becoming a champion because that is going to take hours of practice and commitment. I want to score in the seventies and once in a while shoot par. If I use what I know correctly, I can play pretty well.

LIGUORI: What is your best round of golf?

BROWN: Last year, I shot a sixty-nine at Western Avenue golf course in Los Angeles.

LIGUORI: Can you recall one of your most memorable rounds of golf?

BROWN: Playing with Bill Russell at Pebble Beach. We played thirty-six holes a day at Spyglass, Cypress Point, Pebble and we stayed at Del Monte Lodge. I always enjoy playing with Bill because he is a very bright guy and one of my dear friends. He is a competitor.

LIGUORI: Do you enjoy playing with fellow athletes because they share your intensity and competitive spirit?

BROWN: Oh yes. Most great athletes are that way. There is a mental wall you can't usually penetrate. They have very strong mentalities. So when you mess with them, you just have to beat them because they are very competitive. More so than the average person because the average person is used to making a lot of excuses. The athletes' excuses are on a different level. The mental toughness is different.

LIGUORI: What do you bring from the football experience to the golf course?

BROWN: I got more in the classroom than on the football field and I emphasize education more that I emphasize sports. So when I went to football, the game did not offer me anything except an opportunity to use all the things that I could use. I brought psychocybernetics to football, visualization and all of that. For me to perform on a weekly basis and keep up a standard of some kind of excellence, I had to do things that had nothing to do with football. I studied other football players. I dealt with the physical understanding of my own body. All that is a mental process. I did not bring anything from football. I brought the football experience. I brought the confidence of having been a champion and having competed against the best. Football gave me that. It gave me an arena that I could apply my ability to test it out. Because until I played in that arena, I did not know if all these theories would work in that arena. But they did work. And I was a champion. I know if I work hard, think hard and if I'm tenacious and do things I know how to do, I can win.

LIGUORI: Do you find golf the ultimate competition? In golf, the challenge lies between you and the ball. In football, you had to battle the opponent.

BROWN: The level of competition in professional football was the highest level of competition I was in. I'm with fine tuned instruments who are out there with no fear of me, most of them. Ready to compete forever. That's like holding your breath for nine years. There is more pressure when you are playing with the team because you have got to fit in, perform at a certain time. You can not have it your way. It's not an individual performance. It doesn't work that way. Sometimes I wanted the ball but it was time to throw a pass.

LIGUORI: So the variables in football were much more challenging to you?

BROWN: On that level, yes. In golf, you do have to execute and deal with the variable of shot making. But they are consistent from the standpoint of the game itself. The level of competition would be different. So golf is my favorite game because of all those individual things that I can enjoy and I don't have to be on the top level to enjoy.

If I were to pick a sport to be the toughest to compete on in the highest level, it would be baseball. For me, there are so many fascinating elements in golf. The elements in football are not that fascinating. The game of golf, having all those clubs, having a wind factor, a rain factor, a green speed factor, having sand, having water, having luck, having bad luck, making choices, that's exciting.

LIGUORI: How did you feel [laughing] about my beating you in the long drive competition [at the Ernie Davis Heisman Memorial Golf Tournament]?

BROWN: Where I saw the ball seemed impossible. I don't know where the red tees were, but it was evidently great driving. I think you are a great athlete and I'm glad to see you playing golf because golf is far superior to tennis.

LIGUORI: You enjoy betting on the golf course. Have you ever played with anybody who's cheated and what have you done about it?

BROWN: In golf, I don't believe that there is a human being who won't cheat. I'm not claiming that everybody has cheated, I'm just saying that I don't think that there is a human being that won't cheat because of the nature of the game. The rules of the game are so intricate that you can cheat and not really feel you are cheating. If the person goes in a divot in the middle of a fairway, after hitting a wonderful drive, they might move out of the divot. That's cheating. But in their mind, the divot should not be there. I don't follow anybody around and watch them. What they do is their business. I don't expect perfection out of my opponents in golf.

LIGUORI: Have you ever played golf with O.J. Simpson?

BROWN: Yes, I have played golf with him at Riviera.

LIGUORI: Before the trial?

BROWN: Of course before the trial. I wouldn't play with him now. O.J. was always nice to me. He was always honest about making money. He was learning how to play at the time I played with him. I played as a guest at his club with him and some of his friends. It was very enjoyable.

LIGUORI: Have you seen him since the trial?

BROWN: No.

LIGUORI: I know early in the trial you said on my WFAN radio show and on other shows that you thought O.J. Simpson was guilty. What is going through your mind now that this entire case is over and he is playing golf somewhere?

BROWN: In this case, I think most of the people should shut up. I don't think there are any heroes. I don't think Johnnie [Cochran] is a hero. I think Marcia Clark should shut up. I think Chris Darden should shut up. I think they all should basically let it go. There is no way that whatever they say is going to make it better unless there is a confession. I think it is a tragic situation with no winners. When I think about it, I just think of tragedy, a bunch of losers. I don't know one winner. I don't see anybody that I admire who came out of the case.

I was looking for justice because I detested the hypocrisy of a false hero, which I wrote about in my book [*Out of Bounds*, 1989].

I thought that White America was fooling themselves, because they pick black folks who don't rock the boat and I thought that was false. And then to watch a trial and listen to people and see it switch all the way around, to now he's [O.J.] dealing with the black community, was crazy to me. I wanted people to look at individuals who would have an opinion. I wanted people to look at the *real* part of black athletes, not wanting you to be a puppet to be popular. In my book I said O.J. was a phony. He didn't care that I said it. He laughed at me saying that he was going to make money and I'm not. If you're phony enough in America you can make money because then you can be popular. But if you tell the truth, people aren't going to like you so you can't make money.

LIGUORI: I know you've been critical of Michael Jordan in the past for not speaking out on certain issues.

BROWN: I think Michael is a nice human being. I think he carries himself well. He is a great athlete and I think he is smart. But he is the perfect example of corporate America, the marriage between a black athlete and corporate America. Which means that he can not comment on things in a certain way because it would mess that image up. I don't think he can be in the company of certain people. He is limited and he has bought into that because on one hand, he is one of the most popular Americans alive so he can hold that up to you and say, "Look man, people love me, black, white, everybody loves me so what are you talking about?" I'm saying, yeah, but the way to be popular is to know how to talk out of all sides of your mouth. That's how you get popular. Popularity is not a sign of greatness. In fact, in most cases, it's just the opposite. Usually people become popular later because people understand what they were saying. Usually when somebody is talking a higher truth, the general public doesn't understand it at first and it takes them a while to catch up. And usually the person is dead.

LIGUORI: And then on the other end of the spectrum, Dennis Rodman will say and do anything to bring attention to himself. How do you feel about him?

BROWN: Dennis is obviously making a lot of money. It is unfortunate he has nothing to say. God help him if he doesn't come out of a slump. All of that purple hair and all that stuff will suddenly turn off the world. Dennis was a dedicated defensive player, a dedicated rebounder, a role player that makes the team better, he is smart in a game, he hustles, he is in shape, he runs the floor.

That makes everything else work. But if you want to see a tragic figure, let him have two more bad games and Utah win[2], and you'll see basically the end of Dennis Rodman because that hairstyle is looking nastier and nastier.

LIGUORI: You've played golf with everyone from Jack Nicklaus to Lawrence Taylor. Who haven't you played with who would give you a thrill?

BROWN: I would like to play with some fine female [laughing]. I'd like to play with Annika Sorenstam. I like to see her hitting the ball. She has a demeanor about her that I admire. She has style and class. She has a look on her face that I like that probably masks who she really is. There is probably steel inside, but she looks so innocent.

The guy that really is tragic to me is [Greg] Norman. In The Masters he wouldn't say he choked. He said he had a couple of bad shots. That's choke-o-rino. The only way you can't hold onto six strokes *is* a choke. That's what we do in golf. It illustrates the choke more than any other sport. In basketball, you can miss a free throw. But in golf, you hook that sucker dead left, that arm stiffens up on you.

LIGUORI: How do you feel about the Fuzzy Zoeller comments directed toward Tiger Woods [host of the 1998 Champions Dinner at The Masters] in which he said, "[Tell] him not to serve fried chicken next year. Got it? Or collard greens or whatever the hell they serve."

BROWN: It was a media-made thing and I love the media. But frankly I don't care too much about what anybody says. I'm sure Tiger could care less. But it's a media-driven thing and you have to respond to the media. Fuzzy and Tiger just couldn't get together. Tiger had to make a statement for the general public and Fuzzy had to pay for it.

LIGUORI: So his comments didn't bother you?

BROWN: It had nothing to do with me [laughing]. I like seafood. I don't wear my blackness on my shoulder, I wear my human thing on my shoulder. I don't think there are too many people superior to me because in the eyes of God, I'm pretty cool and I'm satisfied with that.

[2] At the time of this interview the Chicago Bulls and Utah Jazz were tied 2–2 in the 1997 NBA Finals. Dennis Rodman's production was minimal.

Hollywood

Sylvester Stallone

Sylvester Stallone knows how to be a star. Seconds before the cameras rolled for our sit-down interview, he adjusted his chair to a preferred angle and subtly showed me who was in control. "You know," he said, those eyes staring at me, "I can leave whenever I like." Ouch. I'd come to talk about golf, and here he was landing a verbal jab. Fortunately, I was ready. Everything that led up to this interview had conditioned me to take a punch. It was what made talking with Sylvester Stallone exciting as well as nerve-racking.

There, sitting before me, was Rocky I, II, III, IV, and V, not to mention three Rambos and an assortment of other larger-than-life action heroes. Exercise and surgery has allowed Stallone to maintain his Popeye-like biceps and chiseled frame. The tough but sweet face, the droopy brown eyes were all there, qualities as familiar as the *Rocky* theme song.

After hundreds of interviews with athletes over the last thirteen years, including legendary sports figures like Joe DiMaggio, Mickey Mantle, Nancy Lopez, Martina Navratilova, and Jim Brown, there was a special excitement to Stallone. Here was an underdog who'd made art out of sport. He'd done it his way. He'd been a struggling actor-writer who stubbornly insisted on starring in his own film. And then he'd pulled it off, taking talent, enterprise, and most pleasing to us mortals, persistence, to turn the story of Rocky Balboa into a raging success—a cultural icon.

On the other hand, life in the public eye has jaded his initial spirit of refreshing innocence. No matter how far he and Rocky Balboa had come from those mythical Philadelphia streets, no matter how much money he'd made, there was still this edge to Stallone that cried out to be taken seriously. The invasion of tabloid journalism has made him leery of interviews. Stallone's media persona is now governed by control. He will participate in the culture of celebrity, but strictly on *his* terms.

Consequently, when golf pro Jim McLean [of the Jim McLean Golf Academy at the Doral Resort and Spa in Miami] and his then assistant Nannette Lopuszynski, mutual friends of Stallone and myself, asked Stallone if he'd talk with me about his newfound passion for golf, Stallone took control. He would talk with me—in less than twenty-four hours. It was like one of those pop quizzes you get in school. Flying from New York to Miami, I quickly studied my Stallone file, rustled up a production crew, and strategized the line of questioning. I was ready and more excited than I'd ever been for any interview.

The paranoia was quickly justified. Stallone's feet were getting colder than a nervous groom's. He wanted to shoot the interview in another setting. He had second thoughts about the thirty-minute length. He didn't want us shooting certain things that we usually shot with every subject. Nannette told me he had almost decided to bag the whole thing. But like a true Rocky aficionado, I remained persistent, determined to, as Stallone's pugilistic alter ego had said, "Go the distance." With gentle tenacity, we overcame his objections and agreed to fair terms.

K. WINTER/PLANET HOLLYWOOD/REUTERS/ARCHIVE PHOTOS

When Stallone finally showed up in the beautiful room we had spent hours lighting and preparing, I felt I was having an out-of-body experience. Here was my chance to meet the man and the mind behind the celluloid image. I reacted to his initial jab by slipping the punch. "Sure, no problem, but I think you are going to enjoy this." Trying to put him at ease, my opening line introduced Stallone as a Renaissance man. Grinning that familiar aw-shucks grin, Stallone melted comfortably into his armchair.

What followed was a delightful candid discussion about his life and its relationship to golf. Just as boxing had once given meaning to a challenging phase of his life, so has golf emerged as the working metaphor for his current struggles. And I mean working. He approaches his golf game diligently, putting in more time and dedication than many professionals. Any free moment, whether on a movie set in full costume or at home in his recreation room, is spent hitting balls into the net. Golf instructors show up at venues all over the world to keep him straight. Though at the time he'd been playing for only two years, Stallone was already down to a twelve handicap, with his sights set on reaching single digits.

Watching him crush the ball on the range with his Taylor-made Burner Bubble was both entertaining and compelling. I've seen many professionals up close, but I've seldom heard a louder sound of club connecting with ball than when Stallone smacked his drives. At a surprisingly diminutive five-foot-eight, he just killed every ball. His drives average 270 yards, and the sound was even more amplified under the covered driving range.

But just as movie stars favor one side of their face for a profile, so does

Stallone prefer to keep the rest of his game carefully guarded. At the time, he kindly requested we not watch him play his round.

He did admit that his short game still needs lots of work. That was understandable. Looking at his bulging biceps, it's hard to imagine him executing a delicate pitch shot. Stallone's game is "still in production," but given his track record, there's no question he'll orchestrate another Cinderella story. Maybe it will be titled, *Yo, Golf!*

▽

LIGUORI: Sylvester, you're a movie man extraordinaire, you collect art, you write novels, you play polo and now golf. You're such a Renaissance man.

STALLONE: Ah, well, I don't know about that.

LIGUORI: Tell me about your passion for golf.

STALLONE: Well, I just thought that, eventually, I was so curious about the game of golf because I'd grown up watching hours and hours of it on television and never really understanding it. And then after I played polo for well over twenty years, I thought I can't go much further in that sport. I've enjoyed it, and I've taken my falls and my lumps, so I started golf. I mean, there's got to be something to it. So just out of sheer curiosity and an overdeveloped sense of masochism, I decided to take it up, and here I am.

LIGUORI: Is it frustrating for you? I mean, I saw you hit some. You hit the ball very well, but when you get out there, are you frustrated sometimes or do you just have fun with it?

STALLONE: It is. I'll tell you what. I thought marriage is tough. That's just a walk in the park, believe me. This is like going over Niagara Falls in a barrel. What people don't understand and I almost take exception to it—but then I have to consider the source—"It's an old man's sport." It's "this" sport, it's slow, it's boring. I say, equate it to chess. If you're watching a chess game, I'll bet it's really boring. If you're playing it, your mind is spinning, it's burning, your hair is almost on fire with constant anxiety and anticipation. The same is true of golf. It's a very, very psychological game that gets into your blood because it's you against you, and there's no one else to blame. And that takes its toll.

LIGUORI: You're very intense about everything you do. I remember reading, when you were nineteen, you would hone your vocabulary by picking a word from the dictionary and using it every day. Do you approach your golf game with that kind of diligence?

STALLONE: Very much so. I think that having played just a little bit over two years, the biggest problem that one has is their ambitions or their sense of ability, as far as seeing their inability to do it. I mean, it's a sport that really preys on extraordinary dexterity. Maybe it's the hardest hand-eye coordination sport in the world. I mean, I played polo, which is tough, hitting a ball at forty miles an hour, seven feet off the ground, on a galloping horse while people are trying to kill you! But this is even worse! You know what the difference is in polo and in any other sport is there's an excuse factor. You have guilt maintenance and an excuse factor built in. "The ball bounced this way," "It was the horse who stepped on it." In golf, you're blameless, folks, and that's the beauty of it.

LIGUORI: And you have so much time to think between shots, and a great shot keeps you coming back. There's a great quote here that Mickey the trainer in one of the *Rocky* movies said, "You're going to eat lightning and crap thunder. You're going to become a very dangerous person." Could he have been referring to your golf game?

STALLONE: Very much so. One of my greatest fears is when people say, "Why don't you wanna play in somebody's tournament?" I say, "Because if the people stand down that fairway, my lawsuits are gonna go through the roof." It'll look like the Blitzkrieg in Russia in 1942. There'd be bodies littering the golf course. I'm a little hesitant about actually taking it [my game] to the course itself. Also, the mere fact that it's Rocky and Rambo—every time you get up, they're expecting you to rip the hide off the ball. You just can't play a normal game. You have to be kind of like movie magic-ish.

LIGUORI: Do you find that it's tough to live that down?

STALLONE: Oh, yeah. It puts undue pressure [on me]. I think that golf itself is tough, just peer pressure. When you have an image of a super boxer or a super warrior that is basically a celluloid image, people automatically equate you to be that good in everything. It's just not so.

LIGUORI: What about your physique, because obviously you're very diligent about working out, and in golf, you don't see a lot of guys out there who have the great build that you have.

STALLONE: Here's what I believe. I believe, for example, like if I'm working in the gym, I have a golf club with me usually, and between sets, you are constantly swinging so the muscle [is] building. And you literally build an entire new set of muscles every six months, so they're all completely refreshed that you are educating them. It isn't what I call "dumb muscle." You have many bodybuilders who come out with twenty-inch arms, but the only thing they can do is this and this. I'm not degrading that. That's their sport. Now if they wanted to take that and move it into any sport, they would have to lift weights, and as soon as the muscle is still in its heated form, if it's bowling, if it's basketball, then the muscle starts to develop an intelligence. Actually that's an odd thing. The muscle is stupid and always will be. The mind will now be able to focus in and educate the muscle to do pretty much what it wants to do. That's why boxing has gone through such a revelation lately. Weights have always been passé; [people say] they slow you down. No, it doesn't, it speeds you up. It's more horsepower. You just have to know how to use it. And I think that a lot of golfers would benefit, most probably from leg exercises. The biggest problem I have is in the chest area because when I hold the club, I can not get it flat like some of the great golfers. [Stallone holds his arms out in front of him and shows how his chest gets in the way.] I'm in a position where I have to play it a little bit more unorthodox to get through it.

LIGUORI: I hear you practice your swing everywhere.

STALLONE: In every movie, I have to practice in the uniform. In *Demolition Man* [1993], I'd play golf during the day in the net, in the *Demolition* outfit. In *Cliffhanger* [1993], I'm covered in cleats and spikes and rope, and in *Judge Dredd* [1995], it's basically a suit of armor. Now you try swinging in that.

LIGUORI: It's good training. Now tell me, do you get the same feeling in golf or can you equate any of the feeling that you got in *Rocky* when you ran up to the top of the Philadelphia Art Museum and it was just so exhilarating, so inspirational? Have you experienced that feeling in golf yet?

STALLONE: Oh yes. It is a game of imperfection, and when you happen to have a momentary slice of glory, you almost feel immortal for a few seconds. You just savor because there's so much work and the mere fact that this extraordinary occurrence—the stars align, the planets just lined up perfectly, and it all works. I've worked harder at this than any facet of my career, which is a sad statement, but it's true. I mean, I really have found myself to be absorbed by the psychology of the game. Really, that's what it's all about.

LIGUORI: There's a great quote here that I read where you said, "Art is like playing football in the dark, you don't know when you're gonna get tackled. You just go for it." In golf, do you go for it? Are you the kind of guy in golf where you just lay it up to play it safe or would you go for it?

STALLONE: My nature, I tend to go for it. I think that again is probably not the smartest way to play golf, but it's kind of the way I've played my life. I automatically play every hole like it's a birdie hole. If it's a par three, I play it like it's a par two. If it's a par four, I play it as a par three. In other words, I try to put those barriers up which make me a little bit less inhibited and makes me go for something that normally you would be a little tentative. And if you blow it, you blow it, but at least something happens. At least with me you develop a dampened fear factor. You become a little bit more bold. But there will be a time when you will have that decision and you kind of, like, adapted yourself to go with the fear.

LIGUORI: Much like Rocky. He always lived up to the challenge.

STALLONE: Always, yeah.

LIGUORI: But I know you're different from him. Some similarities, a lot of differences.

STALLONE: Yo, golf! [Stallone says with a smile.]

LIGUORI: Now tell me, is there one player out there on the Tour whom you admire the most? Do you have a favorite player?

STALLONE: I'd like to get to know 'em. One of them I played one round with, which I'll never forget, was Ray Floyd. I think he's really fantastic because Ray, besides being a brilliant technician, he brings about a philosophy that has kept him at the height of his game for many, many years. That I enjoy. John Daly and I have met a few times, and I really like John. I think that he brings a certain kind of controversy which is kind of exciting, I think, in an otherwise very staid game. He's an explosive character on and off the course, which to me seems kind of mythic in a way.

LIGUORI: Any favorite teacher?

STALLONE: At first—this is interesting—Jim McLean, I'm working with now, is a fantastic coach. He's a very gentle soul and extremely instructive and knows how to pinpoint areas and not be, as I would be heavy-handed. It's a real gift. I also have taken lessons with, in the beginning from David Leadbetter, who is also a brilliant teacher and needs no introduction. His technique is extraordinary. I was in no way ready for him. It's like, excuse me, you're gonna learn to box and your first fight will be Mike Tyson. It's a little much. These teachers, Jim McLean and David

Leadbetter, these guys are real masters. They really are.

LIGUORI: You certainly have the mental game for it. And the athletic talents, too.

STALLONE: Well, I'm trying. I really want to do well at it. I think it's a lifetime commitment. It really is a marriage between yourself, and there's no divorcing it. You'd better make it work.

[On the range at the Jim McLean Golf Academy at the Doral Resort and Spa in Miami, Florida.]

LIGUORI: What's your drive average, Sylvester?

STALLONE: About 265, 270. I wouldn't mind, I'd be happy at 240 if they were okay.

LIGUORI: Would you say driving is the best part of your game?

STALLONE: The best part of my game, I think, is the amount of money I spend on lessons. It's keeping the economy going. I think that's it.

[Golf instructor Jim McLean walks over and watches Stallone slice a drive.]

MCLEAN: When he hits it well, he hits it 280, 290. It's really not 240. I've been trying, for one thing, to get him to smooth out a little bit, like that drive right there. That's easy 280 right there. Very supple with his swing, and very strong. The next goal of course is to work really on the short game. Sometimes he opens up a little quick, and the ball goes to the right, so when he does this little drill where he drops his right foot back [McLean demonstrates], closes his stance, freezes the left side, or he can feel himself hit against a real firm left side, his body doesn't open up so quick, and it's easy to hook the ball. So it's a good deal.

STALLONE: It has a tendency to go left, which I like.

MCLEAN: Most people that begin are definitely going to be on the outside of the ball, slicing the ball.

STALLONE: So if I can get this thing radically going in that direction, then eventually I'll find a happy medium.

[Stallone hits another drive and then adjusts his stance.]

STALLONE: Now I'll try to go back to a normal thing.

[He blasts another one, this time straight.]

MCLEAN: You see that? Gorgeous.

LIGUORI: That's about 260, 270.

[They all laugh. He departs with a smile, holding his driver in front of the camera to show off his Sylvester the Cat head cover.]

STALLONE: Over and out. Thank you very much. The next club you'll see me at is a nightclub.

Joe Pesci

I was quite nervous. Joe Pesci has a way of intimidating people. I wouldn't want to meet the characters he played in films like *GoodFellas* and *Raging Bull*, a little too unhinged for my taste. Could it all be acting? God forbid I piss him off. He might grab my pen and stab me to death, like he did to that poor sucker in *Casino*. He can't be that explosive in real life, I thought, reassuring myself with deep breathing and the knowledge that my chances of getting him for an in-depth interview were slim. I told myself that Joe Pesci is a superb actor, not the lunatic of Martin Scorcese's celluloid imagination. He liked to play golf, so how bad could he be? My competitive spirit returned. I knew it would be a challenge to book Pesci, but it would be a lively show if I could get to him. I was right on both accounts.

I soon found that getting Joe Pesci to agree to a thirty-minute interview was like making sense of a Ross Perot speech. Almost impossible. His films sell themselves, so you don't find him out there making the rounds of the promotional circuit. He's up there in the major leagues with the likes of Tom Cruise and Michael Jordan. We were going to have to be more than resourceful to nail him. It took some time and serious perseverance, but finally Pesci agreed to the interview, and we headed for Palm Springs.

It was my coproducer Steve Geller's job to ensure no last minute change of plans might prevent Pesci from making our appointment. We needed Steve to hang with Pesci as he golfed, and be right there to escort him to our interview location. He was never to let Pesci out of his sight. Steve walked eighteen holes with the actor, videotaping the entire round of golf, on the lookout for intruders that might steal away our reluctant interviewee. Once Pesci finished his game, it was Steve's mission to separate him from the throng of fans, spectators, and the curious that shadow a movie star in public. With the timing and bravado of a wise guy, Steve hustled Pesci away from the mob and onto his golf cart, hightailing it to our interview site.

Once in the golf cart, the actor lived up to his screen persona, protesting in salty language the ten-minute cart ride from the golf course to our location. "We're driving twenty minutes for a fuckin' five minute interview," Pesci wisecracked. Steve did his best to assure the impatient Oscar winner that the interview wouldn't take too long. Oh boy, this was not going to be easy.

PAUL LESTER

When they arrived, I quickly offered him a beer. We settled ourselves outside under the late afternoon sun, where palm trees and mountains served as our backdrop. It was peaceful and lovely, much too tranquil a setting for the pugnacious personality that sat across from me. As he spoke, I realized that the fervor he brings to his acting roles is evident in his passion for golf. When I mentioned Arnold Palmer's name, Pesci really loosened up. Before long, all those characters from his films, Jake LaMotta's brother in *Raging Bull*, the fast-talking mob accountant Leo Getz from the *Lethal Weapon* series, were all right there with me — reminiscing, storytelling, and slipping in the necessary quantity of "fuckin' this," "fuckin' that" expected of the legendary bad man.

This was a special interview for me. I always like a challenge, and Joe Pesci was certainly that. The intensity and feistiness we love in his movie characters carries over in abundance to his real life and person. But the equalizer in his life is the golf course, the place when he can take his mind off everything and relax. He swears that he never loses his temper when he golfs. As is often the case, the links have calmed the beast. Discovering the man behind the marquee name more than compensated for all those stressful hours preparing for the interview.

The next day, I followed Pesci on the golf course. I knew it was going to be a wild ride as soon as Pesci was introduced on the first tee to a gallery of a couple hundred people. "Ladies and gentlemen," the public address announcer started. "Star of *Raging Bull*, *GoodFellas*, *Casino*, *Lethal Weapon II*, *Lethal Weapon III*, Mr. Joe Pesci." With this, Pesci walked up to the guy, blew cigar smoke in his face, and uttered, "You forgot *My Cousin Vinny*." The P.A. announcer then shot back, "Oh, I forgot to mention *his* cousin Vinny." Everyone broke out in laughter.

He was thrilled to be playing with Annika Sorenstam, who would win her second straight U.S. Open title a few weeks later. The contrast of the quiet and shy Annika alongside the irascible Pesci was a show in itself. But they share a mutual intensity. It was quite interesting to watch the explosive actor, puffing a cigar, and spewing one-liners, next to the dignified, Swedish golf goddess.

By the end of our day together on the golf course, Pesci and I had bonded. We walked side by side over the fairways and talked for hours. He even had me smoking one of his big, smelly cigars. I felt silly over my initial apprehension towards the psychopath of the silver screen. I became so comfortable I was waiting for Robert De Niro and Martin Scorcese to join us and complete the foursome.

LIGUORI: Joe, you're such a versatile actor. Are you as versatile on the golf course as you have become in your acting career?

PESCI: I think so. I think I have a potpourri of shots.

LIGUORI: What's the best part of your game?

PESCI: I don't know. I chip and pitch and putt pretty good.

LIGUORI: The short game is your strong point?

PESCI: Yeah, but my long game's not bad. I guess you could say I'm all-around terrific.

LIGUORI: What's your handicap these days?

PESCI: Sixteen.

LIGUORI: That's not bad.

PESCI: I spread it around.

LIGUORI: I don't know how you get a chance to play, because you're always working. Every time I turn around, you're in another movie. Not just any movie, a strong movie.

PESCI: Well, thanks. Well, when I'm not working, I play golf.

LIGUORI: Do you practice?

PESCI: No, I just like to play. I hate practicing. I play practice rounds.

LIGUORI: When did you pick up the sport?

PESCI: I think I was about seventeen years old. I started banging it around. Then in and out. Six year layoffs, three years off, that kind of thing.

LIGUORI: Did somebody around you play? Why did you take up golf?

PESCI: All my friends played, so I started playing, you know.

LIGUORI: Newark, New Jersey? They play golf there?

PESCI: In Belleville, New Jersey, I started playing. I was born in Newark, then I moved to Belleville, and then in Belleville we played a lot.

LIGUORI: If you could choose any course in the world to play, which one would you select?

PESCI: Well, if I say one, other ones I want to play are going to say, "Hell with him, let him go play the other one."

LIGUORI: How about your top five courses?

PESCI: That's better. Probably Augusta. Pebble Beach is great. Cypress is great. I don't want to rush into this now and miss something.

LIGUORI: Have you played Augusta?

PESCI: I haven't played Augusta. Cypress I haven't played. Played Pebble Beach. Umm, what else? Shadow Creek is great in Vegas—I played there. I'm a member there.

LIGUORI: Do you have a locker? Very few have memberships at Steve Wynn's private oasis!

PESCI: Yeah. I play there.

LIGUORI: What would be the fifth?

PESCI: Pinehurst, that would do. I mean, there's a lot of great courses, it's hard to say. And they keep making great ones, so . . .

LIGUORI: When you're shooting a film, can you play a little bit? Do you get out? Can you work on your game?

PESCI: It depends. When I did *Gone Fishing*, [filmed in 1996 and released in 1997] in Florida, we shot in the Everglades and I stayed in Naples. So I rented a home right on a golf course. And if I got done early, I would go out and play three holes, and I would play on Sunday, maybe. Usually, when I make a movie, I don't play. We did *Casino* in Las Vegas [1995]. I went there a month ahead of time, in August I think it was, and I played with Robert Gamez [of the PGA Tour]. We played every day, almost every day, at Shadow Creek and TPC. But then when I start work, I don't play.

LIGUORI: Is it distracting? Or you just don't want to get out of character?

PESCI: They don't go together.

LIGUORI: Why?

PESCI: Well, they just don't. Unless the character I'm playing happens to play golf. Then I'll try to sneak it in a little bit. To keep it going. If the character doesn't play golf and it's not about that, then I try to stay away from it.

LIGUORI: Tell me about how you connected with Martin Scorsese and Robert De Niro. I read where they found you in a restaurant.

PESCI: Uh-huh, in a restaurant in the Bronx. I was managing it, and they found me and called me. I had quit acting and show business totally.

LIGUORI: Why is that?

PESCI: Just tired of trying. Tired of failing I should say.

LIGUORI: Was it after the movie *Death Collector* [1975]?

PESCI: Oh yeah.

LIGUORI: So you had done that. So they had seen you in *Death Collector*?

PESCI: *Death Collector*. Right. Right.

LIGUORI: And they said, "I want this guy. I want this guy for this film"?

PESCI: Well, it wasn't that easy. They thought that I was interesting as an actor and wanted to meet me and talk to me about *Raging Bull*. So that's how it came about.

LIGUORI: And isn't it amazing that *Raging Bull* didn't win Best Picture in 1980, but some people consider it the picture of the decade?

PESCI: Right. That was really something.

LIGUORI: And you received your first nomination, and it was for Best Supporting Actor.

PESCI: Nomination for an Oscar. Yeah, it was great.

LIGUORI: When Robert De Niro and Martin Scorsese went into the restaurant to find you, to ask you to audition for the part, or if you were interested in the part, how did you feel about that? As you said, you spent all those years trying.

PESCI: Well, in the beginning, it was incredulous, just unbelievable. I didn't believe it when I got the call from Robert De Niro. There were a couple of calls back and forth, from California to New York. And finally he said, "Could we come talk to you about it?" And I said, "Yeah, but I can't come to California, I'm working." And he says, "No, we'll come to the restaurant and have dinner." And they came on a Sunday and we had dinner and we spoke about it. I wasn't that sure that I wanted to. They told me, "Well, why don't you try and see," and so we read some things together. Robert and I clicked right away. And Marty—we all just seemed to click right away and do well together, and it got better and better and the part got bigger and bigger until it was the co-starring part.

LIGUORI: And why wouldn't you have wanted that?

PESCI: Well, because after all of the years of trying. I'd been in show business since I was five years old, and it just gets, you know, too trying after a while. I'd get discouraged too many times, and you don't want any part of it. You just don't want any part of failure anymore.

LIGUORI: The amount of energy that it must have taken for that particular role! I mean, that's you, though; you bring that kind of energy to everything.

PESCI: Well, that's because I'm a bore in my own life. I mean, all of my friends and everybody tell me that I'm a bore.

LIGUORI: No, get out. I can't imagine that.

PESCI: All I do is play golf, and eat and go to bed. So that's a boring life, and I save all my energy for when I do a film or something.

LIGUORI: Arnold Palmer told me you two have played together.

PESCI: Yes, I did. It was a great experience. Arnold is the King. When I played with Arnold, even the kids on Tour—there was a time at AT&T. We came up to I think it was the thirteenth tee or something, and there was a backup. There was a bunch of us all just sitting there, and I never forgot this one. When Arnie's group came up, all the kids that were sitting down got up and were bowing. And it wasn't meant to be a joke or anything. They did it in a light manner, but it was in his honor. They honor him. They really love him.

LIGUORI: He's just amazing

PESCI: He is really loved. Not only by golf fans, but by the kids that are on Tour, and when I played with him down here in the desert at the Bob Hope Classic, the people along the way—he doesn't just wave if they yell his name. He goes over, he says hi, he shakes hands. I mean, he's so personable and takes the time to greet people, look them in the eye, and say hi to them. And a lot of celebrities don't do that. Not just golf celebrities but other ones also. If you're going to say hello, I would think you'd want to look the person in the eye and shake their hand. And a lot of people don't do it. But Arnie does, and I can tell you from being in that arena, it's not easy to do. And to play golf and to keep your concentration. So he does a great job of it and he is loved.

LIGUORI: He has one of the most charismatic smiles ever.

PESCI: Well, it's real. It's real. Want to hear my Arnold Palmer story?

LIGUORI: Sure.

PESCI: We were playing in the desert. First hole I birdie. Everybody says nothing. Arnie says nothing, he's into his game. Second hole, I birdie. He says nothing. Third hole, par five, I forget what course we were playing. I hit the ball onto the green and have an enormous putt for birdie. And I knock it all the way across the green to where he's standing, towards him. The putt goes in and from the other part of the green. After saying nothing to me for three holes and three birdies, the putt goes in. He's on the other side of the green; he looks at me and says, "Let me see that putter, Joe." Now if you know Arnie, he's putter crazy, and it was one of his own putters.

LIGUORI: Way to go!

PESCI: Three birdies before he said anything to me, and what he said was, "Let me see that putter."

LIGUORI: I don't know if you watched him play his last British Open in

1995, but when he took that last walk down the eighteenth fairway and crossed the bridge, turned around and waved, that had to be one of the most memorable moments in sports. He has such a great smile.

PESCI: He's the King, I'm telling you. He really is.

LIGUORI: Did he give you any pointers when you played with him?

PESCI: Ah, you know I never bother the pros because I realize after playing with them so much, that it's hard enough playing golf, period. But to play golf professionally for a living is insane. The amount of concentration it must take to play. Because I know how much concentration it would take me to play without people asking me for autographs and asking me about movies while I'm trying to play golf. It's impossible. So I wouldn't bother any of the pros when they're playing. I mean, they make a living doing it. I watch and I pick up things that way. Because it's really got to be hard for these guys, and I don't know how they do it.

LIGUORI: Have you taken formal lessons?

PESCI: Once in a while, here and there I will. But basically I'm just self-taught. I watch, and I have a lot of friends that play well. I pick up things here and there. I have nine million swings that get in my way.

LIGUORI: Are you the kind of guy that has nine million clubs in your garage as well?

PESCI: Yes, oh yeah.

LIGUORI: Do you try everything that comes out?

PESCI: I have sets of golf clubs that you can't believe.

LIGUORI: Why are you so passionate about golf?

PESCI: It's very relaxing, and it's a way of life after a while. Golf is just a whole way of life.

LIGUORI: Why do you play?

PESCI: I play for relaxation and to take my mind off of everything else in life. I don't think about anything except trying to play golf. So it helps. A lot of other people I know in my situation or are even more successful in my business, you know, they see psychologists and psychiatrists and analysts all the time or once a week. Me, I don't have to do that. I go to a golf course and that's my equalizer.

LIGUORI: Do any of your roles come out when you're playing? Say you get into a really bad mood. You get into a really bad mood and all of a sudden, what was his name, Leo Getz, from *Lethal Weapon II* [1989] emerges.

PESCI: No, I don't.

LIGUORI: You don't carry that over?

PESCI: I don't get angry when I play golf. I can play bad and just laugh at myself and laugh at the shot. I know that it's coming. I know enough. I've played golf long enough and with enough really great players to know that everybody's gonna hit bad shots. If you're going to get angry about it, it's ridiculous. You can't hit perfect shots all the time. You may do it for one day or one half a day, but nobody does it all the time. So I know it's coming so why get upset?

LIGUORI: You never lose your temper?

PESCI: No, I really don't. I don't get upset at all. I feel bad, but I don't get angry.

LIGUORI: How about playing in an event like the Dinah Shore Pro-Am with players from the LPGA? Does it help your game? A lot of amateurs say that they prefer watching the women play because they can relate to their games a little more than they do watching the pro guys play.

PESCI: Well, they're smooth. They're very smooth, and they don't overswing. A majority of them don't overswing. They swing very smooth and graceful. I think the golf swing is a thing of grace and beauty. It's supposed to be done that way. And timing and the bigger the arc and stuff like that, the farther you hit it. I don't think it has anything to do with size.

LIGUORI: Or strength.

PESCI: Or strength, I really don't. There are some people that, if you are bigger and you swing more graceful, then you will hit it further. And you have a bigger arc and you probably will hit it farther than someone smaller.

LIGUORI: If you had to describe your golf game, how would you? Are you a finesse player? A scrappy player? A power hitter?

PESCI: Well, if you gave me those three words, finesse, scrappy, or power, I'd have to jump into scrappy. I'm not a finesse player, except around the green I have a good touch, you know, with the flop shots, pitching, things like that. I have those shots. I have good hands for those. So I guess I have a little finesse there. And a pretty good trouble shot player, because I'm in trouble more than most people. So you get to be good at those shots. I have little tricks. And power, I don't think I'm a power player, but once in a while I can hit it pretty long off the tee. I can get lucky and start banging it if my timing gets good.

LIGUORI: What's your best trick shot?

PESCI: At the AT&T one time, I hit a putter at Spyglass. I hit a putter about two hundred yards through the trees. I took a swing with a putter. And I remember, it came out low, went right out on the fairway, and just ran great.

LIGUORI: That's some distance with a putter!

PESCI: I used a putter because I knew I wanted to keep the ball low. I wanted to hit it as straight as I could, and I did it as a kid. I knew I could do the shot. And when I did it, I remember Billy Ray Brown says to me, "What did you hit there? Did you hit a putter?" I said, "Yeah, I swung the putter." He said, "Where did you learn that?' I said, "Well, it's something I did as a kid and I think it's a good shot sometimes when you're in trouble." You want to keep the ball low, you know. You just pop down on it and just swing.

LIGUORI: I bet the next week Billy Ray used the same shot [joking].

PESCI: Well, I doubt it. Billy Ray knows how to do that with two-irons and three-irons and other clubs I'm sure. Everybody's got their own little gimmicks.

LIGUORI: The Putt-meister, Joe Pesci. Joe, your acting roles have been so diverse. *Home Alone*, which was one of the most successful comedies of all time. *JFK*, quite serious. *My Cousin Vinny*, quite funny. *Home Alone II: Lost in New York*, quite funny. *The Super*, *Raging Bull*, *Casino*, and *GoodFellas*, the one you won your Academy Award in. You were so nasty in *Casino* and *GoodFellas*, but you're not anything like those nasty characters.

PESCI: How do you know?

LIGUORI: You could be, I don't know. How much of you do you bring to say, *GoodFellas*?

PESCI: I think you bring yourself to everything. Those kind of things are in everybody. Anger and craziness. Everybody gets crazy and wants to fly off the handle. Some people don't, and so if you get a chance to do it in a film, well, you're not hurting anyone really. You're just portraying someone else's anger and showing your own in it. It's okay, it's fun.

LIGUORI: What's it like to work with Martin Scorsese?

PESCI: Oh, it's just great. It's a spiritual experience. Marty was going to be a priest when he was young, and he still has a lot of that in him. It's a real peacefulness to be around him sometimes. He can be talking on the set, and you'll see people sitting around and listening like he's the shepherd with his flocks. It's more than just what he's saying. There's a comfortable thing being around him that people like. He's very spiritual.

LIGUORI: Does he bring out your best work, do you think?

PESCI: I would think so. He's very complimentary with everything. He enjoys everything I do. When I have suggestions, he loves them. So he gives you a lot of confidence, and he lets me write scenes, direct them.

LIGUORI: Really?

PESCI: Yeah.

LIGUORI: Does he play golf?

PESCI: No, he doesn't.

LIGUORI: He wouldn't be the type to take it up?

PESCI: I don't think he would. Neither does Robert De Niro.

LIGUORI: Why? I wonder.

PESCI: Well, I don't know. Robert has asked me about golf a lot because he's intrigued by the dedication to the sport that golfers have. He always asks me about it. I promised to get him a set of clubs. And I want him to get lessons from a pro. I just don't want to take him out and let him bang the ball around, so he doesn't get discouraged. You know, it's very hard to play. Al Pacino told me one time he thought he could just play. I said, "Al, it's a different game." He said, "No, I was a good ballplayer, Joe. I was a great ballplayer. I can pick it up, I'm very athletic." I said, "Not this game." And he tried to hit the ball and he couldn't hit the ball. And so I don't want that to happen to Bob. I would like him to get a decent set of golf clubs and get lessons from a pro. But he's not ready to play and spend the time.

LIGUORI: Can you imagine a foursome with you, Robert De Niro, Al Pacino . . . Who would round out that foursome and make it outrageous?

PESCI: Probably Jack Nicholson. Make it totally insane.

LIGUORI: But Jack can play golf. He loves the sport.

PESCI: Jack can hit it, and he can putt. I mean he can hit the hole no matter where it is. He's just amazing with that.

LIGUORI: Tell me about some of the sports personalities you've played with. I know you're friends with former golf analyst Ben Wright.

PESCI: I'm friends with Ben Wright and Gary McCord. I've played with them in Arizona. And I've played with Ben and Jim Nantz.

LIGUORI: Jim Nantz, CBS Sports announcer.

PESCI: Jim Nantz, right. We played at Riviera one time. And I remember playing with Ben last time, and we were discussing, as a matter of fact, women golfers.

LIGUORI: Yes, what about women golfers?

PESCI: Well, I bring this up because of the unfortunate thing that has happened with Ben.[1] I like Ben, he's a great guy. And we were talking about women golfers and different things, and I said to him that because of their big boobs, some of them that have big boobs have a hard time swinging. They have to lay their arms on top this way and then swing. I don't know if Nancy Lopez has big boobs.

LIGUORI: So you're the one that planted that into his mind. It was all your fault!

PESCI: I did. It's not all my fault, now wait a minute.

LIGUORI: He didn't credit you with those comments.

PESCI: He should have, because rather than see him get in trouble, I would take the heat, because it was not meant in a bad way. I think it was just an observation because we were talking about golf in general and saying how you would have to swing, because I was saying that I was barrel-chested. I have a big chest, and I said, "Maybe if I do that, because the women golfers that have big boobs have to lay their arms down over their chest first before they swing." So we were talking about that, and it was just an observation. And as you mentioned before, we were talking that men have big bellies, they have to swing. Well, you don't have to swing around your belly—I mean you're up here, it's different.

LIGUORI: Well, in reality, it was JoAnne Carner [LPGA Hall of Famer] who said—she was joking around with Ben and she said that she originally used the line about women golfers and boobs.

PESCI: Oh, I didn't know.

LIGUORI: He gave JoAnne the credit and not you.

PESCI: Well, that's great. If he wants to. I just feel bad.

LIGUORI: Meanwhile, he's suspended from CBS.

---

[1] Ben Wright was quoted in the *News Journal*, a Delaware newspaper, by reporter Valerie Helmbreck, as saying, "Women are handicapped by having boobs . . . their boobs get in the way." Wright was also quoted as saying, "Let's face facts here. Lesbians in the sport hurt Women's golf." The controversial quotes created an uproar, and Wright in a statement denied much of it, saying, "I am disgusted at the pack of lies and distortion that was attributed to me. . . ." He called Helmbeck's story, "inaccurate." Months later, soon after a *Sports Illustrated* article (1/96) unveiled more information on the story and reactivated the controversy, CBS suspended Ben Wright.

PESCI: I can't believe he just mentioned it and it came out another way, that's all. I feel bad because it wasn't mean-spirited in any way and he's a terrific guy. You know he's not that kind of person at all.

LIGUORI: Have you talked to him since he got fired for those comments?

PESCI: I haven't spoken to him at all. The guy is really a gentleman. He wouldn't insult anybody that way. He's not like that. So I'm sure it just came out all wrong and he was trying to hold his ground the right way. It's unfortunate. I feel bad. He's not that way, and it wasn't meant to be anything that way. But it is true they have to swing different.

LIGUORI: Now wait a minute.

PESCI: I think you can get away with it, Ann. Swing any way you want.

LIGUORI: I was going to say I take exception to that, but I don't have to worry.

PESCI: No, you don't have that problem. I have to worry about it more than you do!

LIGUORI: You know, Joe, had he admitted to saying what he said and apologized immediately, it probably would have had a different ending.

PESCI: Well, maybe that was his macho side or whatever and being a gentleman in a different way. Sometimes when someone might say something to me, and I'll say, "What is this? I heard you said this thing." And they say, "Oh, I'm sorry." And I'll say, "Oh, well, then if you're apologizing then you did say something wrong." Well, you know what I'm saying. I call people on that a lot of times. If they say something and I call them on it and they say, "Well, I didn't mean that . . . I'm sorry. I'm sorry." Well, if you're sorry then what are you apologizing for if you didn't do anything? That's another way to look at it. If he feels like he did not do anything wrong, he has nothing to apologize for. He didn't say anything in a bad way. He didn't mean it in a bad way. And there's nothing to apologize for. It was just an observation about golf in general, not male, female. It was just the swing we were talking about. Barrel-chested with men and big boobs with women—that's the way he and I were talking about it. So that's probably the way it started, and then it got out of hand. I don't know what else took place. But maybe that's why he didn't apologize, because he didn't do anything wrong.

LIGUORI: But beyond that, he was saying that the writer made up a lot of it, took him out of context, and then when questioned about his comments, he refused to admit what he said and then started making things up about the writer.

PESCI: Well, there you go. That happens a lot in this business. We say something and next thing you know, a writer puts something in the paper and it's taken out of context. They say it another way, and we get a bad rap. It happens. So why apologize? "I didn't say that, the writer said that. I'm not going to apologize."

LIGUORI: Ben Wright has a true friend in you, that's for sure.

PESCI: It's not only being a friend. It's being fair. He's not that kind of person. Besides, we were going to work together. And we need people like Ben Wright in golf because he says things like, "Uh-oh. Nicklaus has consigned to the deep." You know I've had neighborhood guys look at me and say, "What'd he say?" And I say, "He said he went in the fuckin' water!" You know, you need somebody to translate. So I was telling Frank Chirkinian [long-time CBS Sports golf producer-director] and we were going to do a telecast that way. I was going to translate for Ben. When he went to Westchester, in New York, whatever Ben said, I was going to translate for the average public people because he would use these big words.

LIGUORI: Half the people don't have any idea what he's talking about.

PESCI: Well, they don't, but it's very educational sometimes. Because of Ben, sometimes I can finish crossword puzzles. He comes up with words.

LIGUORI: Thanks so much, Joe, for being with me. And the cigar is a big part of your game, I bet. How many have you puffed on today?

PESCI: Three. One on the front, one on the back, and one when I'm done.

Cheryl Ladd

Back in the seventies, everyone I knew watched *Charlie's Angels*. There was something in it for both sexes. While the men ogled the sexy, female detectives, women could appreciate seeing women in roles other than the housewives and victims we were raised on in the early days of television. When I met Cheryl Ladd at a hotel ranch near her home in Solvang, California, in my eyes I was meeting a woman who helped break down some gender barriers in prime-time television.

Ladd had come a long way from Huron, South Dakota, where the actress grew up as Cheryl Stoppelmoor. She started singing at an early age and performed in a local band before moving to Hollywood. She got a break as the lead singer in the cartoon *Josie and the Pussycats* and eventually landed the role in *Charlie's Angels*, the number-one rated show at the time, replacing Farrah Fawcett when she left after the second season. Cheryl went on to star in feature films and television movies. She now dreams of the day she'll have the time to golf nonstop, with no distractions.

We set up the interview at the Alisal Ranch in the rolling hills of Solvang, California, a very low-key resort where Hollywood types sneak away for rest and relaxation. I arrived a day early with my friend, Therese Flaherty, who does my makeup, to soak up the fresh air and sunshine. We were in high spirits that evening at dinner, checking out the celebrities and enjoying an unexpected floor show by photographer David Garvey. Confronted by the "men in jackets" policy, the usually irreverent David, accepted the maitre d's offer of a jacket three sizes too small, then made the most of the moment. David had us falling off of our chairs laughing as he pranced before our table in the miniature jacket with sleeves barely covering his elbows and length just reaching his waist. Our laughter was infectious, and soon the entire restaurant, including the waiters, joined in.

The following morning after a nice run in the hills, Therese and I set out for the interview. I entered the room where the interview was to take place and walking right past Cheryl without recognizing her. I quickly realized my mistake, turned back, and introduced myself. She was very petite and looked quite different without makeup, but most surprising was her unusual golf attire. She was wearing a tight tan skirt, black leggings, and a black turtleneck, not your standard golf garb. Later on the course, she added a straw hat and granny glasses to complete the Katherine Hepburn look. Cheryl definitely has her own style when it comes to fashion on the links, and she looked terrific.

Cheryl was friendly and approachable, and won me over quickly with her love for golf. As is the case with most of the female golfers I interview, we became fast friends. We were joined by her husband, composer Brian Russell, another golf nut, and a very enthusiastic audience during the interview. Brian was the person who first exposed Cheryl to the sport, and in the best tradition of golf marriages, Cheryl and Brian plan all their vacations around the game.

Later that day, after lunch, we met at the Alisal Golf Club, where Cheryl and Brian are regulars, and I walked the course with them. Cheryl had a nice smooth swing. She did not hit the ball long, but was fairly consistent in hitting the ball straight and down the middle. On the course, Cheryl and Brian were a handsome couple. With her offbeat fashion look and his long hair pulled back into a ponytail, they don't have the look of "typical" golfers. But looks are deceiving. The interest they showed in one another's shots and the obvious joy they had playing together, left no question that golf was an important part of their relationship.

LIGUORI: Cheryl, you've developed quite a passion for golf.

LADD: More than a passion. An obsession I think is the word.

LIGUORI: Really? Why are *you* obsessed with golf?

LADD: Well, I played a lot of sports in high school, and all my life I played baseball and basketball and softball and volleyball. All kinds of ball sports, and enjoyed each one of them. But no game is as difficult or as challenging or as fun and rewarding as golf is to me. I'm just crazy about it.

LIGUORI: When did you start to play?

LADD: I started golf in 1980 or 1981.

LIGUORI: Don't you wish you played when you were young? I was very athletic when I was a kid. I played every sport, earned sixteen letters in high school, and the only sport I did not play was golf.

LADD: I know. I wish I had, too. I guess at the time, when you're a teenager, golf seems very uncool. It's not active enough. It's not aggressive enough when you're a teenager. You have all this energy, and it seems a bit sedate to you. I couldn't imagine chasing a little white ball over the countryside, but now my children not only cannot believe that we play, they can't believe we watch it on television obsessively. It gets under your skin. It really

DAVID GARVEY

becomes, for me, it's really a part of my life. It's something I look forward to. All the time, our vacations are planned around certain golf courses and things. My husband and I, sometimes we play thirty-six holes a day. When we go on vacation, we really go to play golf.

LIGUORI: That's great! You choose your vacation spot based on the golf course.

LADD: Right. Well, I think, you know, my husband's given me some beautiful things, jewelry and beautiful gifts, but I think the greatest gift he gave me was getting my butt on the golf course and giving me golf. I really do. It's such a gift.

LIGUORI: It's such a life-style, too. I mean, you guys plan your vacations around golf. Sometimes you play two rounds a day when you're out there?

LADD: Sure. You know what the hard part is? Finding another couple that you get along with. You know how hard that is anyway. But you all like each other and then to also have another couple that plays golf, where both of them play.

LIGUORI: My husband and I love to play together.

LADD: Yeah, there you go. Get your husband out there.

LIGUORI: So tell me some of your favorite golf spots.

LADD: I think the Mauna Lani Hotel and golf course on the big island in Hawaii is my favorite because it was the first time I ever shot in the 80s. And I guess I had so many wonderful experiences on that golf course. I had the opportunity to play in the Senior Skins

Pro-Am. I mean, you know, to be there with them when they were playing, and to play in some of the practice rounds with them. To play with Arnie and Chi Chi, and to have that experience and then of course watch them play and go along the course with them in the Senior Skins. That was amazing. I like The Boulders in Arizona. That's very different. It's an entirely different feeling.

LIGUORI: You have an eighteen handicap?

LADD: My goal in life is to be a single-digit handicap. In a way, I can't wait to retire as an actress. When time goes by, I'm sure I'll be doing less and less, and be choosier about things I wanna leave the house or get off the golf course to do, so I'm hoping that as I get older and I get the chance to play more and more regularly, I'll have the opportunity to really fight for that single digit.

LIGUORI: You play with your husband, which is great. Is it competitive with you two out there on the golf course?

LADD: Oh, sure. Oh, please, that's what makes it fun. And we each have our handicaps, but I would never have golfed if it hadn't been for him. We took it up together. He had played a bit as a boy, and he said one Sunday afternoon in Los Angeles—we had the day and nothing to do—and he said, "Come on, we're gonna go play golf." And I said, "I've never played golf," and he said, "You are going to today." So out we went. We rented some clubs and hacked around a golf course in Los Angeles, and I was hooked from the very beginning. By the time I rented clubs three times, I was ready to buy my own clubs. I was ready to go out and really try. Unfortunately, I made a big mistake, because what happened is from dancing lessons, I could sort of copy what it was I was supposed to do when I observed someone else doing it correctly. But I never had a lesson. I should've had gotten lessons sooner. I would advise anyone who wants to play golf to start with lessons. You have to play your own game, whatever that may be, you know, and try not to overhit the ball. And I play with a lot of men, so I really have to keep that thought in mind. I play with a lot of big hitters and I just don't hit the ball that far. But that doesn't mean I can't be competitive. I just stay in my own game.

LIGUORI: Your athletic background must have helped because you said you were so involved in sports. It probably helped you pick up the sport easier when you first started.

LADD: I think I did because I truly learned how to swing a club from watching, from observing, and having had dancing lessons all my life and being a gymnast, I kind of knew how to tell those muscles where to go. But that doesn't necessarily give you a swing. My swing kind of looked correct. It looked kind of pretty, but it was highly ineffective. That took a while.

LIGUORI: Has your music and acting background performing in front of so many people helped calm your nerves on the course?

LADD: No. I sang the "Star-Spangled Banner" at the Super Bowl, and it's not as difficult as trying to swing a golf club when there's a camera on you. And that's the other thing about the pros. Not only do they play brilliantly, they play brilliantly on camera.

LIGUORI: How frustrating was it when you first started playing?

LADD: I had enough good shots right away with this sort of jerry-rigged swing that I have. But I really like the game. I really felt the challenge of it, and I like being outdoors. I liked everything about it, and as I started to actually get to a place where I played regularly enough to get a handicap and all of that started to happen, I really felt like this was my game. It sort of, I don't know if I claimed it or it claimed me, but I really started to feel like this was it for me. This was the game I've been waiting for.

LIGUORI: So you learned quickly?

LADD: Starting out, I would have holes where I was shooting bogey.

LIGUORI: That's very good!

LADD: Bogey holes when you're first starting out is very encouraging. I have a lot of tens and twelves, but there were a few bogey holes which made me see the possibilities. If I could do it once or twice, I could do it more than that.

LIGUORI: Do you remember the very first course you played?

LADD: Yes. It was El Rancho. It was a public course in Los Angeles. A lot of weeds, I remember. Finding the ball was the hard part [laughs].

LIGUORI: You remember those awful neon yellow balls?

LADD: I used every color. I now only use white balls. You know you've really become a golfer when you only use white balls.

LIGUORI: Do you two get along on the golf course, because I know my husband and I sometimes have our best arguments playing golf. We're so competitive.

LADD: We actually get along very well. We are quite competitive. I'll beat him occasionally. He beats me more often, but we just have such a great time. We're so encouraging with each other. Part of the reason is because we learned to play together, and we both went through very frustrating times together.

LIGUORI: Brian was a beginner when you learned?

LADD: He had played as a child a little bit, but hadn't played for years and years, so when we started again, we sort of started together. So we have been through the good and the bad, the ups and the downs. It's sort of like the whole relationship. Golf is like our whole relationship.

LIGUORI: That's wonderful.

LADD: We just are very competitive, but compatible.

LIGUORI: Good. I'll have to take lessons from you two because we're so competitive. If I'm playing well, my husband gets upset because he's not playing well. When we're both playing well, there's nothing like it.

LADD: Yeah, that's great. It's sort of like sex, isn't it [laughs]? When it's good, it's really good, and when it's bad, it's still good.

LIGUORI: Actually, some people think it's better than sex. Now, you say you watch a lot of golf on television. I could never watch golf until I started playing. It's difficult to appreciate watching golf unless you play golf.

LADD: They don't get it at all. They can't quite figure it out. Watching the Masters [in 1995], I have to tell you that I burst into tears at the end of it. [Ben Crenshaw won the 1995 Masters and dedicated his win to teaching legend Harvey Penick, his mentor.]

LIGUORI: I did, too.

LADD: I just burst into tears. I was there at every hole. I was there at every shot as if I were doing it. I was so with him, you know. When he burst into tears, so did I.

LIGUORI: It must be interesting when you're the token woman, so to speak, at a lot of these Pro-Ams and celebrity tournaments. There's really not that many women in Hollywood who play.

LADD: There really aren't very many celebrity women golfers. I don't know why. There are a handful. Joanna Kerns plays, and Cathy Lee Crosby I think plays, although I haven't played with her. There are just very few.

LIGUORI: You would think there would be more. Maybe because golf is so time consuming.

LADD: Maybe because it's time consuming, and I know that some of the women think the clothes are kind of funky [laughs].

LIGUORI: They don't have to wear those plaid knickers. I'm sure you have a really nice golf wardrobe.

LADD: I'm trying to kind of just wear my own thing. A lot of those kind of little pink and blue polyester shorts outfits are just not gonna fly. They're gonna keep a lot of women away from the golf circuit if they think that's what you're supposed to wear.

LIGUORI: So tell me about some of the events you've played in. I understand that you were among those who opened Gleneagles in Scotland.

LADD: This was such an honor. We were invited by Jackie Stewart, I think he was hosting the tournament to open Jack Nicklaus's course at Gleneagles, and Jack of course was there, and Sean Connery and Prince Andrew and, let's see, Gene Hackman, and I was the woman that got to play. I was so thrilled. Are you kidding me? It was such a thrill to play.

LIGUORI: What an honor to be invited to something like that.

LADD: It was. It really, really was.

LIGUORI: How did they treat you?

LADD: They treat me like one of the boys, actually. It's great. It's just great. They have a few little side bets here and there. Got the putting yips a few times in the betting. I'm not too good when it comes to betting. I have a hard enough time; a little friendly wager here and there makes it even more interesting. It helps you concentrate. But what was interesting when we were playing at Gleneagles, the morning we woke up to play, we had gotten up very, very early to have plenty of breakfast and be able to warm up, and Scotland is notoriously damp and a bit chilled. That morning when we woke up, there was snow all over the ground, so we had to wait till the snow melted. Playing golf in Scotland is like going duck hunting. Same outfit, just different essentials.

LIGUORI: It takes some time to warm up, huh?

LADD: It was unbelievable.

LIGUORI: Are you the kind of golfer who will play in any weather?

LADD: Through rain, through sleet, through hail. I've got my rain clothes on, my proper clothes. I'll be out there.

LIGUORI: So you're a real diehard.

LADD: Sure.

LIGUORI: Who have been some of the more interesting players who have been in your foursomes?

LADD: We were playing at Bighorn [Golf Club in Palm Desert, California], and I was in a foursome with Arnold Palmer, and it was he and I and we had two other guys. The two other guys were okay players, but they were so nervous to be playing with Arnie.

LIGUORI: I'll bet.

LADD: They couldn't see straight. Bless their hearts. So was I, but when you're the woman, they also don't expect so much from you, so the pressure was not quite what these men feel when they're playing with Arnold Palmer. So I kind of relaxed and had a good time. Arnie was wonderful, and he was fun, and we were having a great day and we came up to this par three and the other two fellas were playing okay. Not great but not bad either. I was surprised. Some wonderful shots, some really funky shots. So we come to this par three, and there are thousands of people around the green at the par three. So Arnie hits his shot, and he puts it about fifteen feet from the pin. Then our next guy comes up, and he plays it to the left in the rocks. It's a gone ball; forget it. Then the other goes and he sprays it off to the right, and now the green is sort of like an island green because it's just rocks all the way down. So I go up. Now we need this birdie desperately, right? So I go up and I hit my shot, and I landed about three feet from the cup. Well, Arnold Palmer just went crazy. He was so thrilled for me. So we went out there, and of course he makes this little announcement that this is my shot, and everybody applauded. It was so fun. It was so funny. It was like a dream come true.

LIGUORI: With Arnold watching.

LADD: Like when you dream about golf, there's Arnold Palmer bowing to you and saying go ahead.

LIGUORI: Do you know how many people would do anything to play with Arnold Palmer?

LADD: I'm still pinching myself.

LIGUORI: I'm telling you. You gave me goose bumps with that story. So many people I've interviewed said, "Oh, by the way, can you get me a foursome with Arnold?"

LADD: Just to get his autograph. I'm such a fan, so that's why it was thrilling. I know it's a bit of a braggadocio's story but the fact that it happened when Arnold Palmer was there, and he was very proud of me. And nobody could talk to me for two weeks. Everybody would sit still for two minutes while I told them the story. It was great.

LIGUORI: When you look back, would you say that was the best shot or your favorite shot?

LADD: It was my favorite shot probably. And this was really interesting. I was playing in this tournament and Peter Jacobsen—and speaking of fun, he is a hoot and a half and so nice. So I was talking to him about my game, and Peter said, "Do you want me to come and look at you?" And I said, "Would you?" And he said, "Sure." So he played this whole thing and worked and did this whole commentary thing, and he joined me after it was [over] and gave me some tips and really worked with me. He was so helpful and so fun and so nice. While he was working with me, I see another pair of shoes arrive, and he turns and I heard him say, "So, Fred, what do you think?" I look up and there's Fred Couples. I go, "Oh no, Peter Jacobsen is bad enough. Now I have Peter Jacobsen and Fred Couples watching me try to swing this golf club." Okay. Fred said, "Go ahead, Cheryl. Let me see your swing." So I'm swinging the club and I'm trying to get a swing happening, and Fred goes, "Oh."

LIGUORI: That's it?

LADD: And I go, "Uh-huh, what does 'oh' mean?" And he talks to Peter, and I hear him and Peter. I go, I might as well just give up, this is terrible. I'm awful, I can't play, why am I bothering, I'm taking up their time, feeling so negative. Then Peter Jacobsen goes, "Fred said he was looking at your thumb." And I go, "Excuse me, my thumb?" And he said, "Yeah, when you bring your club up here, why don't you set your thumb a little harder on the club. You're moving your thumb around and your club is kind of wobbly." I said, "He watched my whole swing and noticed my thumb?" This is a guy who knows what a golf swing is supposed to look like, and he saw that my thumb was doing something weird. And you know, he was absolutely right. So from now on, every time I bring a club up, I set my thumb so my club is really in my hand. I have a real sense of it instead of kind of flying around. So there you go.

LIGUORI: Tell me about the *Charlie's Angels* series. You became an overnight sensation.

LADD: I was a seven-year overnight success. I had been pounding the pavement for seven years.

LIGUORI: I know when you first started with *Charlie's Angels*, because you replaced Farrah Fawcett, there were always those comparisons. How did you handle that? That must have been tough.

LADD: It was very tough. I wasn't sure what I was walking into. As a matter of fact, when they first asked me to do the show, I turned it down. I was not sure that I wanted to do that show, and I wasn't sure I wanted to try to replace her. She was a phenomenon. Then I went in and, you know, finally came to senses and said, "This is the opportunity that had come. Jump on the train and let's go." So off I went. So the first day I went to work, I had a T-shirt that said "Farrah Fawcett minor." At the time, she was Farrah Fawcett-Majors. So I got everybody laughing, and I laughed, and I just tried to have a sense of humor about it and just do my work. And I just figured people are either gonna like me or they're not gonna like me. I can't do much about that. I'll just do what I think I should do.

LIGUORI: That was an interesting series in many ways. At the time when it was so popular, it really was more progressive for women than most of the series out there.

LADD: Well, you know what was interesting. It got all the attention it did and it got sort of the following it did partly because of how we looked, but at the same time, there were a lot of real positive role models. Before *Charlie's Angels*, most of the women on television were teachers and housewives and really fit into all these little categories. What *Charlie's Angels* did was really open all kinds of doors and say, "Wait a minute. We can be much more than that. We can even be private detectives!"

Chris O'Donnell

The breathtaking Mountain Course designed by Pete Dye at La Quinta is a jewel tucked away in the California desert. It is sculpted out of a mountain that imposes its will on the players, seducing them with its beauty. While attending the Lexus Challenge, a tournament for professionals and celebrities, my husband, Steve Geller, and I played a practice round in the late afternoon. In a whimsical mood that morning, I had put on a pair of goofy bright blue and flowery pink pants—golf pants that looked so silly I wore them for a laugh. I was dressed for fun and riveted by the peace and serenity that I'd come to anticipate whenever I play La Quinta. We were the only people on the course. The mountains, the wildlife, the desert and our clubs—a player's heaven.

On the fourteenth hole, a sand trap hijacked my approach shot, and while in the process of scooping it out, I saw two men off in the distance. As I struggled in the trap, the men drew closer. When my ball finally found its way to the green, Steve and I decided to let the men play through. They made their way up to our green, and we exchanged hellos. I really didn't pay them much attention. The gentleman closest to me smiled as he attempted a long putt. I smiled back and asked, "How's it going?" His response, "Great, I'm playing with some Boy Wonder," seemed odd. He made his putt, and the two went on. I was so into my game that I didn't recognize that one of the men was a rising young motion picture star.

Later that evening, Steve and I attended the pairings party for the tournament. We had arranged to do interviews with several of the celebrities in attendance over the weekend. While making the rounds, I spotted Chris O'Donnell with his family. I introduced myself, and he smiled and said, "You were the one in the bright blue flowery pants on the course!" It hit me—Chris O'Donnell, who played Robin in *Batman Forever*, was the Boy Wonder the man referred to earlier that day. We shared a good laugh over my outfit and agreed on a time for an interview the following day.

Chris O'Donnell is the boy next-door, or the boy you would want next-door. O'Donnell was raised and continues to live in Chicago. His wholesome midwestern upbringing makes him a mainstream dream. It's easy to understand his tremendous success at such an early age; he's sexy, the unspoken reason the boy next-door is so appealing. More important, he's a genuine talent, with an unusual amount of savvy for his age, who has picked excellent vehicles for himself.

PAUL LESTER

At the time of our interview, Chris had made nine movies in seven years. He had made his film debut at seventeen as the young son of Jessica Lange in the film *Men Don't Leave*. He played the older brother of Mary Stuart Masterson in *Fried Green Tomatoes* and an uptight WASP who rooms with a Jew in *School Ties*. His most impressive performance was in *Scent of a Woman*, sharing the screen with Oscar winner, Al Pacino. In 1995, he donned the Boy Wonder's tights in the blockbuster *Batman Forever*.

In our sit-down interview, O'Donnell answered my questions carefully, using bits of sarcasm to punctuate his thoughts. His youth and charm, sprinkled with droplets of immaturity, crystallize into a form of cockiness that he uses as a shield to protect himself.

One of Chris' favorite perks of stardom are the many invitations to celebrity golf tournaments. He moves easily with the likes of Clint Eastwood, Joe Pesci, and Julius Erving, but it's his fascination with the sport of golf that brings him to the tournaments. He truly loves the game and contends that no matter where he is in the world, if he gets on a golf course, he feels like he's home.

LIGUORI: I understand that you're a fifteen handicap and have been playing for most of your life.

O'DONNELL: Fifteen handicap; I'm thinking of going pro. Yeah, I've been playing since I was a little kid. I had a summer house on the golf course, and I grew up kind of, you know, playing all the time as a little kid. I got to a point when I was about thirteen or fourteen where I'd gotten pretty good, but then I didn't play as much because I was working a lot and so that kind of cuts into your game.

LIGUORI: You worked as a model in your early teens, right?

O'DONNELL: Yeah, exactly, and that kind of destroyed my game.

LIGUORI: So you pursued the modeling assignments at an early age over golf?

O'DONNELL: I did, I did.

LIGUORI: And you gradually got into acting?

O'DONNELL: I guess so. I don't know. I really hadn't any experience. I mean I'd done a few commercials, but I'd never even spoken in any of them, and I guess I just was kind of at the right place at the right time. And you know, once I got my first film, that was a big break, and I kind of took advantage of it.

LIGUORI: So the acting profession kind of found you.

O'DONNELL: You know, in a way, yeah.

LIGUORI: So did your golf game come that easily? I mean, it seems as if the acting thing kind of just happened.

O'DONNELL: I mean, everybody in my family plays golf. My brother John is really good. He played a year at UCLA. He's a scratch golfer. But you know I never got near his game. I look better than I am. I have a nice swing, but I always blow up on a few holes so that's my problem.

LIGUORI: What's your best score?

O'DONNELL: Today was my best score, I had an 81.

LIGUORI: Get out of here!

O'DONNELL: Yeah, an 81. I double-bogeyed eighteen. I could have broken 80 for the first time.

LIGUORI: Sounds like you play like Boy Wonder on the links.

O'DONNELL: Yes, yes, I have supernatural abilities on the golf course. I can hit my driver 485 yards.

LIGUORI: Wouldn't that be great? Just for a day?

O'DONNELL: Absolutely.

LIGUORI: Most kids in the Midwest don't grow up playing golf. They play other sports.

O'DONNELL: Well, I was fortunate. We belonged to a country club growing up, so I was kind of a spoiled little country club kid for a while there. They kind of had me in the junior golf, junior tennis, swim team, stuff like that, but I always liked golf the best.

LIGUORI: You've done nine movies in seven years. That's a lot of work for a golfer.

O'DONNELL: For a golfer, yeah, exactly. And I've had a lot of good rounds of golf in there.

LIGUORI: How do you find time to play?

O'DONNELL: Actually, it's the only thing I do when I'm working 'cause when I work, I tend not to go out at night. I just kind of get focused.

It's only temporary. Most movies take about three or four months, so if you just kind of stick it out for three or four months and don't go out partying all the time, and you just kind of stay focused, its a lot easier. I've actually been fortunate. I've worked in Vienna, Austria, and Ireland, and both times whenever I had a free day, I was always on the golf course. In Vienna, we were working six days a week and on my only day off, I would go play golf. And it's just because it doesn't matter where you are in the world. If you get on a golf course, it makes you feel like you're back home again. You kind of have the same smells and you're doing the same thing.

LIGUORI: It must have been gorgeous playing golf in Austria.

O'DONNELL: Yeah, it was. We played this one place, Schoenbrun, which was an old castle, and they built a golf course on the property around it. It's an incredible layout, and if somebody ever went over there with a lot of money and put a great greenskeeper with it, it would be incredible.

LIGUORI: You're quite young to have worked in so many big films with such a variety of actors and directors. Do you feel that people in the business resent you because of what seems like quick success?

O'DONNELL: Resentment?

LIGUORI: Yes, because most actors and actresses spend *years* going to acting school, waiting on tables, auditioning, overcoming rejection . . .

O'DONNELL: Yeah, oh, I'm sure there's a lot.

LIGUORI: It took Jim Carrey ten years of doing the small stuff before he made it big.

O'DONNELL: I'm sure there are a lot of people who resent my success. But what can I say? I was very fortunate to be in the right place at the right time, and I've worked as hard as anyone else has in the meantime—you know, since then. So I don't feel bad at all.

LIGUORI: So who do you study on the course? Who do you watch?

O'DONNELL: I think Ernie Els has an amazing swing. I like watching his swing. Golf is really relaxing to watch because most of the time you kind of sleep through half of it and then you get to the end and, if it's close, you kind of pay attention. I enjoy playing golf a lot more than I do watching it. It's kind of like baseball.

LIGUORI: You wouldn't say you're a student of the game?

O'DONNELL: Not as much as I probably should be. My brother gave me that *Little Red Book*, the Harvey Penick manual.

LIGUORI: Harvey Penick's *The Little Red Book* and *The Little Green Book*. I have them both.

O'DONNELL: My dad is so funny. My dad's the one who's really into studying his game and stuff. I get confused when I start getting tips from people 'cause then I start thinking about different things. I mean, I hit the ball fine. It's more a matter of game management for me. And, you know, just figuring out the right shots and not doing stupid shots.

LIGUORI: Course management.

O'DONNELL: Yeah, exactly.

LIGUORI: Something John Daly's been trying to figure out himself.

O'DONNELL: Exactly. And if I get somebody coming in with a new swing theory, it usually screws me up. An occasional point here and there I like to hear but, umm . . . You know, my dad's funny. I got him one of those little mirrors that you put on the floor and you can kind of see yourself, and he sits in his basement and works out every morning in the freezing winter, and he does his golf swings. And he's got an index card of tips that he has to go through, and then he gets out on the range at our club and he gets all these things. My brother can imitate his swing perfectly. He stops on top. He's just so stiff and mechanical. He doesn't even enjoy himself anymore 'cause he's too serious about it.

LIGUORI: What does he shoot?

O'DONNELL: He's about an eighteen handicap or so.

LIGUORI: Eighteen handicap. Well, you have to give him credit for practicing.

O'DONNELL: He never hit a good shot in his life. [O'Donnell starts imitating his father.] "Ah, didn't get it." "Ah, topped it a little." "Nope, didn't get it." The guy's never hit a good shot.

LIGUORI: Well, he's a perfectionist.

O'DONNELL: Never. It's so funny.

LIGUORI: Do you ever have a fantasy of being a pro golfer?

O'DONNELL: Well, yeah, that would be a great life if you could be good. You know, I wouldn't want to be driving around the Tour in a Winnebago, trying to make every cut, but you've got your own plane and you're going to all your tournaments. That's a pretty good life-style, yeah.

LIGUORI: How would you describe your game? Does it reflect your personality?

O'DONNELL: I have one of those games where I go out and play and I'll do great for the first couple of holes and the guys will say, "You're not a fifteen," and they'll get all pissed off at me and then I'll screw up. And then they'll say, "Okay, yeah, he made two triples. Okay, fine. He is a fifteen."

LIGUORI: "You sure he's not a twenty?"

O'DONNELL: Exactly.

LIGUORI: Well, that's golf. I mean, you have some nice shots. . . .

O'DONNELL: I'm just inconsistent. I'm inconsistent.

LIGUORI: Do you lose your temper out there?

O'DONNELL: No, I used to, when I was little. Always. Especially when I played with my dad, you know, 'cause your dad will always say, "You tried to kill it." "You swung too hard." "Swung too hard, trying to kill it out there."

LIGUORI: It must be tough to play with your dad.

O'DONNELL: Oh, it's brutal. It's brutal. I mean I love to play with my dad, but you know. I think everybody's that way.

LIGUORI: If you could have your choice of playing with any three players, who would you choose?

O'DONNELL: Who would I play with? Oh, geez, I would play with probably . . . anybody living or dead?

LIGUORI: Anybody.

O'DONNELL: Probably play with Bobby Jones.

LIGUORI: You appreciate legendary golfers. Good for you.

O'DONNELL: Ben Hogan, and uh, geez, I guess you'd have to throw Nicklaus in there. Yeah, throw the Golden Bear in there. That'd be a pretty good foursome there.

LIGUORI: Jones, Nicklaus, Hogan, and the Boy Wonder.

Robert Stack

In television's first two decades—when the good guys and the bad guys were easy to distinguish, when the cops were above reproach, providing a comforting shield impervious to corruption or bullets—the most memorable protector of the common good was Eliot Ness of *The Untouchables*. This tall, dark, and handsome paragon of violent righteousness sent millions of Americans to bed feeling safer every week. Buoyed by Walter Winchell's melodramatic, staccato preamble—if you were a bad guy Ness was going to get you—the impression made on the public was so deep that the actor who played the lead role was viewed as one and the same. Thirty years after *The Untouchables* went off the air, Robert Stack was still Eliot Ness.

In his late seventies, Robert Stack has the look of a much younger man, handsome and physically fit. But what distinguishes him from the rest of his brethren is his rich, melodic voice. Play an audio of Stack's voice for any criminal over forty, and they immediately begin to peer over their shoulders, scurrying to rid themselves of incriminating evidence. Such is the legacy of this prime-time crime fighter. Robert Stack has been an actor for over sixty years, and although he made many theatrical films, television is where he made his mark. In addition to *The Untouchables*, his credits include *Strike Force* and *The Name of the Game*. In 1987, Stack had come full circle. Using his staunch presence and his legendary voice for the common good, he began hosting the popular *Unsolved Mysteries*, a program that often helps bring real criminals to justice.

Robert was one of my first celebrity interviews for The Golf Channel in 1995. Until that time, my forte for the previous fifteen years had been interviewing top sports personalities. Sitting down to talk with a prominent actor was new territory for me. My first impression was that the man has style. He wore his grace and elegance with a comfort that you don't often see in these times of in-your-face-ism. His voice and mannerisms took me back to a more proper world when people were kind and polite to one another. We could have started filming a period piece right there, I imagined, with Robert dressed in tuxedo and top hat. He brought forth a simpler, more congenial time—the golden days of Hollywood.

Robert Stack was born in Hollywood in 1919 to a family who had lived in that community of dreams for four generations. When Stack was three, his parents divorced, and his mother took Robert to Europe, where he spent his early childhood in Italy and France. These two countries provided his first language skills. When he returned to California four years later, he learned English, his third language. By 1938, Stack was a striking, young, privileged student at the University of Southern California. He excelled in polo and was a member of five all-American skeet shooting teams, earning two individual world records in the sport. He also answered the call of duty as a lieutenant in the army during World War II.

MARC GLASSMAN

After the war, he became a fixture in Hollywood's inner circle. He spoke of Clark Gable as a surrogate father and of his close friendship with the likes of Gary Cooper. Acting was a natural choice for Stack. With his looks and charm, he moved easily in the community, his career building steadily to the point where he received an Oscar nomination for the film *Written on the Wind* in 1956. By this time, television was beginning to take over America's consciousness. Stack was ripe to make the big leap to the little screen. In 1959, he accepted the role as the famed Treasury agent, Eliot Ness. The show aired for four years, completing its final season in 1963.

Daring exploits in speedboat racing and motorcycling provided Robert with a release from the overwhelming pressures of his career in Hollywood. Golf offered a different outlet, an introspective experience that brought him closer to serenity, while still maintaining a competitive edge. Robert finds a purity on the golf course that has eluded him in his other sporting endeavors. The challenge of the game and the intimate relationship between player, ball, and course are the reasons Stack works the links. His swing is hampered by a back injury incurred during a speedboat accident, but the inner peace, as well as the engaging social atmosphere of the course, renders his diminished mobility irrelevant. He plays in a number of celebrity tournaments and is a gallery favorite.

After the interview, Steve and I joined Robert for dinner where we shared in his stories and laughter. His patience and good humor bolstered my confidence as I set out to explore the personalities of stars beyond the athletic fields. I'll never forget the warmth and class that he exhibited. Robert made it so easy and enjoyable.

LIGUORI: Robert, along with everything else you do, you've managed to become a golfer.

STACK: I've been around it all my life and, as a kid, I grew up with people, like walking around with Lawson Little [won the British and US Amateur championships in 1934 and 1935]. It was before your time. And in the pro-ams, you'd get a chance to play with people like Sam Snead and Johnny Miller. You learn to associate with greatness, and the only sorry part is you have to hit the ball. You are the "before" and they are the "after."

LIGUORI: What's it like when you go out there and you're expected to do well because people know your face? They know you from so much of your work.

STACK: Only one thing, Ann, they like you and they don't mind it when you really scuff the ball because that makes you one of them. I remember Jack Lemmon in his drinking days was up all night at Club 19, and he went to tee off at Pebble Beach—Crosby's Clambake we used to call it—and he took a wild swing at the ball and just hit the very top of it, and it fell off the tee and went about three feet. He started to walk, and he told the caddie, "Don't pick it up." The announcer said, "He must've knocked it down the middle." And the ball was right down, period [laughing].

LIGUORI: Meanwhile, he stepped on it very conveniently so nobody would see it, right?

STACK: Yes! [He continues to laugh.]

LIGUORI: When people come up to you when you're playing in these celebrity tournaments, do they approach you as if you're Eliot Ness from *The Untouchables*? [The television series ran from 1959 to 1963.]

STACK: The mothers, maybe. You must remember there are now three Eliot Nesses. Me and Kevin Costner and there's an Italian kid playing Eliot Ness in syndication, which would make Eliot Ness turn over in his grave. But you could always tell by going through an airport if your show is successful because they kind of scatter around you and all. When you go there and nobody pays any attention, you know the television show isn't doing too well. It happens now to be *Unsolved Mysteries* [debuted in 1988, syndicated]. I can remember with David Janssen once, I went out on the golf course and these girls were running across and I was all ready to take out the pen and sign, and they ran right past me right to David Janssen because he had just done *The Fugitive*, which was brand new. And *The Untouchables* had been on for three years, so I was old hat and he was *it.*

LIGUORI: Such short memories these fans have. You thought they were coming after you because your golf game was so superb.

STACK: Of course. Yes, maybe that's what it was. They saw me try to hit the ball.

LIGUORI: You've made references to *The Untouchables.* What did you think about Kevin Costner in the movie playing the same role, Eliot Ness? [*The Untouchables* in 1987.]

STACK: It's actually two different questions. Kevin Costner is a friend of mine and a very nice man and a fine actor. And David Mamet, who wrote the script of the movie, is somebody I know and a wonderful writer. The first answer is it was a good motion picture. The second answer is it had nothing to do with Eliot Ness or the book. [Mamet] wrote sort of a Greek tragedy, and he made Ness a wimp at the beginning, which he never was. He had to be a wimp so Sean Connery, who never existed in the book, would come in and teach him street smarts and also would involve Connery in trying to get Capone. In the process, Connery is killed, then Ness goes out and revenges Malone [Connery's character]. Well, Malone never existed, so that already is wrong. Frank Nitti [Capone's Chicago enforcer, a character on the show] did not jump off the building. He was killed near a train.

LIGUORI: So you were amazed with all the changes in the script?

STACK: They could've called it anything else. They could've called him Harry Johnson instead of Eliot Ness, but it was a well-done movie and Robert DeNiro was very good as Capone and there you are. It took me a long time to go see it. It took me three months [laughs].

LIGUORI: What was your initial reaction when you found out that they were even making a movie?

STACK: It was kind of like, hey, you know, I'm the so-called original. The thing that bothered me, the thing that kind of hit me—I know Kevin, as I say, and a very nice man—there was a full bleed all the way out to the edge of the paper saying Kevin Costner is Eliot Ness. And there he is with the badge. I said, "No, he ain't. I'm Eliot Ness!" [He laughs.]

LIGUORI: You're passionate about polo and boat racing—action-packed sports compared to golf.

STACK: Golf, you gotta take sort of a psychological tranquilizer, and people keep saying you gotta smell the flowers. I must say, even if I was a good golfer, you get some of those guys who plumb-bob every putt, and it was like Walter Hagen [one of the great characters of golf in the twenties, Hagen won eleven major championships in his career] said, "If you're going to miss it, miss it fast." And the really good ones don't take forever. It's like you watch [Lee] Trevino. Trevino lines a shot up on his way to the ball.

LIGUORI: I love watching him.

STACK: I think that too many people who've watched a magnificent golfer who used to take a lot of time, like Jack Nicklaus, they watched the real pros and think they should copy them. They don't have the talent. That's the big difference.

LIGUORI: You are in the Skeet Shooting Hall of Fame. How did you make the transition to golf?

STACK: Golf is a social game, and it's a shared experience. You can sit around later and laugh about the terrible things that happened to you, except I hate to see grown men cry when you miss a three-foot putt and it cost them a hundred dollars. That I don't like.

LIGUORI: You have some interesting stories. I know Jerry West [NBA Hall of Famer] plays at Bel Air Country Club [located in Los Angeles, California], and you've played with him.

STACK: Jerry got so good. He got to be a scratch golfer. You got some guy who's an eight handicap, who's a hustler, and there goes the house and the kids.

LIGUORI: Does the skeet shooting—the skills that it takes to do that, the focus, the diligence—does that transfer over at all to your golf skills?

STACK: Not really. It should in the putting. It's more reactive. It's like playing tennis at net or playing Ping-Pong or playing badminton or anything else that moves fast. It's eye-hand coordination. That's what the game is about. It's quite different. It's just like golf and tennis. Tennis is like shotgun shooting; golf is like rifle shooting. One is precision, one is reactive. Golf is precision like tennis is reactive. Shooting is reactive, and it doesn't take any brains. Your body knows the answer, and all you have to do is be a good athlete and get out of the way of your body. Golf is different. Golf you have that one second and you lose it the next. Remember Tom Watson, and I saw it that one year—he couldn't make a mistake. He had the replication of Ben Hogan's swing. Never gonna lose it. Next year he lost it. Whatever it is. It's like only God can make a tree. Someone said on a three-par only God can make a three [laughs].

LIGUORI: Robert, along with excelling as a skeet shooter and in polo, you also became quite good in speedboat racing. Wasn't that dangerous?

STACK: Well, when you're very young, you're never gonna hurt, you're never gonna get old, you're never gonna go to the great beyond. And this is why all the fighter pilots who are any good are about eighteen or nineteen years of age. It's only until you have the first really major accident that you realize that you are not indomitable. You may be up there with a harp and wings before you know it. People told me when I was racing—it's happening now with people like Paul Newman at an advanced age—but when I was doing this, they used to come to me and say, "You've got a death wish." I say, "No, I have a life wish." I said, "Because on that razor edge, the excitement there is like none other, and you can jam a whole day's living in about three or four or five minutes." It's exciting. It's really a kick. You can talk about drugs—I don't know about them, I never took those—but I'll tell you that's a real high.

LIGUORI: And you are still racing now?

STACK: No, I don't do that anymore. I can't jounce around as much as I could with my back. But I understand the compulsion. It's a great escape from our profession. Paul Newman does it and does it so well. It's a complete encapsulation. It's you and it, "it" being the car or the race boat or motorcycle or whatever. It's between you and that, and there is a very unknown person—I won't say death—but a very unknown something over here that if you screw up, you're gonna have to pay a penalty.

LIGUORI: What in golf could possibly give you the same thrill? Have you experienced anything in golf to give you anything near that same thrill?

STACK: Oh, there's a purity in golf that there is in very few sports. It's when it comes together proprioceptively; that's when the body works absolutely perfectly and pure. And it works in that wonderful arc and the sound when the club hits the ball and it goes exactly where you want it to, that's ecstasy [laughing].

LIGUORI: I can see it all over your face. And you obviously have experienced a few of those times.

STACK: I've had a few of those times, yes. I played with Arnie [Arnold Palmer] at the opening of a golf course in Texas and with Gene Cernan, the astronaut, and I actually outdrove them on one hole. There was a hurricane blowing, and I cut across. I thought I could get over some trees, and they went the other way around.

And the wind blew it and I was about ten or fifteen feet ahead of Palmer, but Palmer took the long way around with the hook. I said, "After you short knockers are finished, come up here and we'll try and figure out how far it is to the green" [laughs]. That's something else that happens in our profession. We're fans of athletes, and when you get out there and you play with Palmer, with Trevino, you know them. So we're fans of theirs, and in a strange sort of way, sometimes they are of us. It's a great symbiotic relationship. It's fun. It's a fun game.

LIGUORI: What do you attribute the popularity of golf within the Hollywood community?

STACK: Number one, it's a social game of course. And you interact and you suffer together and tell lies later on and look forward to the entire week. You look forward to the foursome on Saturday or Sunday. Not too many sports like that. It's always been a popular game. My gosh, going back on the walls of the Bel Air Country Club, you've got Gary Cooper and Clark Gable and Carole Lombard. It was really Hollywood's game.

LIGUORI: You mentioned some legendary names. Is there a foursome in your memory that shines above all the others whom you've played in?

STACK: I was never really invited. I shot skeet with Clark Gable and shot ducks with him. In fact, he was like my surrogate father, Gable. Gary Cooper, I used to shoot rifles with. Hollywood used to adopt a sport called skeet shooting along with—they were all very golf oriented in those days. They're coming back to it now. You got a lot of guys like Joe Pesci and a whole lot of other characters at Bel Air now, and that's good. It was Hollywood's game and still should be.

LIGUORI: They allowed Joe Pesci into Bel Air with the long hair, bearded look he sported for *With Honors*.

STACK: He looked like a renegade off the streets. My, he looked like a street person. "I'm supporting my family looking like a street person," he said. "Okay."

LIGUORI: You were talking earlier about the similarities of what it takes to be great at skeet shooting and how that might translate to golf.

STACK: There is one big analogy, and one is tunnel vision. It's like Bobby Jones said. The reason [he became] a good golfer is because he was a caddie and never saw anything but good golfers play, so he never had the chance to be a bad golfer. So if you see that and the proprioceptive sense picks it up and sees the image of that perfect golf swing all the time, that's what your body is going to do. You must have a concentration so that nothing bothers you at all. You can just tunnel vision and turn it on and that's it. The world is there and the ball is all that matters, and you're thinking about forty-seven different things.

LIGUORI: It's almost like you're in a zone. I remember reading that Loren Roberts, one of the best putters on the Tour, doesn't even look at the hole. He sees it almost peripherally, and he just wants to get the speed of the putt down and the direction and he doesn't even look at the hole. He doesn't have to.

STACK: We used to have a test, when I was a kid growing up, at the World Championships of skeet shooting. You could do everything, but you couldn't touch a person. You could throw confetti in the air, you could yell in their ear, you could do anything. You would not be phased by it, and sure enough, you'd go to the Nationals and the World Championships and the bull horns [calling] "gray field five" just as you're calling for the bird. I had a guy walk up to me on the toughest station on the field with a movie camera going "eeerrr, eeerrr, eeerrr," and what you do is the same thing in golf. What you do is take that challenge. I'm gonna concentrate more on this than I've ever concentrated before in my life on this target. I don't care what you're doing, pow! And so you use all of the things that can be interferences and use them as a challenge, and that's how you get to be good.

LIGUORI: What's your best round of golf?

STACK: I've shot a 74 once. In fact, that was when we went out with Arnold [Palmer]. He says, "This young man is one of the best golfers in the movie business." I didn't dare tell him that I shot a 74. Then I played with him a year later and I was back to normal, my horrible hacking, and he said, "A little off your stick, aren't you?' I said, "Yeah, I really am a little off my stick" [laughs].

LIGUORI: You rose to the occasion when you had to.

STACK: I was insane with that 74 anyway.

LIGUORI: Which one of your characters shows up at the golf course? Who is the real Robert Stack?

STACK: I don't know. I'm just a guy that, on the golf course, I am continually trying to be something I'm not. You know, it's a very difficult game. It's a really fun game, but somebody said, "I'm humiliated enough in my profession. I get paid for it. I come out on the golf course and do it for free."

LIGUORI: Robert, in the original *Untouchables*, I understand the Mafia intruded during those tapings. What was that like?

STACK: Desi was threatened by a gentleman whose name I will not mention [Desi Arnaz of Desilu Studios produced *The Untouchables*]. He grew up in the precincts and he knew Al Capone's son, Capone Jr. Anyway, somebody from Las Vegas came down and told him to lay off, and Desi said, "Hey, amigo," he was half bagged, "the gig swings two ways. She swings in, she swings out. You don't like what I do." Three days later, somebody shot three holes right through the main dining room door of Indian Wells because he used to own Indian Wells. Desi Arnaz. Jimmy "The Weasel" Fratiano, who was an informer, wrote a book, and in it he mentioned the fact there was a contract to kill Desi, but they decided not to because they thought it was too much trouble and would get too much publicity. That's how close he came to being killed.

LIGUORI: Just from his involvement with the series?

STACK: But the series began with stuff they didn't want to have publicized. And remember, you have generations. They may wear different clothes, but the same stuff goes on. Look at *Pulp Fiction*, *Wiseguys*, same thing. And you watch the life and death situation. The eeriest show we ever did on *The Untouchables* was "The Kiss of Death." I laughed when I read it, when two men kiss on the mouth. And when it played, we had this ugly tough guy and we had Frank Nitti, and Nitti kicks his hat back and grabs him and kisses him on the mouth. Well, what that means is you have been delegated to go kill this guy. Instead of laughter, there was this tension on the set. It was eerie because you were getting into some of the mafiosi ritual. The black hand.

LIGUORI: And you had some personal experiences with the Mafia?

STACK: They came to me. Actors and ballplayers and hookers they considered hired help. If you read *The Godfather*, you'd know what I mean. If they're gonna go scare somebody, they're gonna get the guy to talk. Desi Arnaz is the guy who owns the studio, but not some dumbbell like me who puts makeup on and makes funny faces.

Susan Anton and Jeff Lester

Actress-singer Susan Anton and her husband-manager Jeff Lester started their marriage out right—they learned to play golf on their honeymoon. Three years later, they are both golf enthusiasts and enjoy a healthy husband-wife rivalry on the links. In the segregated world of golf, it is still unusual to see men and women playing together, so it was nice to meet a couple that play as much golf as my husband and I. We had a lot of fun sharing war stories on the pleasures and the pitfalls of playing the game with your spouse.

When I sat down with Susan and Jeff, they were taking a few weeks off from a show Susan was doing in Vegas to play in the Frank Sinatra Celebrity Tournament. Like Steve and I, Susan and Jeff are pretty close in ability. Golf is one of the few sports that a man and a woman can play together on a level playing field. Susan and I both hit a long ball and thus keep up with our husbands' distances when we tee off from the forward tees.

We compared notes on some of the hazardous ground a couple has to travel on the links if they are to avoid marital conflict and found that the "cart dilemma" was at the top of the list. There is something about husbands when they are in the driver's seat, they focus on their own ball and bypass their spouse's ball even when it makes geographical sense to go to her ball first. I've had the "selfishness" discussion with my husband more times than I care to remember. Another problem for golf couples is learning how to deal with the intense competition. Steve and I can't quite root for each other unless we are both playing well. Unfortunately, it is rare when we both play well on the same day or even on the same hole. The marriage improves when we both play bad, since we share our frustration and curse the game together. In those rare moments when we both are playing great golf at the same time, it's better than sex.

Though Susan and Jeff downplayed their rivalry, once we were on the course, I could spot it a mile away. Even practice chip shots and putts were a series of contests to be won, but they have learned to appreciate their competitive spirit and blow off the friction once the clubs are put away. Susan and Jeff share a great enthusiasm for the sport, and golf has strengthened their union.

The golf addict that I am could never fathom a marriage in which one person had the bug and the other didn't. My theory for a happy golf couple is for them to be well-matched in ability and to play together. Unfortunately,

PAUL LESTER

this is not always possible due to the discriminatory policies at many private clubs that restrict tee times for women.

Susan is a popular celebrity at golf events. She is always smiling and knows how to have fun, brings a respectable game, and often entertains at the charity dinner following the tournaments. Golf is her passion and the centerpiece around which her life revolves, influencing even her performance schedule and selection of projects. She and Jeff have found a serenity in golf, which attracts so many show business people to the links. Susan and Jeff—a match made in fairway heaven.

ANN: Susan and Jeff, golf has kept your marriage strong.

SUSAN: Well, we learned to play golf on our honeymoon. Actually, I had been introduced to the game. The very first time was when I graduated from high school. My mom and dad gave me golf lessons for a graduation present, and I tried it for a little bit and got frustrated much too fast. I wasn't mature enough to appreciate the quality of the gift they had given me. And so years and years passed, we got married, and we were on our honeymoon up in the San Juan Islands on an island called Orcas Island, and they had this funky little golf course there.

ANN: Funky?

SUSAN: Funky. And we got out there, though, because it looked like great fun, so we got out there with some rented clubs and whacked it around and really had great fun and took it up.

ANN: And Jeff, did you feel the same way?

JEFF: It was one of those moments where I, because I've always been athletic, I tried this game and I thought, I can't play this game. This just must be one of those things I just absolutely cannot do. But we stayed with it. We kept working at it.

SUSAN: And he still can't play now [laughing]!

JEFF: And I still can't play. Nothing's working.

SUSAN: He's very good actually. He's very good.

ANN: Jeff, you're a twelve handicap and, Susan, you're a sixteen handicap. It must still be competitive between you two out there when you play.

JEFF: It gets competitive out there.

SUSAN: Well, what's good is we've gotten to the point where we've played enough that we really appreciate every golfer doing well. It's not like you're in competition with one another as much as it is that you really appreciate a good shot, when somebody has really been able to manage something that's really miraculous. So it's not as competitive. However, he is supposed to know where my ball is at all times.

JEFF: If we're in the cart and I'm just kind of basically driving down to where the balls probably are, Susan gets kind of upset if I . . .

ANN: And what if he doesn't find your ball?

SUSAN: Well, this could be big trouble. I mean, I've outgrown it. Really, it's been very good because now I just have to keep it in the fairway to avoid family arguments.

JEFF: In the beginning, she would actually jump out of the golf cart, mad at me, if I drove anywhere past her ball. Now we've worked out a lot of that.

SUSAN: Chivalry is not dead. You wait . . .

JEFF: That's right.

SUSAN: . . . till she's hit the ball.

ANN: But maybe you drive the ball longer than Jeff?

JEFF: She does sometimes.

SUSAN: Sometimes from the red tees.

JEFF: Yeah, she's a killer.

SUSAN: Yeah, but I can get it out there pretty well, sometimes.

ANN: Well, I know your golf course, the TPC Summerlin in Vegas, because that's where the VH1 *Fairway to Heaven* gig was. So we got familiar with that course.

SUSAN: We love this course. We looked at a lot of different courses when we moved out to Las Vegas, and they're building a lot of them out there now. It's really going to be, I think, a major golf destination, not just gambling. And one of the things that we loved about this TPC course is that it's an Audubon Society course, so they really preserve the wildlife and they're real cautious about overseeding. There's no harsh chemicals, and so environmentally it's safe.

JEFF: There's only forty courses like that in the country that are rated that way, and they really make sure that all the animals are protected, and they don't use, like Susan said, any of the bad fertilizer and all that kind of stuff.

SUSAN: We're proud of it. It is nice.

ANN: And how often do you get to play?

SUSAN: Every day. Well, it depends. If I'm getting ready to play in a tournament or something, I'll try to get out and at least practice every day and play a couple or three rounds a week.

JEFF: The guys at the course call her the Vijay Singh of the TPC because she's out there practicing all the time. [Singh is on the PGA Tour.]

SUSAN: I am. I'm the Vijay Singh of TPC. I'm a range rat.

JEFF: She'll go out there, I swear, like six hours at a time.

ANN: Really?

SUSAN: I'm a range rat. I don't know when to come in.

ANN: It's great to have that discipline and determination to practice.

SUSAN: I love it. I just love it. I wish it showed up more, but I think it's starting to. I feel like I'm on a plateau there. I'm starting to get a better understanding. It's coming together more.

JEFF: I love to hit the range. I don't quite do it like Susan. I mean, I swear to you it's amazing. She'll come back with blisters, she hits so many balls.

ANN: Wow, and you just love it. You're really motivated to improve.

SUSAN: But there really is something about the range, unlike the golf course. For me, it's very liberating because it's endless opportunities. You're not keeping score, so you can really live in a world of denial. You know, you've got this giant, giant area that you're hitting into.

ANN: That's right. Hitting balls on the range, if done well, can give you a false sense of confidence.

SUSAN: Yeah. And so you hit these balls out there and you feel like you're really good. Then you take it out on the course, and now it's narrowed down to "here," and then you get close to the green, it's smaller yet. Now the hole is yet smaller, and it really starts to show up.

ANN: The course becomes an illusion. Susan Anton psychoanalyzing the game.

SUSAN: Anton and Zen golf. Yes, I love it.

ANN: So tell me the truth. Have you ever had a huge argument on the course?

SUSAN: Oh yes, yesterday.

JEFF: I think that carts maybe should just be abolished because I think that carts really get in the way. Because there's a thing about carts. You should be driving a certain way.

SUSAN: I hate carts. Golfers aren't supposed to travel in pairs.

ANN: It's very distracting. The cart's behind you, and you've got to think about keeping the cart up with the twosome.

SUSAN: Golfers aren't supposed to travel in pairs. It's a solitary thing that's played in groups, and you hit your ball and your thought is not about everybody else out there. You want to go to your ball; you want to figure out what your distance is and how you want to go about taking care of business. Now when you're in a cart, you have to wonder where the other person is. Are you behind? Do you have the club that you need? When can I go to my ball?

ANN: You travel so much, performing, Susan. Can you keep up the golf while you're on the road?

SUSAN: All across America. We've played some of the best golf courses that America has.

JEFF: See, we've got this down because I've got the top one hundred *Golf Digest* courses in the U.S., and then we start plotting our course. What city are we going to be in next and what's that close to?

ANN: Do you one day hope to be invited to play in the AT&T Pebble Beach Pro-Am?

SUSAN: That's one of the reasons I've really started playing from the white tees, because you have to play from the white tees if you ever are going to get in that, and I'm a bit of a way from being there. But I would love to get invited to the AT&T, and I think there are a lot of gals out there who could get out there and lose the ball just as well as some of those guys.

ANN: How far do you drive the ball?

SUSAN: I can get it out there about 200, 210.

ANN: That's great.

JEFF: She can hit it well.

SUSAN: You know that's just with my three-wood. I still don't feel that strong with my driver yet.

JEFF: I've seen her hit the ball 260.

ANN: Is that right?

SUSAN: Yeah. I mean, I got a good roll. And I did win a long drive contest with a 242 once.

ANN: That's fabulous. What do you play with?

SUSAN: Cobras!

ANN: How did you hook up with Cobra Golf?

SUSAN: Cobra is truly—it's like serendipity. It's destiny in our lives because the very first tournament I ever played in, we'd just started playing golf and I was invited to participate in what was the Greater Greensboro Open. I think Chrysler took it over now. I'm not sure who's sponsoring it, but K-Mart used to sponsor the Greater Greensboro Pro-Am. And I was just supposed to sign autographs. I said, "I can't play yet but I'll show up."

Well, I showed up and they needed a celebrity because somebody didn't make it. They said, "We really need you to play." And I said, "I don't have any clubs." And they said, "You can use these from the pro shop." And they brought out the King Cobra Oversized Graphite because I needed the length. They said, "How about these?" and I said, "The Greg Norman? Sure, I'll play with these."

ANN: No problem.

SUSAN: Sure, I'll play just like Greg. Well, they teamed me up with John Daly.

ANN: Oh my goodness.

SUSAN: And we're walking up to the very first tee, and I'm making a deal with God you won't believe. Like, "Please, dear God," because his galleries . . .

ANN: They're huge.

SUSAN: Thousands.

JEFF: Just a wall of people.

SUSAN: And I've never played in a tournament, let alone one of these with John Daly and galleries like this one.

ANN: This is your first event?

SUSAN: Very first event, and so I said, "Dear God, please just let me get it out on the fairway." And all I could hit was my five-wood at that time. Well, of course, John teed it up in Greensboro and I teed it up in Alabama, but I teed it up, and I got it straight, flew it right out there. And I ended up beating them by about twenty yards.

ANN: Unbelievable!

JEFF: She played really well.

SUSAN: It was a good beginning. It was amazing.

ANN: To beat John Daly's drive, even from the red tees.

SUSAN: It was pretty exciting.

ANN: Yeah, you can say you beat John Daly.

SUSAN: And those are the clubs I play with today.

ANN: Well, it's good to see, from a woman's perspective, that golf is now thinking of women when they design clothing. Because it used to be you'd go into a store and the clothes for women were hideous.

SUSAN: I hated it.

ANN: You just couldn't find any stylish golf clothes. You'd have to come up with your own style and your own kind of wardrobe because there was nothing appropriate.

SUSAN: Yeah, quite honestly, when there was a PGA show in Vegas that we went to and I saw the Como sports line, and I told them, "This stuff is so beautiful." I said, "I would love to get involved with you guys with this because women need this kind of high-quality, beautiful, timeless fashion." For some reason, they thought that all women who play golf want to wear pink shorts with a little shirt that has rhinestones on it that says "golfer on board" or something. I said, "Give me a break." And what's with these hats and things? I said, "Give me a break."

ANN: Wait a second. Michelle McGann might get upset.

SUSAN: No, Ann, if you hit a ball like Michelle, you can wear whatever you want. But that's how we got hooked up with Como, because I think they are really beautiful clothes.

ANN: And with so many more women, especially executive women playing, they should be able to have a wide selection of styles to choose from.

SUSAN: Absolutely.

ANN: Golf clothing lines are finally designing clothes for the serious female golfer. So many more business women are taking up the game. They're realizing the advantages of networking on the course and doing business on the course. More and more working women are learning how to incorporate golf into their life-style.

SUSAN: The majority of great things in our lives have come from golf. Great friendships, business opportunities.

JEFF: We've met great people through golf.

SUSAN: Our personal life is all from golf.

JEFF: And a lot of the things that we are spinning our lives and work into has a lot to do with golf.

ANN: It's all golf related.

SUSAN: It's all such a common denominator. You get out on a golf course and it doesn't matter if you're the CEO of any of the biggest corporations, and the guy that keeps the greens clean, whatever. You get out there with your handicaps and you tee that ball up—it's a level playing field.

JEFF: That's one of the greatest things. Hit it and play.

SUSAN: And it's fabulous.

ANN: And obviously, it's even more meaningful if husband and wife can share it.

SUSAN: That's right.

JEFF: Just a few arguments here and there.

SUSAN: Hey, probably fewer than if we didn't play, because then we wouldn't have anything to distract us.

ANN: Susan, I read a piece written on you in which you talked about turning forty and how, instead of it being traumatic, it was quite uplifting. You have a whole different perspective now on your business, on life overall, and on your philosophy about golf.

SUSAN: There's so many levels of golf as to why I love it, and you can really start to see how it shows up in your life, and every time you're out there, I think you get a new life lesson. But it's so true because you've got to play what the moment is. You can't be ahead or behind. You've got to really appreciate where you are at the time you're there, and assess the situation and see what your next move is. And you've got a lot of options. And also, the thing about golf that I love is that you need to always stop and look around and see where you are because golf courses are always set in God's arena. It's the only game that you play in God's arena. Man helps it out a little bit here and there but you carve it in and lay it out right there in the earth and there's nothing like that. So, yeah, I think it teaches you patience, and it also teaches you a lot of acceptance. Sometimes you may be over there in the rough, thinking that it's over, and it's not.

JEFF: Yeah, that's a lesson.

SUSAN: You know, you've got to hang in there.

JEFF: When you can. Because it's very humbling, but you really do. You just have to stay with that next shot.

SUSAN: Hang in there.

ANN: Golf can be a metaphor for so much in life.

JEFF: It is, and I think that's part of what people are drawn to about this game is that you never quite know what you're going to get and you always feel like you're going to learn something. And you might just do this amazing thing. And that one shot in the round, you can remember it for years. "Oh, my God!"

SUSAN: It's true. And I read something great in one of my acts. I tell a golf story and then I sing "The Glory of Love." It reads, "You gotta win a little, live a little." Because it really says the whole thing, and the beauty of golf is that it's always that one or two great shots that make you want to—you can't wait to tee it up the next day. And it's just like life. You can go through a day of nothing but bogeys, but you might have one or two moments in the course of that day that are just so perfect that you feel like, "I can't wait to tee it up tomorrow and see what the day is going to bring me." So the metaphors really are endless.

ANN: Well, keep having fun with it.

SUSAN: And with each other.

Kevin Costner

Word was out in the golf world for a year prior to the premier of *Tin Cup* that Kevin Costner was working on a movie about a golf pro who falls in love with one of his students (played by Rene Russo). Costner had little use for golf before the film and had seldom made the rounds of the major celebrity tournaments. The film sparked his interest in the sport, and as the talented actor hit the links, the golf world was buzzing.

And for me, it meant getting him on the show. Twist my arm. I'd always been a big fan of Costner. What woman in this country isn't? For months, in the back of my mind, I strategized on how to land Kevin Costner as a guest on my show.

Timing is everything in this business. When I heard that they were having the premier of *Tin Cup* in Louisville the Tuesday prior to the PGA Championship, I knew that this was my best shot at organizing an interview with Costner. There was only one problem. I was in Atlanta covering the Olympics for Westwood One Radio, hosting a three-hour, daily talk show and reporting on basketball and gymnastics. Working the Olympic Games is an all-consuming and physically draining assignment. Luckily, the screening and interview were scheduled for the day after the Closing Ceremonies. But I was completely exhausted. After three weeks in Atlanta, all I wanted to do was go home to my husband, Steve, and my dog Max. I considered that cozy possibility for a while, then reminded myself that Costner was going to be in Louisville and so must I. It was my only chance.

I have great admiration for Kevin Costner and the guts he shows in choosing movie roles that are meaningful for him, even when they are commercially risky. There was little encouragement and much speculation when he decided to direct and star in a three-hour Western with Indian dialogue and subtitles, but *Dances with Wolves* was a huge success, earning several Oscars including Best Picture and Best Director. *Waterworld*, the most expensive film ever made—over $175 million—was expected to be the biggest flop in movie history. Instead, it went on to become an international box office success with profits of over $100 million.

I was also impressed with Costner's ability to hit a golf ball. He has always been a good athlete, but prior to the filming of this movie, Costner

REUTERS/BLAKE SELL/ARCHIVE PHOTOS

had neither the time nor the inclination to play. He did not want to use a double for the movie, so if he was going to be plausible as a professional golfer, he needed a crash course in a hurry. Enter Gary McCord, whose book, *Golf for Dummies*, is still on my nightstand. He is the professional most credited with teaching Costner. He came out looking like a genius. In a very short period of time, he transformed the actor into a decent player, enhancing his own reputation in the process.

I was most enamored of Costner in his early days when he was the devoted husband and father. He still is very close to his kids, but his marriage ended in divorce several years ago. When we sat down, Costner looked tired and unhappy. It was my impression that he was worn down living the life that feeds the tabloid monster. I could not avoid asking about his personal life, and he told me he identified with the character he played in *Tin Cup*, Roy McAvoy, a "mess" personality.

Costner is as charming and seductive in person as he is on the big screen, not always the case when you meet film celebrities. The smile and appeal that have captivated audiences and propelled him to the upper reaches of movie stardom are the real thing. Kevin Costner doesn't have to act sexy. He is sexy. After our interview, having checked my vital responses to see that I was still breathing, still functioning, still relevant in my own little world, I tried to comprehend the mystery of this most flirtatious man with enough magnetism to attract any woman.

Months later, we both played in a celebrity golf tournament. I watched him from a distance as all the women flocked around him and all the men positioned themselves to golf and party with him, sucking up the rays of his starlight. Tomorrow they would brag about hanging with the sensational movie star. I watched him as he left the dinner party with the most beautiful woman in the room, a trophy amongst the macho eyes looking on. What is it like to be in his position? I wondered. Does he ever tire of the relentless adoration? Does he often question who his real friends are? Does he get sick of these questions?

LIGUORI: I understand you went from a twenty-eight handicap in real life to playing a golf pro in the movie, *Tin Cup* [1996], refusing to use a double for the golf shots.

COSTNER: I don't know what it was. I'd lose about twelve sleeves of balls a day.

LIGUORI: It's unbelievable that you were able to improve in such a short period of time.

COSTNER: Yeah, well, there was a certain amount of panic that occurred, plus I knew a whole bunch of people were going to be watching, so there was reason to try to get there.

LIGUORI: Are you passionate now about the sport, having made *Tin Cup*, a romantic comedy set in a golf environment, and spending so much time learning to play?

COSTNER: I wouldn't say passionate, but it represents a really good outlet for me now that I didn't experience. I was introduced to golf early and it wasn't something that I was going to do, and then as an adult, it was something I didn't feel I had time for, you know. So the once-a-year kind of thing just actually easily confirmed why I didn't like golf.

LIGUORI: How about a spiritual connection to golf? So many golfers make some kind of connection to golf that your character in *Tin Cup* had. Do you experience that with the game?

COSTNER: No, no.

LIGUORI: So, it's just on to the next sport—you've conquered this one onscreen?

COSTNER: Why I like the game is that it's competitive, and I found it to be a really good release for me to be with friends and find myself in kind of private situations for three or four hours. And so, not only do I get the game and the competitive thing, but I also get a chance for things to come out on a personal level that maybe don't come out at a restaurant when you're interrupted or moving or that sort of thing. It's still an angry sport. You know, I try to describe it a couple of times and I think Ron Shelton [the director of *Tin Cup*] and I—I don't know about Cheech [Marin, Costner's caddie in the movie] and Craig [Stadler, a PGA tour player who's also in the movie]—but we grew up playing basketball, baseball, and football. We didn't have a country club kind of mentality in terms of tennis and golf, or in something that we were playing. And in all my experience of playing sport, I've lost and I've won, but I've never been angry at the end of the game. I've always felt really good. Eight pickup games—you know, "hold the court" or something like that. But at the end of the day, I felt great, had a great day of playing. And I've had days of golf where I just hated it. It was very different than anything else I'd ever played, and I thought, great, why the hell did I even go out there and play? So that's never been an experience for me in a sport, to have that kind of frustration and anger.

LIGUORI: Your character in this movie seemed to be more like you than other roles you have played. Did you identify with this character more than in other roles?

COSTNER: Not really, but I understand this character and there is a lot of him in me. But I loved *Wyatt Earp* [1994], you know, but what it is, is Wyatt Earp is a more difficult character to watch. *Perfect World* [1993, Butch Haynes] is a more difficult character to watch. But I identified with both of those men, and I identified with Roy [his character in *Tin Cup*], who is like a mess. Who is just a complete emotional mess—funny and full of poetry and bluster and everything else. So, yeah, it's a more enjoyable character for people to watch on the surface because he is as flawed as we know we are inside. At some point, I cannot let what other people think about the movie override what I think about it, and to me this is just graduated refrigerator art. I mean my mom would put up any painting or any drawing I did on the refrigerator whether it was good or not, and because she did that, I kept making them, I kept making them. And in my professional career, I keep making these movies that I think have a value, have a sense of drama to them, and you know we looked at the movie, and I don't depend on the world to tell me what's right and wrong, or what's good and bad. I think we live too much in a world that does this, that does that, that says who is the best dressed, who is the worst dressed. I think we live in a world that's constantly trying to tell us what to think. And I already know what I think about *Tin Cup*, and so my expectation has been met. The idea that other people like it, that's the refrigerator art. I hope so.

LIGUORI: Making *Tin Cup* must have been refreshing after all the challenges associated with making *Waterworld*.

COSTNER: Well, it's a different kind of movie, to be sure. You know, I mean that's a big costume movie, and a big action movie, and there's hundreds and hundreds of people. And while this is a movie that seems to be about golf, it's not. It's about men and women. Movies will always be great when they are about men and women for the most part, if you ask me. And so here is this classic American movie, set against the world of golf, and really what Ron [Shelton] and Johnny [Norville, the cowriter] did is they made golf real to those people who know about golf and they made it accessible to people who think that they don't want to have anything to do with golf. It's heavy on the humor and the drama.

LIGUORI: Well, the romantic comedy roles are perfect for you, I think. Talk a little about this.

COSTNER: [Laughing] You mean I'm a funny lover? What are you trying to say?

LIGUORI: [Laughing with him] No, I mean your charm! Romantic comedies best showcase your charm. You know what I mean. On to another subject, the scene in *Tin Cup* where you are in the bar and you are challenged to hit the ball through the bar, out the door, over the water to knock the pelican off its perch—how tough was that to do?

COSTNER: Well, it was tough staging, because you know you wanted to find the right jocular thing between me and Don Johnson [playing a rival golfer], the right staging, the challenge, and I need a fairway. And it takes a while to find the movement because you have the words on the paper. And then really what happens is when people start drinking scotch and walking up and down, and you get the extras going back and forth with trays, and you get that locker-room feeling inside the clubhouse of a big tournament, you know, suddenly things start to come alive and then you start to find your rhythms about how this can work. A bet gets made in front of a lot of people—it's just a sucker bet, but then what you do is you rise to the challenge.

LIGUORI: I understand that someone once challenged Gary McCord [professional golfer and TV commentator] to that very same scenario and that is how the scene found its way into the script. Is that true?

COSTNER: Well, you know, these guys get rained out like ballplayers. You see ballplayers go out and do ridiculous things when they get rained out, and sometimes the mood just hits you. And you know you put a bunch of guys who all they've done is just play sports, and then you coup them up in a room and you get alcohol going. People get bored and they make up dumb games.

LIGUORI: Your image has always been this regular guy who has resisted the temptations of superstardom. Is that still you, or do you think you've come full circle since then?

COSTNER: Well, I have the benefits of superstardom, so for me to indulge myself—I mean, how can I indulge myself more than things that are already given to me? The things that are important to me are my family, my friends, the people I will meet. You know you just have to keep yourself on some kind of even keel there. I've always been surprised at people who become monsters after they are successful, because I guess if you're going to become a monster, the time to become one is when you don't have anything. When so many things are given to you, it's easy to be generous and charitable. That's an easy thing. What you have to realize is that when you get to that point, all the people that are around you are there to help you. And what happens is that sometimes people start to look at the people around them who helped them and start looking at them as privileges. That person is very vital to you, and if you appreciate him and understand him, that's one thing, but over time, people start to think, "I'm entitled to that." Not true.

LIGUORI: Are you happy now?

COSTNER: No. You know, I tell you either your professional career is where you want it to be or it's not, and your personal life—and I think a lot of people relate to the idea that I can't get my professional and my personal life balanced. I wish my personal life was in a stronger order, but it's what it is, and you deal with that like a bad lie. You know, you just go up to it and you think about it and then you can make the best play that you can make. How did you like that? I turned that into a little golf analogy.

Joanna Kerns

The image of Joanna Kerns as the quintessential mom was firmly etched into my brain. The star of the television series *Growing Pains* personified the notion of clean-cut vitality in the modern American woman. Though I wasn't a regular viewer of her hit show, it was impossible to miss her as television's favorite woman in distress in a multitude of made-for-television movies over the past decade. I admired the decency and humanity that Kerns brought to her characters in crisis, as they cope with their tales of misfortune. Then I saw her pictured in *People* magazine in a special feature on Hollywood golfers. One of television's paragons of motherhood was an avid golfer, too. I had to interview her.

I found out she was playing in a tournament at Ballymeade Country Club in Falmouth, Massachusetts, and made arrangements to have her on the show. The "Queen of television movies," as she has often been described, was completely cooperative as preparations were made for her appearance. When we finally met on the Cape, we found we had much in common.

Kerns has her own production company and, in addition to her acting, has gone behind the camera to direct. Like myself, Joanna has been an athlete all of her life. In high school, she was a gymnast who tried out for the 1968 Olympic team. Kerns athleticism is homegrown. Her father was an all-American football player, her brother is a golf instructor, and her sister is Donna DeVarona, a gold medal-winning Olympic swimmer. Joanna discovered a passion for the links ten years ago and is now a dedicated student of the game, with strong opinions on the special issues that affect women in golf.

We swapped war stories about the discrimination that women continue to abide as this once white male fortress slowly cracks open its doors to women, African-Americans and other minorities. We commiserated over the distressing fact that women are still prevented from joining country clubs independent of their husbands. Kerns was turned down by three private clubs before gaining membership into the Riviera Country Club in Los Angeles. Female members' tee times are often limited to off-hours on the course. We have both been restricted from playing on Saturday and Sunday mornings before 11 AM and at some clubs prior to 2 PM. We know well the condescending looks and the subtle complaints of men when women are

MARC GLASSMAN

playing in front of them. The stereotypical notion that women golfers are slow has grown tiresome and insulting. Joanna and I both share a very competitive drive and love for the game. We agreed that there is no greater satisfaction than outdriving men from the reds and scoring better than the guys in our foursome. Our gripe session was great therapy, an opportunity to share our concerns over the brutal underbelly of the world of golf. We settled on the hope that Tiger Woods shall free us all.

There is certainly a symmetry, a microcosm of harmony, that golf disciples can tune into when the vibes are working. Joanna's honesty and willingness to share her heartfelt feelings and opinions allowed us to establish a rapport. While walking the fairway, Joanna admitted that in her career the two greatest hurdles in her path were fear and the difficulty of living up to other people's expectations. In between golf shots, we found our way to one of my favorite topics, the parallel relationship between life and golf, and how the course reveals one's strengths and vulnerabilities. In the short time we knew each other, Joanna and I, through our mutual infatuation with the sport, were able to forge the beginnings of a friendship.

Joanna Kerns impressed me as an individual at peace with herself, confident and unafraid to speak from the heart. As my husband and I made plans to play golf with Joanna and her husband, Marc Appleton, I knew that we would remain good friends. Golf certainly has a way of bringing people together.

LIGUORI: Joanna, you're an actress, a producer, director, writer . . .

KERNS: Golfer.

LIGUORI: Golfer. Well, maybe we should put golf at the top of the list because I know you are playing so much golf.

KERNS: Well, I play whenever I can. In fact, I've been accused of being on the golf course when I should be other places, but we really won't talk about that.

LIGUORI: Is that why you play golf—to get away from the hectic pace of Hollywood?

KERNS: You know, I think it's one of the few times that I get away from it all and that I can only think about the game and I can only "be." And the minute I start thinking about the last shot or the shot ahead, my game goes away, but I kind of have to be in the moment. It's very similar [to] acting that way. If you're in the moment, your work is much better than if you're thinking about what you just did or what you're going to say or whatever. It suits me. I like it a lot.

LIGUORI: Joanna, how much of your acting technique can you bring to golf?

KERNS: Well, I think my work as an actress is on the mark when I'm not really thinking about it. You do kind of all your work ahead of time—it's the same as golf. If you take lessons and you have some technique, and you practice, then when you get out to play the game you should just be playing the game. You shouldn't be thinking about any of that other stuff. And that's where it's similar to acting. You also have to be in the moment as an actor. The minute when you see somebody on the air, and you see where they're gonna go, and you know they've said that line forty times before, and they're kind of wooden. Well, golf is similar. I mean you have to erase everything you're thinking about, just be clear and in the moment, and you can usually hit a pretty good shot that way.

LIGUORI: Joanna, more and more young women are playing golf. But back when I was a kid, women didn't play golf when they were kids. It was a sport for the older women at the country clubs.

KERNS: Older women, or men. I mean it still is, it still is a man's sport. It's very, very tough for women to join country clubs.

LIGUORI: Absolutely.

KERNS: There are very few clubs that will take them. My club is one of the few.

LIGUORI: And you're where?

KERNS: I'm at Riviera in Los Angeles, and across country, it gets worse. I mean it's one of the few elite institutions left, I think, in this country. It's very tough to qualify for certain club standards, and it makes me mad, but it's still out there. It's still going on. We were talking, my husband and I, about what Tiger Woods might do for all of us in a way. I mean, not only will Blacks and minorities be allowed to get into country clubs, but maybe it will help women, too.

LIGUORI: Was it tough for you to join a club? I mean, in your whole process of looking for a private club?

KERNS: It was my fourth club that I tried to join, and I was always turned down for other reasons. But friends of mine, guys that I played with, got in before me, or were accepted, and I wasn't.

LIGUORI: That is maddening, isn't it? That's just so awful.

KERNS: It was infuriating, and I was surprised. I've grown up my whole life—my father always told all of us that we could do anything we wanted to do as long as we worked hard enough and we were honest about what we were doing and our effort was real. And you go to join a country club and suddenly because you're a woman, you can't join. Or because you're a woman, you can't play before eleven o'clock, because somewhere women didn't work. Somewhere in someone's mind, women didn't work, so men get the early hours. I mean, that's what they say.

LIGUORI: So many clubs discriminate against women. As more and more business women play and demand equality, maybe membership rules and the time restrictions will change.

KERNS: See, I think they're worried about slow play, which is a reality in country clubs. If you have . . .

LIGUORI: But, how many guys play so slow [laughing]?

KERNS: They do, they do [agreeing and laughing].

LIGUORI: No offense, guys, but really. Guys seem to have summit meetings on the greens.

KERNS: They do because of their betting. But, I think that if you are above a certain handicap, maybe you shouldn't play until later in the day, and you should only play nine holes so that you get out of the way. I mean, when we take our son out, my stepson and Marc's son, out to play, we go out later in the day so he can hit a few balls.

LIGUORI: And not have to worry about the foursome behind you.

KERNS: And if somebody's behind us, we make him pick it up and keep going.

LIGUORI: It really comes down to being courteous. It's really being aware of golf etiquette and being courteous and letting the guys behind you, or the ladies behind you, pass you if you're playing with a beginner.

KERNS: That's right.

LIGUORI: Women are learning the benefits of playing golf for business reasons.

KERNS: I've often wondered if that's why men don't really want us in country clubs. And that may or may not be true. But I also think women need to learn how to network better and help each other because I think men, through sports like golf and all the other team sports that men grew up doing, they do learn how to be team players and help each other.

LIGUORI: They learn about competition. They learn about winning, about losing. You acquire a lot of knowledge as to how to handle certain situations as an athlete.

KERNS: And how to separate the personal from business.

LIGUORI: That's right.

KERNS: I think games like this and networking like this allow them to do that.

LIGUORI: Tell me about the pilot that you did that involved women golfers.

KERNS: Well, the pilot that I just wish had gone. I did a pilot for ABC actually a year out of *Growing Pains*, and it was called *The Long Game*. It was about a woman who was the John McEnroe of the Ladies Tour at the end of her career, and she's one game out of the Hall of Fame and can't win that tournament, and she is a little crazy. So really it was about a woman who is reinventing herself and a woman who didn't know who she was without a golf club in her hand.

LIGUORI: That was a great idea.

KERNS: A great character. She was a great character; she was really a brat. It was a real departure for me because, although Maggie [her role in *Growing Pains*] could be combative and definitely had her own opinions, she was still nice. And this character was not nice. This was a club thrower, so it was a fun show. I had a great time making it. I had a lot of support from ABC and the network, and it just didn't—it was just one of those things that didn't go. It was before its time I think.

LIGUORI: That's too bad.

KERNS: What I loved about it is you had a character who had misbehaved, you know like McEnroe did and got away with it. But if you had been a woman on the Tour who had misbehaved, what do you do after you quit? What happens when the celebrity isn't there anymore? Do you have to go and teach in a club that maybe you did something bad at? Everybody knows how bad you were. I liked that idea. It was great fun.

LIGUORI: You were talking about the discrimination that women face with joining country clubs.

KERNS: We've still got a long way to go. We've come a great distance, I think. But I think a lot of what must go on to change is just education. People need to know that these things are happening. Like when I went to go join a country club, I didn't know that women couldn't join. It never occurred to me that women couldn't join. But there are clubs in Los Angeles that I can't join because I'm an actor, I'm in the industry. They say, "We don't want entertainment people."

LIGUORI: That's probably the excuse most of them use.

KERNS: Yes.

LIGUORI: The real reason was your gender.

KERNS: Different ones for different reasons. Some clubs said lack of charitable contributions, but it was to their charity.

LIGUORI: It can be very nasty.

KERNS: It's very nasty. And unfair. I just want to play golf.

LIGUORI: Joanna, has any of the mental preparation and training you utilize in acting carried over to your golf?

KERNS: I think actors are incredibly focused. I think actors have to learn because you can be all alone in a scene but there are about forty people around you staring at you in that moment. You have to be able to block everything out and be right there, and that's what you do with golf. And that's maybe why so many actors get so crazy about it and like it so much. I think doctors, too. It used to be doctors play on Wednesdays, but doctors have to do this incredibly intense work. [Marc hits his drive.] That was a beautiful shot, and I talked right through it. But they get to come out to the golf course and they have to focus in the same way, but nobody is going to die if they make a mistake.

LIGUORI: You were saying earlier about how in your acting career, when you let things go and you moved on to, say, directing, all of a sudden all these acting jobs . . .

KERNS: Started coming my way.

LIGUORI: Can you do that in golf as well? Can you let go of a shot that you're struggling with and all of a sudden it comes to you?

KERNS: Usually around the eighteenth hole and I've played terribly and I go, "Oh . . ." I can't swear on camera, but I go, "Just forget it, forget it. I'm just going to play." Then I hit it, so I think it's the same thing.

LIGUORI: It's amazing how the philosophies are so similar.

KERNS: I think one of the things as a kid that I didn't understand about golf was that there was this interior game, this wonderful game that you don't understand when you watch it. I think television coverage has brought that kind of out now, because you're really getting close and you get to see some of the strategy that goes on. Letting go is definitely the way to go in life as well as golf. It is like life, because everything gets in the way in life. Life is what's happening when you're making other plans. It's all these other things that come in when you're expecting to be doing something else, and golf is the same way. You always expect to be in the middle of the fairway after a perfect shot.

LIGUORI: Joanna, what do you think has been the most difficult obstacle to overcome in your acting career? The most challenging aspect that you've had to overcome as a working mom, as a professional?

KERNS: Oh, besides fear? I don't know if there's an actor out there that truly understands where their talent comes from. And I think that it's something that every time you go into an audition, some new situation comes up. You really have to get past what you feel, especially since I've had this wonderful success in my life. It's getting past what other people's perceptions are of you, especially if they know you really well in a certain role. Because in what I do, it's about reinventing yourself every time you go out, and sometimes it's hard to get past the PR and the press, and you have to kind of clear your mind. Clear your mind of not only your expectations but whatever they expect of you and just go out and do the best job you can. And so I think that's the hardest thing as an actor in terms of performing. And that's why actors are so turned on by being on a stage in a theater performance because moment to moment to moment, you're on the line the whole time. It isn't going in for a two-minute scene or a five-minute interval.

Dennis Franz

Dennis Franz, better known as Andy Sipowicz, the volatile police detective on the television series *NYPD Blue*, has a theory about actors and golf: any actor with a low handicap is probably not working very much. Franz's eight handicap of a few years ago has ballooned with his success, but he's not complaining. The fifteen-hour days he puts into taping the hit show don't leave much time for golf or, for that matter, interviews. When I heard that Franz was squeezing the Frank Sinatra Celebrity Golf Tournament into his busy schedule, I called his publicist to arrange an interview and was pleasantly surprised when he quickly agreed.

We flew to Indian Wells, California, and set up in a hotel suite at the Marriott Desert Springs. The first morning of the pro-am, I walked out to the carts with the intention of introducing myself to Franz and confirming our interview for that afternoon. I was excited and ignored my interviewer's sixth sense that whispered to me, rocky waters ahead. There was a buzz in the air as hundreds of fans gathered to soak up the glamour of the star-studded event. I scanned the rows and rows of golf carts occupied by celebrities. My heart sunk. There was no Dennis. Maybe he had canceled at the last moment. Finally, I located his unoccupied cart. His clubs were there, so Franz could not be far behind.

As the tournament director completed the rules and instructions, and the carts were summoned to their holes, Dennis wandered over to his cart looking a little groggy. He had arrived late the night before and had been sidetracked at the bar, visiting with friends until the early hours of the morning. We made our introductions, set the interview time for 5 PM, and I left feeling relieved and looking forward to our meeting.

By 4:30 PM, my excitement had turned to despair after I checked my messages and discovered Dennis had canceled. He was exhausted and needed a nap and would try to do the interview later. That sounded pretty ominous, but having flown all the way to California for the interview, I wasn't going to give up. At 6:30 PM, I went down to the cocktail party in search of Franz. I figured with forty-five minutes before dinner, there was enough time to still do the interview. I found him looking rested, and he good-naturedly agreed to my plan. As we were about to take our leave, his wife, Joannie, approached with a plan of her own. An auction had begun in the ballroom, and she wanted Dennis to help her bid on a few items. I got Dennis and Joannie drinks and reached for my most persuasive sales pitch, explaining to Joannie that I had come a long way to talk with Dennis and would only keep him for a half hour. She didn't seem particularly sympathetic, but Franz convinced her and we were on our way. Now all I had to do was get him up to the interview suite where the cameras were set up.

Tom Watson, Sandy Tatum, Dennis Franz, and Woody Austin. COURTESY OF AT&T PEBBLE BEACH NATIONAL PRO-AM

Another problem: it's never easy ushering a star through a hotel lobby. The fans were out en masse, seeking autographs and pictures with the popular actor. Dennis insisted on accommodating every request, and I cooled my heels for fifteen minutes as he chatted with his admirers. As my half hour dwindled, I did my best to quell my frustration, be polite, and hope Joannie would understand.

Finally, we were seated in front of the cameras, and the interview went smoothly. Franz chose his words carefully—he is a sweet, sensitive, thoughtful man. He displayed none of the well-known mannerisms of his explosive television character. Success came slowly for Franz. When he arrived at his peak, he benefited from a forty-plus maturity that enabled him to handle the pressures of his fame graciously. In the 1993–94 season, Dennis and *NYPD Blue* achieved the grand slam of his profession—an Emmy award (for lead actor in a drama series, he has since won another), a Golden Globe (Best Performance by an actor in a television series), the Screen Actors Guild Award, and a Viewers for Quality Television Award (Best Actor). An hour after we left the cocktail party to do the interview, Dennis was back with his wife, just in time for dinner, and I breathed a sigh of relief.

The next day we filmed Dennis in action on the golf course. He looked miscast in these surroundings. We all agreed that golf seemed out of character for Franz. Sipowicz would look more at home chomping on a pizza and pulling on a Budweiser in between his turn on the lane. What was the blue-collar New York tough guy doing on the carefully tended landscape of the fairway? From the looks of Dennis's game, Sipowicz had taken over. He was rusty and it showed as the actor contended with an assortment of slices and shanks. The consolation prize, according to the Franz theory of actors and golf, is that his rusty swing speaks well for the health of his career.

The same humility Franz showed during the interview transferred over to his golf game. There were no clubs thrown, no four-letter words, or any other displays of temper. And he could not have been sweeter to his team and the fans who followed him from hole to hole. Andy Sipowicz was nowhere to be found.

LIGUORI: It took a long time to escort you through the lobby, amongst all your fans. You certainly showed a lot of patience. It looks like you appreciate your success.

FRANZ: Well, it's going well on a personal level. On a professional level, everything seems to be going in a real positive direction, and life is pretty swell right now.

LIGUORI: There must have been a time obviously when it wasn't like this because you seem to appreciate the accolades. You take time with people, you're patient with everybody who comes up to you, and that to me signifies that there was a "before" to this "after."

FRANZ: I too often see people who are abrupt with the fans and people who want to do nothing but compliment you and pat you on the back. And I see other stars who don't take the time, and I'm sort of offended by that, and I think, why be anything other than cordial to somebody who wants to pay you a compliment?

LIGUORI: How about on the golf course? I mean, can you get even one shot in without getting bombarded by your fans?

FRANZ: I think you may see that me on the golf course is not much to get excited about. I'm certainly not here for my golfing prowess.

LIGUORI: But you love the game. You've been very passionate about golf for a long time now.

FRANZ: I certainly do, yes, I do. You'd think I'd be a good golfer with how much I like it. I just don't have the time. When I do, I really have a pretty together game, but I think it's that whole thing about actors and handicaps. When your handicap is low, you're not working much. And when it gets back up there, it means you're too busy to play, and so it's rising up there. I'm glad on that level. I've got an excuse at least.

LIGUORI: But putting in twelve to fifteen hour days on *NYPD Blue*, how do you have time to do anything?

FRANZ: Sometimes sixteen hours. And, yeah, that'll wear you down. You look forward to the weekend so you can come out and be part of this sort of madness.

LIGUORI: Can you bring your putter to the set to practice?

FRANZ: I got it set up in my trailer: from the kitchen area to the bedroom area, there's a little trail leading to a cup.

LIGUORI: What's your handicap now?

FRANZ: Thirteen. But I'm not playing to a thirteen. I certainly don't. I'm not swinging comfortably. I'm just not hitting the ball correctly. But I was down to an eight. I actually had it down to an eight.

LIGUORI: That's fabulous.

FRANZ: So I was at one time playing well, and then *NYPD Blue* started up, and little by little, it's gradually getting back up to where it should be for the level of play I'm playing at now.

LIGUORI: Now for some reason, I can't imagine Andy Sipowicz playing golf.

FRANZ: I know. Golfing and skiing. That's another thing I like to do, and people say, "Something's wrong with this picture. Sipowicz with a golf club? I don't know."

LIGUORI: Andy Sipowicz would never play golf, in my opinion, but maybe they'll write it in the script one of these days.

FRANZ: I don't think he would. We've talked about different avenues and directions for him to go, but I think Sipowicz is a bowler if he's anything. Maybe a pool stick in his hand or something.

LIGUORI: With a short sleeve shirt and a tie.

FRANZ: Yeah.

LIGUORI: Like that segment on *The Simpsons* where Homer was wearing a short-sleeve shirt and tie, and his wife Marge did not like it.

FRANZ: Isn't that funny? I was just thinking of that!

LIGUORI: Tell that story. What was that all about?

FRANZ: Homer and Marge are going out, and Marge says, "Homer, you can't wear that." He's got a short-sleeve shirt on with a tie. She says, "Homer, you can't wear a short sleeve shirt with a tie on." And he said, "Sipowicz does." And then she says, "You have to go take it off," and he's walking back going, "I wish I was Sipowicz."

LIGUORI: That was funny. If Andy Sipowicz was playing golf and chunked one, how would he react?

FRANZ: He'd show you the fine art of throwing that camera into the water. Probably. This would be after he dropped his pants. Fling a few clubs. Eh, I don't know.

LIGUORI: But you're so even tempered. You're so opposite from that. How would you react?

FRANZ: Well, I've thrown a few clubs in my days. I just don't have the ability enough to qualify to get angry about a bad shot because they're all bad. So I just have to accept it.

LIGUORI: Have there been any police officers on the course rooting you on? Because I know you get that often. They identify with your character on *NYPD Blue*.

FRANZ: We got it on the way in. In fact, we got stopped on the way in, and I was a little exceeding the speed limit. It turned out the registration was a little out-of-date, our seat belts were a little un-on. But he wished us a nice evening, and so there is some benefit to being on a good police show.

LIGUORI: That never works for me, for some reason.

FRANZ: You got a different series. You gotta get a different show.

LIGUORI: Is there one part of your game that needs more work than the other?

FRANZ: I have trouble hitting the ball. That seems to be my problem. No, I don't know. If I don't play enough, my body just becomes inflexible, and so more often than not, I start slicing my drives. But when I'm on my game, I'd say that probably my short game is the one that I'd need the most work on 'cause when I play often, I can drive pretty well.

LIGUORI: Talk a little bit about how involved you get with the show as far as writing.

FRANZ: They're open for every possible suggestion you can come up with. I think that's one of the things that makes the show so special, is that the writers are flexible enough that they encourage and welcome suggestions from cast members, from any fans. I mean, they really have their ears open. They're not closed minded in saying, "Oh, we know where they're going and that's that." People throw in these very odd suggestions, and sometimes they pick up on them and they run with them.

LIGUORI: Didn't you suggest the actual relationship with the district attorney?

FRANZ: Silvia Costas, yeah.

LIGUORI: That's worked out. *NYPD Blue* fans will never forget the infamous shower scene. [Characters Andy Sipowicz and Silvia Costas are showering together, and Franz's behind is exposed to the camera.]

FRANZ: I remember that! One little butt shot and look what happens. Show your butt and win awards, that's what I say.

LIGUORI: I'm telling you. Well, Leno had a good line on that. Do you remember it?

FRANZ: He had many good lines at my expense, I will say.

LIGUORI: Jay Leno on *Late Night* showed a picture of a bottom and said,

"This is a butt," and then he showed your bottom and said, "This is a butt on Twinkies."

FRANZ: The first time I really took an assault was, I think, Thanksgiving night, and he started talking, "Well, *NYPD Blue* finally showed Dennis Franz's ass. Now do we really need to see that?" And then he started a whole barrage of one-liners.

LIGUORI: You know you've made it when you can fill his opening dialogue. Your two main passions in life have been acting and sports.

FRANZ: I actually thought I was going to go into sports. I thought that's where I was headed. My love was baseball. Catching.

LIGUORI: That's right!

FRANZ: I was a catcher. And I used to eat, sleep, and drink baseball. That was my thing. The older I got, somewhere along the line, I auditioned for a play. I used to like to sing also. I was in school choirs and things. But I wasn't even aware that they had a theater department at the high school I was at. And this girl I was going out with was trying out for the play *The Crucible*. I went with her, and I just got sort of competitive about it. I saw the other people auditioning, especially the boys, and they were very meek and quiet and they weren't projecting very loud. And my father—I used to sing, and when I used to sing, my father would always say, "Sing loud, let people hear you." So I thought, "Boy, at least I can be loud, if nothing else." So I just raised my hand and I said, "Could I try this?" And I basically was loud, and I got one of the leads, and that's what started it. Then I did that play, and I had to drop out of one of the sports I was involved in, which was swimming at the time. I was on the swim team, and I dropped out of the swim team for that season and did this play. Loved the experience. Then, one by one, I dropped out of the other school sports I was playing after school and devoted all my time to trying out for plays and I just had a real passion for the theater. I just loved it. I was the kind of guy, I'd just come to the theater at night after school, when it was dark and nobody was in there, and I'd just wander around the stage. I liked being in the theater. I thought, boy, that could be heaven on earth if I could ever make a living at something like that.

Music

Alice Cooper

When I'm asked which guest I've been most surprised by, I immediately answer Alice Cooper, the master of shock rock. Cooper's loud music and controversial lyrics made him a rock star, but his outrageous clothing, makeup, and the crude sexual overtones he used, while hammering the sixties' love generation with his Theatre of the Grotesque, made him a legend. Not only did Alice rebel against conformity, he rewrote the rules of nonconformity.

Alice Cooper is an avid fan of The Golf Channel. His passion for the game has made him a regular on golf courses throughout the country. I was taken aback when Cooper's manager, Toby Mamis, told me that Alice would love to be a guest on my show. Toby wanted to time the interview around something his client was promoting. I assumed Cooper was about to release a CD or maybe embark on a new tour, but to my surprise, Alice was plugging Callaway Clubs. His Callaway commercial, where he co-stars with his boa constrictor on a putting green, was about to air nationally. Cooper's well-documented fondness for reptiles doesn't compare with his lesser known ardor for his five handicap.

In his wild days during the seventies, when a rock star would not be caught dead on the links, Cooper used to sneak out of his hotel with his clubs so that his fans would not catch him indulging in President Ford's favorite pastime. Between concert tours and onstage dramatizations of songs such as "Welcome to My Nightmare," and in the midst of tokes, gulps, and snorts, the king of drag rock was a golf junkie.

The pristine surroundings of the Mission Hills Country Club in Rancho Mirage, California, during the Nabisco Dinah Shore Celebrity Pro-Am, were the backdrop for our interview. Here, captivated by the beautiful desert mountains, under clear skies and palm trees, I was about to interview the grand daddy of rock's chicken abusers about his short game. My experience with celebrity interviews has taken me to some strange places, but this was raising the crossbar to new heights. Only the malleable purity of a golf course could create such surrealism.

To get into the spirit of it all, I wore a leather biker's jacket over my golf outfit. As we settled down to business, I searched Cooper for clues to the bizarre, but his gentle, sane demeanor suggested he had checked his rene-

ANN LIGUORI PRODUCTIONS

gade reputation in the clubhouse. Ironically, the most shocking thing about Alice Cooper was his normalcy. He was simply Vince Furnier, all-American golf addict.

Cooper was thin as a rail, with long dark hair. His gaunt, tanned face acted as a telltale odometer for the many miles of abuse on rock's treacherous freeway. He has been sober for years and credits his obsession with golf for saving his life. He is a bright, articulate, funny man. The guillotines, electric chairs, and other dark symbols he used to turn the music world upside down were simply stage props. He's comfortable separating his image from his reality.

Cooper has been married to Sheryl since 1976, and they have three children, Dash, Calico, and Sonora Rose. The family accompanies him to many celebrity tournaments, and they're *all* gorgeous. Surprises abound from this complicated man. Alice and his family are not only regular church-goers, but he even helps out with the annual Christmas pageant. I discovered that Cooper was the son of a Protestant minister. He played golf a lot with his father and spent a lot of quality time with him on golf courses in Phoenix, Arizona. The game of golf allows one to play well into the later years, and parents and their adult children are often afforded the opportunity to close the generation gap. Golf's timeless quality can even secure a bridge between a minister and his rock and roll son from hell.

These days Vince Furnier's props are his golf clubs, hundreds of them; his favorite performance venue, the fairway. Golf and the shock master are compatible bedfellows.

LIGUORI: Alice, as a shock rocker, how can you be accepted in the conservative world of golf?

COOPER: Golf cuts through lines of everything. Golf cuts right through all social lines. You can walk into the room with the president of U.S. Steel and the president of the United States, and if you're talking about how to correct a little slice just by turning your right hand, that stops conversation right there because they're all interested.

LIGUORI: Golf, the universal language.

COOPER: Yeah, it doesn't matter if you're a hard rocker or a diplomat. When it comes to golf, that's a sort of a common denominator.

LIGUORI: What's been the most outrageous reaction you've gotten from somebody in the golf world?

COOPER: I haven't ever been thrown off a course. But I can think of some people that I could bring on golf courses that I would get thrown off just by bringing them. But I think if you can go out there and play well, they can't really say anything about it. You go out there, and if you can shoot five or six over, you're usually playing better than the person that's bothering you.

LIGUORI: You're a five handicap, which is damn good, and . . .

COOPER: I'm an extremist. I play five times a week—five or six times. When I was on tour, we would tour for three years without a break. When I was an alcoholic, I used to drink two bottles of whiskey a day. I think everything I do is to the extreme. So when I got into golf and I stopped drinking, I became an extremist golfer. I never do anything "sort of." I either do it all the way or not at all.

LIGUORI: Is that why you took up golf, as a rehab for the alcohol?

COOPER: I found it as trading one bad habit for one good habit. My wife would say I traded one bad habit for a worse habit. But yeah, I actually used it—when I stopped drinking, I went to a hospital and stopped. I haven't had a drink in thirteen years now. The day I got out of the hospital, I played thirty-six holes, and then I played every day for a year, eighteen holes to thirty-six holes a day, and it really was a good help.

LIGUORI: Several athletes I've talked to say they use golf as a form of alcohol rehab. Lawrence Taylor's attitude was "Golf is my therapy. I'll rehab on the golf course."

COOPER: I think so, yeah. It's just one of those things. I don't know, there's something so addictive about the game. There's a satisfaction in the game also that, if I don't play golf during the day, then I feel as though I've missed out on something—there's a big part of my life missing. So when I go to Europe and things like that for a week or two weeks, I feel like I gotta be really committed to what I'm doing over there. If it's a TV show or a movie or something like that, I've gotta really want to do that movie because I know I'm gonna not be playing. And I think if you talk to guys like Stallone and a lot of people in the business who like to play golf—Michael Douglas, people like that—they'll tell you the same thing. They'll really have to love the movie in order to sacrifice the golf.

LIGUORI: Can't they find a course to play where they're filming?

COOPER: Stallone tried to have one built in Rome when he was doing a film in Rome and he tried to . . .

LIGUORI: Make it part of the contract. I'm sorry. No golf course, no movie.

COOPER: He actually had them. They were going to have to build a golf course for him. Which I think is very cool. [Cooper turns to his manager, who is watching our interview.] Can I get that in my next contract? Okay? Good.

LIGUORI: What do you like about this game?

COOPER: Well, it's the fact that you get rewarded for good shots and even your bad shots. It's a game of how good are your bad shots. It's such a unique game because of the fact that you get out there, you get to hit the ball, you get to pound the ball, and the better you get at it, the more addicted you become because you know that you can hit 68 good shots. It's possible to hit that many. My best round was 67, and I was unconscious that day because I hit 67 good shots in a row.

LIGUORI: Where did you shoot 67?

COOPER: In Phoenix, at Camelback Country Club. And the next day I shot 84. On the same course. So it shows you just how fast it goes.

LIGUORI: So now, you probably always strive to shoot a 67.

COOPER: Well, I know it's there.

LIGUORI: Sure, you know you can do it.

COOPER: Yeah, I know it's there. I know I'm capable of doing that, and I think that every golfer knows he's capable of shooting par golf. And so it's just a matter of "is this going to be the day when he does it?"

LIGUORI: But Alice Cooper didn't just say, "I'm going to go out and be a five." I mean, it must take constant practice.

COOPER: You know, I never practice. I just play. But I play with a lot of pros, and I play with a lot of assistant pros. I play with my teacher Jim Rooney in Phoenix, Danny Briggs, who's on the Nike tour. I have a lot of guys in Phoenix—Tom Weiskopf helped me, Johnny Miller helped me.

LIGUORI: So you're serious about the lessons?

COOPER: Yeah, when you play with pros, it's sort of like taking a lesson. If you get to go out and play a round with Tom Weiskopf, that's like taking ten lessons because he'll see things that other guys won't see and say, you know, "Don't try to hit it as hard as I am." That makes sense. And as soon as you do that, you're suddenly hitting the ball straight again.

LIGUORI: So you won't go on the range to practice?

COOPER: Oh, I do once in a while.

LIGUORI: How about going to the green to practice?

COOPER: If I'm starting to see a consistency where I'm hitting the ball twenty degrees to the right of the green, maybe five or six times, I say, "Uh-oh." It's like when your car gets out of line—you know you have to go in and get your front end aligned, and they'll say, "what's going on?" I can't figure out what's making me do that. And a pro will look at you and go, "Ah! It's this." And it's usually something as silly as moving your left foot back two inches and suddenly you're back in line again. But amateurs will never be—we can't see that. We get stuck into a rut and we can't see that little adjustment.

LIGUORI: So you surround yourself with pros.

COOPER: Good players, yeah.

LIGUORI: That makes sense. You were very smart with the way you orchestrated your career, and now it has carried over on the golf course—it's very smart. Why waste time? You surround yourself with the best.

COOPER: I think that's a good idea. When you're doing records, you try to surround yourself with the best musicians, the best writers, the best producers, and that's the same thing in golf. You try to. But I have just as much fun going out and getting a pickup game and playing with five guys, or four guys that are like twenty handicaps. I have just as much fun. I'm still playing golf. But if I want to play hard, I want to play good, like today, I'm playing with an LPGA pro. That's going to bring my game up.

LIGUORI: Will you ask the person you're playing with from the LPGA for some advice?

COOPER: Absolutely. If something starts going wrong, if I'm seeing the putt to the left, if I'm pulling the putt, I will absolutely go to her and say, "What do you see? What's going on?" Because I certainly don't have all the answers. I'm one of those guys who says, "Let's ask for directions how to get there." I'm not one of those husbands that says, "I know how to get there."

LIGUORI: Has anybody you've ever played with been intimidated by you? "God, Alice Cooper, I remember the guy with the paint and the nails and the hair and the costumes and the snake and the chicken. . . . "

COOPER: If that comes up I just say, "Let's play five bucks a hole, then we'll talk about it, okay?"

LIGUORI: But you really are much different than your onstage persona.

COOPER: Well, I think anybody that has a character is [different], you know. You'll be surprised, Howard Stern is nothing like Howard Stern on the radio. Most guys—Woody Allen is generally not funny; when you're just talking to him, he's very serious. I think a lot of people create an image, create a character, and they play that character so well that you think that that's what they are. And that's a compliment that I can play that character of Alice so well. I'm nothing like Alice Cooper. I mean, I created him so I wouldn't have to be him. He's really truly my anti-character.

LIGUORI: I know you grew up as a four-year letter man in high school athletics.

COOPER: Well, one of the funniest things was the fact that when Alice Cooper first came out, the band, there's five guys with hair down to their waist, tattoos everywhere, ripped up, makeup, and we really looked like the band from hell. And we looked like, "Oh please, this is the worst bunch of guys ever." Everybody in the band was a four-year letter man. Everybody was an athlete. Everybody finished high school, went on to college.

LIGUORI: Were you angry as a child?

COOPER: Absolutely not. I was an artist. I was an artist. I figured something out. I figured that there were no rock villains, there were only rock heroes, and there needed to be rock villains. So I created Alice as a rock villain. But Alice was always a comical character to me. He was about as villainous as the Joker. I mean, you know he didn't really do these things. And most of Alice's mystique was the audience making up the different rumors about Alice.

LIGUORI: And the critics. . . .

COOPER: And the writers, yeah. But that's the fun of Alice is the fact that people use their imaginations and create this horrific character, and when you really get down to the character, yeah, he does things on stage that are, "What!? How did he do that?" But I created him; he's my Frankenstein. I'm Doctor Frankenstein, and he's my monster.

LIGUORI: Alice, you're a Callaway guy now. You play with the Callaway Big Berthas and the Callaway irons.

COOPER: You know, I'm on their staff now, on the Callaway staff, because I think what they figured was, if Alice can hit them, anyone can hit them. They sent all their clubs to me, and if I can hit them, then the average guy can hit them.

LIGUORI: I love the commercials you do for Callaway. You get the boa constrictor out on the putting green, and the ball winds its way along the snake, into the hole.

COOPER: It took us years to train that snake to putt like that. It's funny that Callaway used the snake and Cobra [another golf club manufacturer] didn't.

LIGUORI: Do people come up to you and say they saw you in that golf spot?

COOPER: Oh yeah. I get a lot of recognition from that, especially from people who aren't rock and roll fans. You have to expand a little bit. I don't want to be known just for rock and roll. I'm forty-eight now. I love golf. I'd love to make golf a semiprofession.

LIGUORI: Have you tried everything out there? Are you the kind of guy that would experiment with every single brand?

COOPER: I am a golf club junkie. My garage looks like Nevada Bobs. When people come into town I say, "Don't bring your clubs." They go, "Why?" I say, "Just come in—what do you play?" They say, "Well, I play this." I say, "What? Stiff? Regular?" Because I've got everything in there.

LIGUORI: "What length of shaft would you like?"

COOPER: Yeah, exactly. No, I am a golf club junkie. I can't help it. I go into golf stores. I love old golf clubs, not old, old ones, but every once in a while, I'll see a set of old Wilson Staffs and I'll just go, "Man, I've got to have those."

LIGUORI: So you're a collector?

COOPER: Yes, and I love yard sales. I've become a yard sales freak.

LIGUORI: Alice Cooper shows up at the yard sale.

COOPER: Oh, I love yard sales. People who won't admit they love yard sales and flea markets and things like that, they're just not alive. Pawn shops—pawn shops are great.

LIGUORI: Do you ever find any good golf clubs at pawn shops?

COOPER: Oh sure, you find great putters at pawn shops.

LIGUORI: Tell me how you broke into the music business because the Frank Zappa story is so funny. You showed up at his house at 7 AM?

COOPER: Well, he said seven; we didn't know he meant seven in the evening. So we figured, we got there in full makeup, full everything, at seven. We were so anxious to get a record contract.

LIGUORI: This was back in Detroit?

COOPER: No, this was in Laurel Canyon [California]. He lived in a big log cabin then. And he had seen us play and he said, "Listen, I want to hear your material. You should come up to my house at seven." And we literally got there at six and set up in the morning, and he came down with his coffee and said, "What are you guys doing?" And it never occurred to me that he didn't mean seven in the morning. So he listened to about four songs and he said, "Okay, okay, okay, okay, I'll sign you. Go, go away."

LIGUORI: Get out of here.

COOPER: "Get out of here."

LIGUORI: Tell me about the time you worked with Salvador Dali.

COOPER: He spoke five languages. He spoke French, Portuguese, Spanish, English, and Italian, but every fifth word was one you could understand. At the end of the press conference that we did, they'd ask me what I thought of Salvador Dali and what he just said. And I'd say, "I don't understand a word of what he is talking about. I enjoy his paintings and his insanity and probably, technically, he is one of the greatest painters of all time. But I don't understand a word he is talking about," and he jumps up and says, "Confusion is the greatest form of communication."

LIGUORI: He gets it!

COOPER: He wasn't unaware of anything we were talking about. He was wearing a pair of socks that Elvis Presley gave him, giraffe skin pants, Aladdin, purple velvet shoes that curl up, a tiger skin coat. He had his sideburns in pin curls, and I was going to ask him, "Why don't we go and play a few holes, Sal?'

LIGUORI: Could you imagine him on the golf course? What kind of golfer would he be?

COOPER: I'd like to see him paint a golf course. His rendition of a golf course would have giraffes coming out of the water, melting trees, and all kinds of stuff.

LIGUORI: Alice, you started golfing when it wasn't cool to golf.

COOPER: You know, that's true. When I was playing golf, it was like we had to hide it. My manager and everyone around me knew I liked to play golf, and it was like getting away with something real underground. It's like I was into some sort of strange ritualistic thing. I was playing golf! But it was not cool because most of the kids at that time, their dads played golf, and it was not cool to play golf. Even though I knew that Iggy [Pop] played golf and some of the guys in Pink Floyd, and there were a few guys out there in rock and roll who played. But for Alice to play golf, it was too conventional.

LIGUORI: How did you sneak away?

COOPER: I used to have to just get away and go to golf courses that were unpublicized. We had to deny it all the time, that I played golf.

LIGUORI: "That wasn't me, I swear."

COOPER: I mean it was very weird. I was doing the most wholesome thing in the world, and we had to deny the wholesomeness of it. Which is kind of funny, just totally opposite. It wasn't like Billy Graham going out and doing something really horrific. It was like some bad guy going out and doing something good.

LIGUORI: Did you play with your band members as well?

COOPER: No, none of the band played. I was the only one.

LIGUORI: They probably thought you were nuts.

COOPER: Yeah, they did. They were all hung over and everything, and I was out at six o'clock in the morning playing golf.

LIGUORI: Was this after you went to detox or before?

COOPER: I had started playing golf before that as just curiosity. I could hit the ball, and I think I had a natural swing so I could play pretty good. When I stopped drinking, I got much better. Suddenly it all got into focus. The same thing happened to me with my stage shows. When I stopped drinking, my stage shows got much better. They got much more clear and much more energetic and focused. So I guess a bottle of whiskey isn't the best idea.

LIGUORI: When your band members saw you playing golf, did they think, God, he's really losing it?

COOPER: First of all, they would never come out there. They would never ever come out there.

LIGUORI: But when they saw you were going out, sneaking out with the clubs?

COOPER: Yeah, they just didn't understand it. And I didn't understand it at the time. I didn't know why I liked it. But it was sort of a natural attraction for me. And in Detroit we didn't have—where I came from we only had three sports. In Detroit, when you were a kid, you had baseball, football, and grand theft auto. That was it. There was no golf; there was no tennis.

LIGUORI: What sports did you letter in?

COOPER: I lettered in track and cross country. I was a distance runner.

LIGUORI: And nobody in your family played golf?

COOPER: No, my dad started playing when he was about sixty. When I started going out and playing, he got interested and he started playing and he got addicted to it. He just loved it. He played five times a week if he could.

LIGUORI: So it was something you could do with Dad?

COOPER: Yeah.

LIGUORI: How uncool, people must have thought, for a rock star.

COOPER: No, it was cool. My dad was cooler than me. That was the problem.

LIGUORI: He inspired all your concerts?

COOPER: No, not at all. He was a pastor.

LIGUORI: He was?

COOPER: But he was the coolest pastor in the world.

LIGUORI: What kind of pastor?

COOPER: Protestant.

COOPER: Did you go to church?

COOPER: Oh, yeah. I grew up in church. I go to church now.

LIGUORI: Every week you were in church? Every Sunday?

COOPER: Yeah.

LIGUORI: Even during your darkest period?

COOPER: Oh no, no, no, not then. I was the original prodigal child. I was the prodigal son who went as far as you could go and got reeled back in.

LIGUORI: What did Dad think during those days?

COOPER: My dad was one of those guys—when I tell my daughter, my daughter's a teenager, I say, "Always remember this. You've got a lot of cool friends, but your dad is Alice Cooper. I'm cooler than any of your friends." She says, "You know what? You're right, you are cooler than my friends. You're hipper than my friends." My dad was always funnier than me. He was always more aware of what was going on out there. He could tell you who played every instrument in the Animals or the Yardbirds, but he could also tell you passages from any scripture in the Bible. He didn't think that rock and roll was necessarily music or was necessarily bad. I think that what he thought was that a lot of the messages were bad. A lot of what it was opening up for us, saying that sex, in other words is okay. Well, he didn't believe that and so he says, "Be careful what you write about." So I think that a lot of Alice Cooper writing was much more satirical. I only wrote about things that were socially critical in places that were appropriate. But really, like I said, never political, and you'll never find anything on our stage that was ever anti-Christian because I came from a Christian background and I was a little too aware of that to be antireligious at all.

LIGUORI: Well, if that's the case, then I think a lot of your songs were probably misperceived. I remember your song "Dead Babies," it was about child abuse.

COOPER: It was the very first anti–child abuse song. If you listen to that song, it's talking about parents that are just not aware of what their kids are doing or dead babies can't take care of themselves. It's not saying, let's go kill babies. It's saying if you leave your kid alone to what kids are going to do, they're going to die. And that was written in 1970. "Only Women Bleed" was the first women's song. In fact, it got picked up later. Tina Turner did it. There were about thirteen different covers on it of women doing that song. And it was talking about women being abused. When you heard the title, "Only Women Bleed," it sounded like we were trying to get away with something, but that's not what the purpose of that song was at all. It was saying that women take a lot of abuse that they don't need to take.

LIGUORI: "I'm Eighteen"—even that had a message.

COOPER: "Eighteen" was a celebration of being eighteen. You know, the idea that when you're eighteen years old, you're not a boy, not a man, you're right in the middle. You're confused and everything is upside down in your life and it's great. For some reason, it's great to be eighteen and to be confused.

LIGUORI: A lot of the misperceptions with your songs benefited you in a promotional way.

COOPER: Yeah, and in a lot of ways I think that now maybe those songs are being relooked at. And now people are looking at them and going, "Oh, now I get it. I understand what he was trying to say." And sometimes it takes ten years before somebody will go back and look at a song and say, "Oh, now I understand that."

LIGUORI: Do you feel as if your music is more appreciated today?

COOPER: I think, at the moment, it was shock value. We were the hottest thing around. For ten years, we were the biggest deal around. Yeah, your time goes in cycles. And then there's the time when the next wave came in and this band here was the hot one. Guns and Roses were the next thing, but I think what lives on is quality. I think if you've written quality material and if you've done quality shows, you can go on as long as you want to go. As soon as you start getting schlock, start getting like, "Ah, who cares," then you're not going to be around very long.

Kenny G

Kenny Gorelick hits a golf ball with the same passion and intelligence that he brings to his music. The number-one selling jazz instrumentalist of all time is very serious about his game and organizes his busy schedule to set aside enough time to play and improve.

Kenny G studied accounting, of all things, at the University of Washington. Upon graduating with honors, he left the numbers behind in search of the perfect chord. Kenny was hired by Jeff Lorber to join a popular Portland-based band, the Jeff Lorber Fusion. After four years with the band, Arista Records offered him his own solo deal. He developed his unique style with his first several albums, then captured the ear of the mainstream listening public with his breakthrough fourth album, *DuoTones*. The hit single, "Songbird," written in 1986 for Lyndie, the woman who would become his wife, emerged as a pop classic. Kenny's seventh album, *Breathless*, released in 1992, combined jazz, rhythm and blues, pop, and funk. It debuted at number nine on *Billboard*'s album chart, breaking Stan Getz's thirty-year record for an instrumentalist's residence in popular music's Top Ten.

Kenny G agreed to meet me in Seattle during his Starlight Foundation Golf Tournament, whose proceeds are used to grant the wishes of children suffering with terminal diseases. I was impressed with how organized he was, juggling a schedule that would rival a secretary of state's. The image of a jazz musician conjures up an atmosphere of late nights and smoky bars, but the very disciplined Kenny G seemed to have brought a touch of new age enlightenment to the genre. On that beautiful weekend in Seattle, Kenny entertained for hours at the gala dinner the evening prior to the tournament. The following day, he spent hours mingling with the children, teaching the rudiments of his lifelong passion, golf.

The day of our interview, Seattle glistened under a rare, bright sun. The Starlight Foundation arranged for a suite at the Four Seasons Hotel. Kenny arrived wearing an oxford shirt and blue jeans, his famous long, wavy hair adding the proper amount of hipness, his musician's entitlement. He was scheduled to do a sound check following the interview, so he carried his horn, which he never let out of his sight. The only instrument that rivals his affection for his horn is a golf club.

Passionate golfers are often very eloquent describing the parallels between golf and life. Kenny has spent a great deal of time and energy thinking about why he plays the game and how it relates to making music. He can describe the beauty of Payne Stewart's golf swing with the same ardor he might feel for a Coltrane riff. Growing up, he pursued the sax and golf with equal fervor. He's been playing golf since he was ten years old and is proud that he captained his high school team.

LGI

It was a pleasure interviewing Kenny G. He said more about the game of golf in ten minutes than most guests say in hours. His love for golf resonated so forcefully that upon seeing the show on The Golf Channel, Arnold Palmer's wife, Winnie, had her secretary call my office to say she loved the show and to request Kenny's phone number so that she might tell him personally.

Kenny G is an original. Although the contemporary jazz and new age world embrace him as one of its masters, he enjoys the blissful moments and the humbling exercises his ego undertakes in the presence of great golfers. Kenny truly feels that golf has made him a better musician. He takes rhythm and tempo very seriously in both worlds.

ANN: Kenny, I know that you are a very passionate golfer.

KENNY: I've been playing since I was in high school, and I just love golf. I love it maybe too much.

ANN: How do you find time because, not only are you one of the best instrumentalists of all time, writing and playing, but you also produce a lot of your own albums, and you are a licensed pilot? When do you have time to do all this and keep your golf game up?

KENNY: Well, when I'm touring, I usually play in the daytime. So when we wake up in the morning, me and my friend, who is also a pilot, fly around in this airplane. And so we fly the plane and pick a spot maybe where there's a good golf course or maybe there's a friend. Fly in there, play a game, then I can fly out, and be on time for my sound check and do the show.

ANN: It's so convenient. Is that why you got your pilot's license?

KENNY: No, it's not why I got my license. I've always wanted to fly, and it just worked out this way. But golf is actually the thing that keeps me sane when I'm out there working because it gives me something that is just so much of a break from reality. And I know golfers—if you talk to nongolfers, they don't understand that when you're on the golf course, it's such a rest. Your mind just goes—at least mine does—in a good way, it goes to rest. Of course you're thinking about your shots and you're trying to challenge the golf course, but I don't think about music when I'm on the golf course. I don't think about any problems that I might have. I just think about my golf game. I come back to my concert refreshed, ready to go, and I think I play my saxophone better now that I'm a golfer.

ANN: So it's not a "good walk spoiled," as Mark Twain described it?

KENNY: Well, I just like being outdoors. I like the beauty of a golf course. I love walking the golf course. There's so much about it that I love, and I think it's one of the only sports where you actually have the sense of competition, not only with your friends or whoever else you're playing, with against the course. And you can hang with your friends. I've gotten to know people on the golf course, and I think if I was out there playing basketball or whatever, you don't get that sense of breaking down walls that most people have on the golf course. You're just a golfer, and if you're a good golfer, everybody likes you. I played in the AT&T Pebble Beach this year for my first time [1995]. I was playing with and hitting on the range with some of the best golfers and realizing it doesn't matter how rich or famous anyone is. When somebody sees an unbelievable golfer, they're humbled, and all they want to do is find out how the guy does it.

ANN: How did the pros there react to you?

KENNY: I was flattered that there were a few pros that came up to me—and I was glad they did—to offer little bits and pieces of constructive criticism. One guy came up and said, "You know, your grip, I was noticing—I couldn't help but notice—try this and that and . . . "

ANN: Who was that? Anybody in particular?

KENNY: Well, Mark O'Meara[1] is actually a guy who I've played golf with a few times, and he, I think, has got a really great way of giving advice.

ANN: It's rare that one finds a great player who is also a fine teacher.

[1] O'Meara is a five-time winner of the AT&T Pebble Beach National Pro-Am as of this writing.

KENNY: It is.

ANN: When you find that great communicator, it can really make a difference with your game.

KENNY: And you're out there when you're getting ready to swing, your neck's out there, and you don't want to lose any confidence by somebody saying, "You've got it all wrong. You've got to start completely over, and here's my first piece of advice." Mark has a way of taking what you've got and making it better. And I've learned a lot by playing with him. I've only played with him twice, and I just love him. I think he's a great guy.

ANN: How often do you take lessons?

KENNY: I take a lesson every week. One day a week. Same time, every week, and I play golf one day a week as well. So I take one day of lesson and play one round a week.

ANN: So that's fairly structured for a schedule as hectic as yours.

KENNY: To me, it's my break. I'm in the studio making music or I'm on the road or whatever, but Tuesday at three o'clock I know where I'm going to be, and I'm not to be found on Friday.

ANN: You're always playing on Fridays?

KENNY: I'm out there on the golf course.

ANN: Kenny, you were *Billboard* magazine's jazz artist of the decade. You've recorded eight albums. The records have sold over thirty million copies. That's amazing when you think about it because you were an accounting major in college. Did you play back then too? What came first, golf or your music?

KENNY: Oh, music first. Actually, I was on my high school golf team. I was the captain of my team. We had the worst team of all the other high schools. I was the number-one golfer on the worst team, but I was shooting anywhere from 77 to 74—my best score in high school. I shot right around 80, in that range, so I was still a decent golfer.

ANN: But why golf? Did you play other sports as well?

KENNY: No, I didn't actually. My brother, when I was ten years old, took me out to the golf course and kind of introduced me to it, and I just loved it. And I was kind of good at it right off the bat. Going to college, you know what, I did not play golf once all through college. I got into music. I got into playing music, and I was studying. It wasn't that I went to college to become an accountant or to become an accounting major. I just did not like the theory part of music. I didn't like the studying of music. I liked the performing of it. I liked the playing of it because it's a labor of love for me. It's an emotional thing. Music is what I did. Studying accounting was partially just a mental exercise and partially my parents kind of—I wanted to give them some legitimate diploma, and I have a Phi Beta Kappa key.

ANN: Were your parents skeptical about your having a career as a performer? Is that why you majored in accounting?

KENNY: No. You know what? She would have been happy for me to major in music. I just didn't enjoy it. I took a music theory class, and I sat there and thought, well, here I am two hours a day in this class. Okay. Add up the number, that's ten hours a week I could be home practicing. And I'll bet you I'll become a better saxophone player if I take those two hours and practice, not to just sit there and theorize what music [is] and what comprises music. Now this is not to say that that's not a legitimate thing to learn. I'm just saying it didn't work for me.

ANN: When did you start playing the saxophone?

KENNY: When I was ten.

ANN: You took private lessons?

KENNY: I took private lessons and also lessons at the elementary school once a week. I just loved it. I was good at it.

ANN: Marching band?

KENNY: Marching band, yes. Marching band, concert band. I played my clarinet in the marching band because I didn't want my sax to get wet.

ANN: My, this has been a love affair.

KENNY: I'm telling ya.

ANN: Way back when. So are you as careful with your golf clubs? Between the sax and the golf clubs, which is a little more special?

KENNY: Oh, my sax.

ANN: Still the sax? You let other people borrow your putters and your Callaways?

KENNY: Oh yeah, yeah. They can take my clubs, but don't take my horn.

ANN: Your music is a combination of pop and R&B, funk, a little bit of everything.

KENNY: I don't know what those labels mean in terms of music. I don't know what "pop" music means. I know what I like. I know what feels good to me, and I do that. But I can't describe music in words just like you probably can't describe that feeling when you hit a great golf shot in words. I mean, well, how did you do it? What did you do differently?' Who knows? It just all came together. How did you sink that putt? I don't know.

ANN: Great analogy.

KENNY: Maybe there are pros who know those things, and then they can analyze themselves and fix it as they're doing it.

ANN: Even pros go through weeks and weeks of slumps where they can't figure out what's going on. And when they do not know what's going on, it's a matter of changing things and getting it right again.

KENNY: Let's face it, golf—well, you know, anything, once you get to a certain level of expertise, whether you are a pro athlete, golfer, musician, whatever, if you're at a certain level, then it's a mental game. Are you going to have a good night? I mean, let's take Andre Agassi. Is he going to win? Well, he's as good as anybody. So is Pete Sampras. Andre's rated number one, but at any given moment any one of those top guys can take the tournament if they feel it.

ANN: Tennis and golf are about 80 percent mental, once you have the mechanics down.

KENNY: And with music. If I feel it and it's really happening, I can play no wrong notes. And other nights I struggle to get through a concert and just walk home going, well, I know people probably thought it was great, but for me, it wasn't great.

ANN: Really? And you feel that way in music?

KENNY: It's normal.

ANN: All great players in golf have those days.

KENNY: Well, otherwise the pro would be able to birdie every hole.

ANN: That's right.

KENNY: You birdied it once, then why can't you do it every time? You played great tonight. Why can't you play great tomorrow night? That is the mystery of these kind of things. That's why they're so intoxicating. That's why golf is just such a thing that brings you in. Because you hit that beautiful shot. Well, same guy, same club, two seconds later, and it goes completely the other way. Same guy playing that beautiful note, a second later it's flat or it's sharp or you missed it or your finger fell off the key. Why? We're human. And that's why these kinds of things are, so you go for them because it's just such a challenge to you and so satisfying when you feel like, you know, I mastered this thing and I did it great. And then tomorrow night, it wasn't so good, so you look forward to the next night to redeem yourself. All right, I know I did that last night. Tonight I'm going to fix it somehow. And you work on it. You know, I get into slumps where I might do a few shows and it just wasn't happening. And then all of a sudden, bam! There's that music and I feel great.

ANN: There's that birdie shot. It's an interesting comparison, making good music and playing good golf. Are there any similarities between the feel of playing the sax, with the feel of golf? I mean, it's hard to describe sometimes, but you know what kind of finesse it takes to have a solid chipping game.

KENNY: It's just translating feel. Golf is a lot of feel, obviously. You know, the short game. You can't really teach how to finesse the ball closer to that hole. I don't really know. I would think that since a lot of what I do is based upon the feel of my fingers on the saxophone and there's a lot of touch involved; it isn't just mechanically doing that. There's a lot of finesse. I would maybe tend to think that some of that—and I'm a great putter, so it carries over.

ANN: Is that your strength in golf? Putting, would you say?

KENNY: Actually, my strength—I got it all. I think my strong point would be off the tee. I'm really good off the tee, and I think my putting has just come along and maybe this is part of it.

[Kenny had brought his sax to the interview, and I could not resist.]

ANN: Let's hear it.

KENNY: Oh, you want to hear it?

ANN: Go for it.

KENNY: I don't know what's appropriate for golf, but . . .

ANN: Have you ever composed a golf song? When you're playing, do you think about golf?

KENNY: I told my partner, Jim McGovern, when I played in the AT&T Pebble Beach tournament, "If we make the cut on Sunday, I'm bringing my horn out and every time you're going for a birdie putt, I'm going to give you a few notes. I'll serenade you and get you in the mind-set for it." Now, we didn't make the cut as a lot of people did. But *if*—you can quote me on it—*if* I ever make the cut in that tournament, I'll bring this out and whoever I'm playing with, paired up with, hopefully this will, as they're lining up their putt, I'll just give them some [plays his sax] and then they just knock it in the hole, and we just roll on and win the trophy.

ANN: Wow. That sounds beautiful. So you would serenade your golf partner?

KENNY: See, I can make birdies with this thing.

ANN: I'm telling ya.

KENNY: I wish golf was that easy. Oh, man.

ANN: What would you play if you were trying to get me to really focus, relax. A lot of times, I bring the office to the golf course.

KENNY: You bring the . . .

ANN: You can't do that.

KENNY: No, you can't.

ANN: You've got to just put it all behind you, and you know, I'm living in New York City, and it's a very hectic pace.

KENNY: If you want to relax on the green, just before you putt, you should listen to this. [He plays a lullaby.] I do that kind of like a bird, so that's a birdie.

ANN: Instant birdie, right there.

KENNY: That's an instant birdie.

ANN: You have such feel. And that has always been you. You can't learn that, that's just your makeup.

KENNY: It developed. You can learn the techniques that are involved in playing it, and to play this properly, you should learn it and be able to play. You should never let technique get in the way of what you're feeling, so get the technique down. It's true in any sport, and once you get the technique down, then get out of the way. Get your mind out of the way and just let it flow. And that's the secret to this thing.

ANN: Would you ever like to take golf even further than you have taken it? What's your goal in this sport?

KENNY: The goal really is I would like to be a five or less. And I mean a real five. There's a lot of guys who say, "I'm a seven." And then you go out on the golf course and they shoot an 85. Oh, was this an exceptionally bad day that you had, or is this your normal game since I won't ever see you again? And I hate that. What's the ego involved? I want to say, "I'm a four," and go out there and either shoot a 69 or a 77, but nothing more than that. And I'd like to do that. But I want to do it in the right way. I want to get the golf swing down. I want to take it and respect it. I don't want to go out there and just whack at it. I want to respect what it takes to be a good golfer, and I'll keep working at it, and if I get there, great, and if not, I've always got this. [He points to his sax.] So I'm happy.

ANN: You probably have played with some incredible golfers. In your memory, who have you most enjoyed playing with? Is there a fabulous foursome or your most favorite foursome that you can talk about?

KENNY: God, you know, I've had so much fun. I played golf one day with Donald Trump.

ANN: What was that like?

KENNY: It was the most fun because if he hits a bad shot, he doesn't really get upset about it. And he's such a competitor that it just brings the best out of you. I shot a 75 at the Atlantic City Country Club, and we went out there, it was hundred degree weather. We're sick. We love golf too much. There wasn't anybody else on the course, but we went out there. I shot a 75. He was like tantalizing me, "I'm gonna beat you. I'm gonna kill you. You're not going to be able to outdrive me." And all this stuff.

ANN: And he was serious when he was doing this?

KENNY: He was probably doing it to just—he just loves that kind of thing. Just the two of us.

ANN: But he wasn't getting upset?

KENNY: No. And we had a great time, and he brought the best out of me. And I love playing golf with him. He's just total fun.

ANN: Any one pro who you love to watch more than anybody else?

KENNY: I love watching Payne Stewart's swing. I just think it's just gorgeous. I mean it's just so beautiful. And, to me, if I ever have the chance to just watch him swing, if they slow it down and you hear, like, Johnny Miller commenting on that swing, to me that would be a blissful moment. To be able to sit in front of the TV and just watch that analysis, that would be like a minivacation.

Amy Grant

Amy Grant caught the golf bug in the early nineties and has since become a fixture on the celebrity golf circuit. By bringing her good-natured attitude and competitive spirit to the links, Grant realizes the impact she can have in the golf world, showing mothers and working women that it's never too late to pick up the sport.

I first saw Amy at the *Fairway to Heaven* golf event I cohosted in 1995 for VH1, and I admired her from a distance. Here was a woman who seemed to have it all. She had sold over eighteen million records, won five Grammy Awards, earned four Artist of the Year awards, and performed everywhere from the White House to the Grand Ole Opry. I watched her music video "House of Blues," in which she sings with Vince Gill, another of my favorite singer-golf addicts, and the chemistry and excitement of their voices brings to mind the word *sensuous*. In addition to all of this, she is a wife and mother of three.

Despite her many accomplishments, I was most impressed by how Amy carries herself. She is who she is. Amy refuses to manufacture a false image. Her healthy self-esteem enables her to avoid the distorted undertow of her industry. No weird lyrics for effect, no strange stage shows or revealing clothes to exploit her good looks. She's as sexy as can be, but what you see is what you get. A proud Christian, Amy has taken Christian music to a wider audience than any artist in the contemporary genre. Her success has opened doors for others by demonstrating the far-reaching appeal of great music with a positive message. She made the transition from gospel to pop as smoothly as the sound of her silky voice.

I was determined to book Amy on my show. She was playing in the Nabisco Dinah Shore Pro-Am in Rancho Mirage, California, and her assistant, Deanna Hemby, said Amy would like to do the show if she could fit it in. That same day Grant was scheduled to perform at the pro-am dinner. Her dress rehearsal with Vince Gill and others reduced my window of opportunity to inches.

I connected with Amy after she completed her round. This included waiting out her swarm of fans, who gathered around for autographs. As I observed this ritual, impressed by her inordinate patience with the throng, she assured me she would do the interview, but her time was limited. My challenge was to get more than enough material in a very short period

ANN LIGUORI PRODUCTIONS

of time—to get to know the "real" Amy Grant and communicate that to my audience.

I like to have at least forty-five minutes with my guests so that I can create a conversational and relaxed atmosphere. Amy was so honest and forthcoming that despite the limitations on time, we were able to cover a lot of ground. We immediately hit it off. The next day, while following her on the course, I felt like we'd been friends for years.

I learned a lot about Amy by watching her on the course. She's extremely determined, very confident, and enjoys the distinction of being one of the few women stars in the music business who has been able to play the celebrity golf circuit. One's handling of good and bad shots, challenging situations, frustration, strategy, and course management will generally reflect many aspects of one's personality. Amy uses her quick wit and sense of humor to handle the shots that go astray. Her expectations about the game are as realistic and honest as she is.

Admittedly, Amy is a newcomer to the sport of golf. At the time I interviewed her, she had been playing for two years. Despite her inexperience, she had a nice, smooth swing, one that mirrors her personality. That was comforting. It would have been disappointing if Grant had an ugly, choppy swing. On the contrary, with a smooth follow-through, she swings with a rhythmic tempo befitting her musical timing. Her ability to connect on 180-yard drives made it obvious she'd taken lessons and was serious about improving. Like most golfers, she is competitive and not above the requisite amount of frustration that goes with the game. How a major star handles the humility forced upon them when their brilliance doesn't transfer to the golf course is a distinct character portrait. Amy was true to my perception—she was cool. It's not that she doesn't play hard and want to become as good as she can, but Amy has it in perspective, preferring to enjoy the process of learning while feasting upon the camaraderie the fairways offer in abundance.

She's fun to be with, driven, focused, and quite reflective about how blessed she's been in her life. If ever I'm asked to recommend a female role model for any young woman, I'd suggest Amy Grant. She juggles an amazing and successful music career with raising a family, and works on her golf game, while keeping a sane and moral head on her shoulders—a rare feat in this day and age.

LIGUORI: Amy, you've won five Grammy awards. Sold over eighteen million records—it could be even higher than that now. What a success story. And on the golf course . . .

GRANT: Not a success story!

LIGUORI: No, no, you're a wonderful story.

GRANT: Oh, well, thanks.

LIGUORI: You haven't been playing that long.

GRANT: Almost two years.

LIGUORI: That's not long at all.

GRANT: It's a great, wonderful game.

LIGUORI: You have a very smooth, natural swing. How did you develop that so quickly?

GRANT: Well, I don't know. I feel like I duff it like everybody else does. I just have gotten some great advice. I think because of music, I've had the chance to play in some really interesting foursomes. Very patient foursomes and with several pros. And a word timely spoken goes a long way. And so I've gotten a lot of good advice, and I have enough friends that play golf. I would like to be good so I wouldn't slow the game down so much.

LIGUORI: You think about slowing everyone else down, really?

GRANT: Sure.

LIGUORI: On the course, there always seems to be that stereotypical, "Oh, it's a girl. She's going to golf so slow." Is that on your mind ever?

GRANT: I'm not thinking, oh, I'm a girl. I'm just thinking, oh God, I'm slow. But, you know, that's all right. I'll learn.

LIGUORI: Do you get advice from the pros who you play with?

GRANT: I don't think I would go out of my way to ask. The first round of golf I played [eighteen holes was in Nashville]. The second eighteen holes, I was invited by some friends to play at the Sara Lee, an LPGA stop in Nashville, and I was a little nervous. It was my second round of golf, and I was just hoping I wouldn't kill anybody in the gallery. And I went out the day before we were going to play the pro-am. I was on the driving range, just kind of working, and Meg Mallon came up and said, "Now here, look, back up a little bit, what we're going to do . . . " And then somebody else came over, and it was such a great, no-pressure, friendly environment. You know, I'm obviously a novice. I'm a singer. I'm never going to be a golfer. It's been that way; people have been very friendly giving advice. If they are not going to give advice, I figure they're thinking, "This cause is so lost, I'm going to stay out of it."

LIGUORI: Sometimes it's just a matter of one word, one little tidbit of advice, and all of a sudden it's a revelation.

GRANT: Yeah, it lasts for a swing or two.

LIGUORI: So you've only been playing for a short time. Does anybody else in the family play? I mean, why golf?

GRANT: Why golf? It's a great job to have while you tour because on the road, I work at night, and I've toured since I was eighteen. I'm thirty-five, and you can only go to the mall so many times. And I don't really like to shop. I have three kids, and I've taken them to every zoo across America. You finally go, "Hmm, golf courses. What a great idea." And the guys in my band love to play, and it's a great focus, that need to focus that everybody has.

LIGUORI: Golf, a walk in the country. It's something that you can do by yourself. If your band plays with you, that's even better because you don't have to shuffle around looking for a foursome or a twosome.

GRANT: It's wonderful, and it's just nice to travel the country and you get to meet people. On a golf course, everybody walks up in golf clothes and you're not aware of somebody's job. You don't care how old people are or how young they are. It's a wonderful, level playing field. And also, even if you're having a real bad day, you're not making anybody else's day bad unless you throw some gosh-awful fit, and even then, you know, carry on.

LIGUORI: It's a great equalizer. You can tee off from the reds and still compete with a stronger or better player. Who do you follow on the women's Tour?

GRANT: My best friend who plays is Kris Tschetter. And we met at that first Sara Lee. The first or second day she was the pro in our group. And I had to leave the golf course that day and go to the recording studio. I was recutting an old Joni Mitchell song, "Big Yellow Taxi." She's just such an easygoing person, and I invited her to the studio.

LIGUORI: She must have loved that.

GRANT: Well, yeah. I felt like she really kind of held me by the hand walking into her world for the first time. And since then, she's come out and joined me on the road and come to some shows, and so I'll probably feel an emotional investment in how she does. Every time you meet somebody, suddenly it's a person and not just a name. And you watch them play and you feel the emotion behind what they're doing. You hear their voice. You imagine how they're reacting to what they've done, good or bad. And because of music I've gotten the chance to play at a lot of celeb pro-ams, and I've just met a lot of wonderful people.

LIGUORI: There's definitely a connection there. Obviously you root for Kris when you see her.

GRANT: Sure. I got a chance to play with Laura Davies. I loved that. Tammie Green, Becky Iverson. I wouldn't say I know them well, but I know them well enough to know that they care about what they do.

LIGUORI: Do you watch a lot of television? Would you follow the Tour on the weekends?

GRANT: I don't watch a lot of TV, period. I just forget to turn it on, and so I'm usually seeing somebody else with the sports section open and I'm going, "Can you help me read?" I'm also kind of blind, so it's hard for me to read it. I just hear it through the grapevine.

LIGUORI: I understand you sung at Betsy King's induction into the LPGA Hall of Fame [1995].

GRANT: I did. I sang and I hosted it.

LIGUORI: The LPGA Hall of Fame is one of the hardest Hall of Fames in any sport to get into.[1] You really have to endure.

GRANT: Sure. Fascinating group of women, too. It was wonderful being there and getting to hear input from these women who were really forerunners, pioneers. Especially the older women. It's a real treat.

LIGUORI: It has not been easy. Now they're finally getting the money they deserve, finally getting the exposure they deserve. It's great to see that women golfers can compete and make a very good living, because it wasn't always like that.

Do you ever golf while you're recording? Will that help you at all? As far as getting away, the therapeutic aspect of playing?

GRANT: Golfing fits more with touring because studio work—it's very focused, and it's not like you're trying to rush through and get it done so you can go play. It's its own fascinating process of watching something unfold.

LIGUORI: Studio work must be very demanding.

GRANT: Well, it's very demanding, but it's very exciting. To hear a song in your head and to walk into a room of great players and they execute your song with all of your expertise and all their creativ-

---

[1] Entry into the LPGA Hall of Fame requires a player to have been a member for ten consecutive years and to have won at least thirty official events, including two major championships, or have won thirty-five official events with one major championship, or have claimed forty official Tour events without a major championship.

ity. You don't really want a distraction from that process because it's pretty wonderful, and right now, I'm getting a chance to do it, but I know that won't last forever. And so I'm just enjoying that. On the weekends, maybe dragging my children out—we usually make it through two or three holes, and then they're bored stiff and want to go home.

LIGUORI: Do they play at all?

GRANT: The eight-year-old struts around a bit with the bag.

LIGUORI: Amy, you've been able to balance a family, a husband, three children, and a very successful music career. That must be difficult, with your travel schedule and with the time that you need creatively to focus on your music. I admire somebody who can do all of that. Well, a lot of women are balancing now, the work and the family.

GRANT: Everybody's balancing. In this day and age, gosh who's *not* balancing? I think you just oil the squeakiest wheel and keep going.

LIGUORI: It seems as if everything in your life is running rather smoothly.

GRANT: You know life is fun, and wonderful, and hard, and dirty, and my life is no different than anybody else's in their wonderful moments. And the most highly publicized things in my life are the most polished things, but you know, I wake up and kind of shuffle down for a first cup of coffee like everybody else and just hit the ground running.

LIGUORI: Does your husband [Gary Chapman] play golf?

GRANT: He does. He's a much better player than I am.

LIGUORI: Do you get out with him at all?

GRANT: Not very often, because he plays his absolute worst golf when he's with me. And it really kind of takes the fun out of it for him.

LIGUORI: Do you fight with him on the golf course?

GRANT: No, it's not really, well, it's not a competition to me. No, and I actually play very well when I play with him.

LIGUORI: What is it about playing with one's spouse? When I play with my husband, if I'm playing well, he's not playing well. If he's playing great, I'm not playing great. It's rare that husband and wife each play well together.

GRANT: We don't get a chance to play together that often.

LIGUORI: Talk about your participation in VH1's *Fairway to Heaven* because the music business is golf crazy. I know Alice Cooper loves to play every day.

GRANT: Well, I think America is golf crazy right now, and who knows why? Maybe it's because it's one thing you can't do fast. And so *Fairway to Heaven*, I think it's fun just because people are thrown together who have a similar job but don't necessarily get to spend a lot of time with each other. You mentioned Alice Cooper. I had a chance to play with him. People were teasing us this particular day—it wasn't at that tournament. They were going, "It's the heaven and hell foursome." And we got out there, and he has the most unbelievable sense of humor. He said, "Amy, I'm the happiest man I've ever been." We talked about touring, and people are just not that different. You know, everybody has different props and different attitudes and different vocabulary, but people are people and that's the fun thing about the *Fairway to Heaven*, getting together.

LIGUORI: If you could put together, perhaps, a fantasy foursome, who would you like to play with? The ultimate foursome?

GRANT: I don't think I could. I don't think I'd plan that hard.

LIGUORI: Who have you played with that might have been your favorite foursome? Or actually, maybe one entertainer? I know you and Vince Gill play together.

GRANT: We do play together.

LIGUORI: What's that like?

GRANT: Well, it depends on how he's playing. If he's playing well, he's so funny and an unbelievable joke teller and does everything with great voices and impersonations. And if he's playing poorly, he throws his toggle switch.

LIGUORI: Just get out of the way?

GRANT: Just give him a little room.

[Ann is walking the course with Amy at the Mission Hills Country Club during the Nabisco Dinah Shore Pro-Am.]

LIGUORI: I read where on your very first day out on a golf course, you had a little trouble in the sand.

GRANT: Oh, um. You want me to retell the story? I don't think so. My first and last fit.

LIGUORI: What brought you back after that first day?

GRANT: Oh, I don't know. I think I was just so ashamed of myself. You know, to pick up golf in your thirties, which I'm sure a lot of people do, you just don't realize by that time in life, you're pretty much doing things you're good at. Why put yourself out? I took a lot of lessons before I went out the first time, and it was so much harder than I dreamed that it was going to be. And the first caddie I played with, he counted everything.

LIGUORI: No mulligans?

GRANT: You know, "Can't we call it a practice swing?" Anyway, I got stuck in a sand trap and couldn't get out. Days later, they send in food and water . . .

LIGUORI: Set up a little tent.

GRANT: Yes, I was half way to China and the sun went down.

[Ann and Amy are walking with Amy's caddie for the event.]

GRANT: I got here at the Nabisco Dinah Shore, and I was rescued right off the bat by David here, my wonderful caddie for these two days. Of course, he walked up and said, "Do you need a caddie for the day?" And I'm thinking, for all I know, this guy is a serial killer. So I asked to see his credentials.

[Ann and Amy look over at a stunned David.]

LIGUORI: Now does he look like a serial killer to you?

GRANT: Well, you know, it's America. Anyway, I just knew it was the greatest setup in the world. We were walking to a green at one point, and I hear him singing a song—it was a Carole King song.

LIGUORI: And you bonded immediately, right?

GRANT: I'm a huge Carole King fan. And so we're kind of picking out different songs and, yeah. The game is about companionship.

[Amy and her caddie are singing parts of Carole King's "Sweet Seasons" from 1971.]

AMY AND CADDIE: "Sometimes you win, sometimes you lose. Sometimes the blues get a hold of you . . . ."

GRANT: I think she wrote that song prophetically about my golf game. You think so?

LIGUORI: I read a story about your husband and how he handles the wilderness out there at the Tennessee Golf Club in Nashville.

GRANT: Yes, especially in the spring when you first open up the club, there are a lot of snakes. My husband carries a sawed-off shotgun in his golf bag. I've killed a bunch of snakes out there. I've killed snakes on the green with my spikes. But we live on a farm. That's really no big deal. Snakes are a part of life.

LIGUORI: Amy, thanks so much. See you on the links.

GRANT: Be sure and duck!

Vince Gill

I first met country music's Grammy Award winner Vince Gill during my interview with Amy Grant at the Nabisco Dinah Shore Pro-Am. I had arranged to pick up Amy at the eighteenth hole when she finished her round and drive her to our interview sight, and was surprised when Gill, who had been observing Amy's finish, got into the car along with Amy and her assistant. He knew exactly who we were and was excited for Amy that she was doing the interview, and I was excited to have the two biggest stars in country and pop music within my grasp. I kidded Vince that his public relations people had blown me off several times when I asked for an interview with him. He laughed and said, "You just have to ask me."

A couple of months later, that's exactly what I did. When Fred Scrutchfield, the producer of Vince Gill's tournament, The Vinny, invited me to Nashville to play in the celebrity tournament to benefit junior golf programs in the state of Tennessee, I was ready to play and to work, and Gill was ready for us. I've never been a country music lover and had never been to Nashville, but this visit made me a fan.

Gill's charisma and charm make him appealing to women of all ages. It was easy to see why Vince is such a successful performer—the same emotion and sensitivity he brings to his singing comes through when he's discussing subjects about which he's passionate. When Gill emotionally recalled playing golf with the late LPGA's Heather Farr, who died of cancer, he became teary-eyed. When he talked about his dedication to junior golf, I *felt* his enthusiasm. When Gill spoke about his daughter, I could see them together—their loving relationship. And when he recounted stories on the golf course, I saw the gleam in his eyes and was right there in the midst of the story.

Vince has been a golfer almost his entire life and plays every day, even when he's on the road. He is such an avid golfer he gets The Golf Channel via satellite on his tour bus. I had heard in golf circles that Gill has an explosive temper on the course. I couldn't imagine this sweet, mild-mannered guy, winner of eleven Grammy Awards for tender love songs, behaving with the kind of fury that rumor suggested.

The day after we sat down for a long chat at the Golf House, I followed Vince for nine holes. We had discussed his temper in the interview, and at first he was playing so well that Vince, the nice guy, was firmly in control, but

ANDY LYONS/ALLSPORT

soon enough, after hooking a drive into the water, his "evil twin" took over. The transformation was swift and undeniable. In an instant, all that Southern, country boy charm evaporated. It was obvious that the water brought out the sailor in Vince, because swear words flew.

The same emotional intensity that makes Gill's music so compelling drives his passion for the game of golf. Vince makes amends for his incivility on the course by helping to bring the game to young players in Tennessee. In a charity concert two nights later, to raise funds to teach, develop, and house young golfers all over the state, Gill commanded the stage at the Grand Ol' Opry with his silky voice and sensitive songs. The memory of his on-course temper tantrum quickly faded.

It was a delightful weekend. An enormous crowd of golf enthusiasts and country music fans who cared little for the sport were all enlivened by the prospect of sharing space with the popular singer. Gill was mobbed by autograph seekers on every hole and did his best to accommodate the throng while keeping his focus on the game. The topper to an already stimulating couple of days was when Vince Gill won his own celebrity tournament.

LIGUORI: Vince, you've won eight Grammy Awards![1]

GILL: Ah, it was rigged.

LIGUORI: Fifteen country music awards as well. The list goes on and on, but you probably cherish another number more than any other.

GILL: My one hole in one.

LIGUORI: That's right. And you're a two handicap!

GILL: Ah, right. I've played this game forever.

LIGUORI: When did you start playing?

GILL: I was a kid. We were in junior golf. I knew I was playing competitive golf from third grade. I've got all the scores and all the play dates that we had when I was a kid, and I was nuts for sports. You know, it didn't matter if it was basketball, baseball, or golf. I wasn't quite big enough in some of those other sports. I was one of the littler kids in school and golf stuck.

[1] Vince Gill won two Grammy Awards in 1997 and two more Country Music Awards since this interview.

LIGUORI: So you started playing golf at a very early age. Did your dad play?

GILL: Yeah, my dad played some and took me out. I remember the first golf course we ever went to play. I remember the first place my dad took me to play was in a little town called Crescent, Oklahoma, and it was a little nine-hole course out in the field somewhere, and the greens were made out of cotton seed holes, very much like sand greens would be, where they have a big rolling pin that comes across and they roll this big flat spot across the middle. And they have a string on the pin, and wherever you land on the green, you take the string and go put down the trough. That was my first memory of playing a big golf course.

LIGUORI: You started playing golf so early, which is unusual. Most kids play baseball, basketball, and everything else, and pick up golf later.

GILL: Yeah, they were much more popular games, and you were kind of, I guess, a squirrel or a dork if you played golf.

LIGUORI: Where did you make your hole in one?

GILL: Hole number sixteen at TPC in Scottsdale, Arizona, at the Phoenix Open, playing with Mark Calcavecchia [of the PGA]. And I just made ten on the hole before so I was not happy, and I walked up to the tee and there was a sign that said, "hole in one wins new house."

LIGUORI: No way!

GILL: Any hole in one wins a new house. A $175,000 house.

LIGUORI: I never play in those kind of tournaments. I only get the car.

GILL: And I was the last guy to hit in the group, and I hit it and it was a good shot, backed up, and went in the hole. And I almost decapitated Glen Campbell, who was playing behind us. It was one of the good reasons I threw my club for a change. And this little guy with his clipboard came down and said, "Congratulations," and I said, "What, did I win a house?" And he goes, "No, but you did for this couple, this young couple." So that's pretty neat. You know sixteen is a really famous hole and a par three where everybody hangs out and screams a lot and has an extra large time, so that was fun.

LIGUORI: Especially after you aced that one. How far was it?

GILL: Just about 115 yards.

LIGUORI: So have you seen the couple since you won them a house?

GILL: Haven't been out, haven't invited me out to dinner or anything like that.

LIGUORI: No?

GILL: I'm kind of hard to find.

LIGUORI: Did they send you a thank you note, at least?

GILL: Yeah.

LIGUORI: You won them a house!

GILL: It's real neat. They're a young couple. The guy worked at Home Depot and so that was kind of neat. And they won some cash to furnish the house and stuff.

LIGUORI: Do you feel that you could have become a professional golfer, at one point?

GILL: Maybe.

LIGUORI: You've thought about it, haven't you?

GILL: Well, you know, I think that question gets posed to me as "what would you do if you weren't musical?" Well, golf's the only other thing I can do, and I really don't know. Maybe if I would have hit 500 balls every day, tried to go to college, tried to do all the things that everybody does who gets out there and plays the Tour, maybe. I think the chances were pretty slim, but I mean it's kind of neat because the career I chose, I would say the percentages of succeeding in the music business are probably equally as slim.

LIGUORI: Is that right?

GILL: So, I didn't, you know, trade something that was really hard for something that was really easy. I was just a little bit better musician.

LIGUORI: Maybe you don't get quite as frustrated as a musician then?

GILL: No, I do.

LIGUORI: Do you?

GILL: Yeah, I'm pretty driven by doing something well, you know. I know I have the talent to do something well. If I don't feel like I measured up to what I think I should do, then it frustrates me a bit.

LIGUORI: Do you see any similarities between music and golf — getting the rhythm down, the tempo, the frustration level, etcetera?

GILL: Sure, there's nights you're playing and you know you feel like you're just flagging it every time you open your mouth or every time you turn up your guitar. You know, it's very similar. I could see a lot of similarities in that. And then there's days where you feel like you've got all thumbs on your hands, when you're trying to play and you miss and you miss, and both are creative type things. I mean, in golf, there certainly are mechanics as well as playing the guitar and stuff. There are mechanics there, but the creativity, when you think up a shot or you think up a lick, there's some similarities and they are both pretty neat.

LIGUORI: Do you ever get into a slump in music?

GILL: Sure. I would think so. I mean I feel like there's periods where I get stagnant and not improving like I wish I could, but you know, a lot of that's due to the fact that you have a lot of demands on your time, like I'm not seventeen or eighteen years old anymore and I can't play four or five hours a day if I want to. You know I just don't have the time to be able to do that, so you have to just tell yourself that this is about as good as your gonna get.

LIGUORI: Like you say on the golf course?

GILL: I never tell myself that on the golf course. I should maybe.

LIGUORI: Weren't you a one handicap at one time?

GILL: I've been a plus-one. I got a plus-one when my career was really suffering and I had nothing to do but play golf everyday. But it's always been around scratch, two, or three or four or whatever. You know it's unbelievable because I have the best job in the world to be able to play as much golf as I want. My work day doesn't start, even when I'm on tour, until eight o'clock at night, with a sound check around four. But I still get up at eight o'clock in the morning and go find a club and say, "Hey, we'll swap you some tickets for some greens fees. Mind if we come out and play?" And I made some of the best friends in the world in the game of golf.

LIGUORI: Which courses are your favorites?

GILL: I've played at Augusta a few times, and that was great. I'm such a fan of golf—with a lot of those places, especially at Augusta, I knew every club to pull. I knew what every shot had to do. And I played really good the first time around it. I went to seventeen even, and I hit a sand wedge on the seventeenth and hit it over the green, made bogey, and then got mad and bogeyed eighteen. But it was so much fun—that's a lot of fun to go play a golf course and then see it on TV.

LIGUORI: Sure. Or see it on TV as many years as you've probably watched the Masters and then go play it.

GILL: Exactly. That was a big highlight, getting to go down there and play.

LIGUORI: Have you gone to watch the Masters in person?

GILL: The year after I played there. I went there and played in the fall, and then that Spring I went to the tournament.

LIGUORI: Any favorite hole there?

GILL: Oh gosh, I'm trying to think what hole I played good. I don't know. They are all really special if you can remember shots, like the putt Jack [Nicklaus] would make on the sixteenth[2] and all the famous eagles you see at thirteen and fifteen,[3] and having the same shot that Chip Beck had that one year.[4] And it makes you respect sometimes what he chose to do. A lot of guys haven't been up there, 240 yards away on fifteen, and wondering what that second shot is like. It's pretty penal if you hit past [the hole], so it really makes you appreciate how good those guys are, especially when you go out there and play some of those tracks.

LIGUORI: Speaking of the Masters, what were you thinking while watching Greg Norman in 1996 lose his six-stroke lead in the final round?

GILL: Unfortunately, I'd like to think of that Masters as the one Nick Faldo won instead of the one that Greg lost. It was not fun to watch, and I bet Nick didn't have fun watching it happen. I think Greg knows those are the kind of things that go on in the game of golf some days. Some days it goes right and some it doesn't. I've gotten to know Greg a little bit. He came to a show or two and came out on the bus and had a few beers. And we had a good time. He's a good guy, and at least he was there.

LIGUORI: A couple of years ago, I cohosted VH1's *Fairway to Heaven*, a golf tournament where music stars team up with professional golf stars. Your team won, and the finish to that golf tournament was outrageous. You and John Daly ended up being thrown in the water.

GILL: Oh yeah, my big idea to throw John in the lake and I kind of went in with him.

LIGUORI: Before that, Daly walked up on the green while the other team was hitting their approach shots.

GILL: That was an impressive display. They were firing wedges, and he just grabbed the balls and threw them in the water.

---

[2] Jack Nicklaus won his sixth Masters in 1986 after a come-from-behind victory. Trailing the leader Seve Ballesteros, Nicklaus eagled the fifteenth, birdied the sixteenth and the seventeenth, and parred the eighteenth to win the tournament. His tee shot on the sixteenth put him three feet from the hole, lining up a putt that would ultimately help him win the tournament.

[3] In 1991, there were eighteen eagles at the fifteenth hole, the most ever on one hole at Augusta. In 1992, there were fifteen eagles at the thirteenth hole. Two years later, Jeff Maggert made history by making a double eagle on the thirteenth after he holed a 222-yard three-iron shot.

[4] At the Masters in 1993, on a par-five, fifteenth hole, Chip Beck was three strokes behind Bernhard Langer but elected not to go for the green on the second shot. He wound up parring the hole. Langer birdied and went on to win the Masters.

LIGUORI: He didn't even flinch as the shots were coming his way. He figured nobody would hit him, right?

GILL: Great hands, threw it right in the lake, every shot that came in.

LIGUORI: Is he your favorite player?

GILL: He's a pretty neat guy, you know. I think some of the stuff people have said about him and some of his rowdier ways and stuff—I think he's got a big heart and I think he does a lot of nice things for people. I went and played in a tournament with him in Memphis. He has a deal for the Make-a-Wish kids, which I do a lot for. He's got a big heart.

LIGUORI: He really does. He's a lot of fun. He's been on the show a couple of times. We are here for your charity tournament, The Vinny. And this is your fourth year. And you've raised a lot of money, and I got a tour of the Tennessee Golf House here, which is beautiful. And you do such wonderful things for young people, really devoting so much time and contributing a lot of money from your performances to develop young golfers.

GILL: Well, we've raised about half a million dollars in just three years, which is pretty remarkable for a pro-am event to be able to raise that kind of money. And I love to see the money go to these kids, but even more so, when we started, I said, "Look, I don't want this to appear to be golf for golf." I really want it to go into the cities, and we've been into the inner cities and got some minorities interested in the game of golf.

LIGUORI: It's a very expensive sport to take up for children who don't come from well-to-do families.

GILL: Well, it is, but even in public golf, you can take care of those kids. We played as juniors when green fees were fifty cents; you could play all day long. I played forty-five holes, fifty-four holes everyday in the summer. I just like 'em. I like those kids. They're a lot of fun. I was just out there today having a little game, you know, a little putting game with three or four of them.

LIGUORI: Great to see you giving back and getting inner-city kids interested in golf.

GILL: Yeah. I didn't want it to look like we were doing a tournament for the country club kids. Because country club kids are fine. They're gonna be involved in golf and get the lessons and have the money for the clubs and all this. What we're doing—we're a little more grass roots oriented, and really it goes across the whole state. My favorite story of all is we took some money that we made through this tournament and just bought them a mower. They needed a mower for the golf course. Those kind of things. A lot of the guys that come and play, they'll get all the clubs they don't need, don't want, and don't have any use for, and we'll cut them down so we have clubs for kids. And I think the neatest thing about this whole place is that once it really is rolling and doing as well as we'd like it to do, adults can't play, unless they're sponsored by a junior.

LIGUORI: What an interesting idea.

GILL: Reverse discrimination, I guess.

LIGUORI: So what aspect of your game needs the most work?

GILL: My attitude.

LIGUORI: Get out of here! You don't get upset on the golf course do you?

GILL: Oh no, you've heard I have!

LIGUORI: No way. Do you really?

GILL: It's legendary. I make Craig Stadler [of the PGA] look like an altar boy.

LIGUORI: You get that upset, huh?

GILL: I do.

LIGUORI: How may clubs have you thrown?

GILL: Oh, whichever one I've got a hold of. I'm getting better. As I get older, I get a lot better. But I've broken my share.

LIGUORI: Really?

GILL: I wish I didn't, but that's my cross to bear.

LIGUORI: You're telling me you lose your temper on the golf course, so my image of you is changing a little bit. What have your learned about yourself on the golf course?

GILL: Well, you know, it finally took somebody to see—nobody ever sees anything positive about the emotion of anger. But all my emotions are right here on my sleeve, whether I cry, whether I laugh, whether I'm sad, any of those kinds of things. And anger is another one of your emotions. It's difficult to control where I want to cry about something that moves me or when I'm gonna laugh. Somebody says you can't control any of the other emotions, so why do you expect to really try to control anger? You know? And it made a lot of sense. That's the reason I try to do so much nice stuff for folks, raise money, and do tournaments, and do all this stuff because they know how evil I am on the golf course.

LIGUORI: Losing your temper—your evil twin.

GILL: Yeah, I have an evil twin that shows up when I play golf, and so I try to compensate for the evil side.

LIGUORI: How often do you get lessons?

GILL: I get help from some of the best players in the world. Peter Kostis [golf pro and analyst for CBS] helps me out from time to time and Gary McCord [golf pro and CBS Sports commentator]. A buddy of mine named Rick Walker who has a teaching school up in northern California. I met a really neat guy from Australia named Jerry Hogan who really has some really good, factual, straight ahead things—no towels under the arm and no magic cures, just kind of straight physics and what the golf swing is about. He was fun to work with a little bit. I played more golf with Bob Walcott then probably anybody, and we'll go hit balls and go to the video room and draw the lines and look at what we're doing and help each other. But he helps me more than I help him.

LIGUORI: Have you ever considered writing a golf song?

GILL: No. There is a great one that's been written by a buddy of mine named Fred Knobloch called "Golf's a Bitch and Then You Die."

LIGUORI: How true.

GILL: "You don't know when and you don't know why." There's some great lyrics.

LIGUORI: You should sing it.

GILL: It's hysterical. I don't know all the words, but I think him and Tom Schuyler wrote it, and it's two of the better song writers in town and both are frustrated golfers. It's very, very funny.

LIGUORI: Have you ever considered playing on the Celebrity Golf Association Tour?

GILL: I've played in one event, but I like amateur golf. I know you could give your prize money away, but then there's not much point in going out there and playing too much of this stuff if you're not going to play for the money. But I, at some point, would like to play some serious amateur golf, you know, when my career slows down and I can go work on my game. I don't care if I ever win or beat anybody, but I love to try. I like to see the true pros on TV.

LIGUORI: Who do you like to watch the most? Who have you learned the most from just by watching?

GILL: Well, I think a lot of people say you should find somebody that their mannerisms are similar to yours. I have a pretty quick swing. I think Nick Price would be somebody that would be a great swing for me to emulate, and you can't argue with Tom Purtzer's swing. Ernie Els. I got to sit at Ernie's feet and watch him hit balls last year in Michigan. And it's always inspiring. I got to do the same thing with Jack Nicklaus and Seve Ballesteros, and just watch him hit balls. You can learn a lot more by watching then you can anything else. Joel Edwards is one of my best buddies. He and Charlie Rymer, they're always coming to town or I'm finding them, and we talk from time to time. Joel has become a real close friend, and he'll call me up and say, "I'm doing *this*, and I can't make *this* putt," and it's a real thrill for me to know those guys. And the fact that they'll come to town and play this tournament, and just be my buddy, man, that's the best.

LIGUORI: What is your best all-time golf shot, if you can quickly think of the one you consider the ultimate?

GILL: I made my hole in one. I was playing with Arnold Palmer in my home town after the bombing in Oklahoma, which was a real emotional tournament. We raised a lot of money for building a new center for the kids, but my favorite shot was a putt. We had a skins game at the LPGA event in Nashville, the Sara Lee, and Heather Farr[5] and I were really, really close friends, and she came back and played in a skins game with me one last time. I think it was three years ago maybe, and we were a team, and I hit a seven-iron on the first hole [Vince's eyes get teary] about five feet away and she made the putt and we won the skin. Nobody thought we'd scratch and win a skin, but that might be my favorite golf shot.

LIGUORI: It was your most memorable shot?

GILL: Very sweet.

LIGUORI: You should write a song about it. Vince, thanks so much.

GILL: You bet.

[5] Heather Farr played on the LPGA Tour and died of breast cancer in 1993 at the age of twenty-eight.

Glenn Frey

The Eagles were the rage when I was a teenager. They were one of the few bands whose lyrics I knew by heart. In fact, the song "Hotel California," the mystique of the lyrics and sound, created a lasting impression on my mind. It was played on the radio in Cleveland, where I grew up, seemingly more often in 1977 than any other song that year. And ironically, the song became a good omen. Every time I heard it in the car traveling to an away varsity tennis match, I'd win. "On a dark, desert highway, cool wind in my hair." It didn't get any cooler than that song.

The Eagles are one of the most popular rock and roll bands of all time. They have sold more than ninety million albums worldwide, have had five number-one albums, four Grammy Awards, and countless sold-out tours throughout the world. Their *Greatest Hits 1971—1975* is the all-time, best-selling greatest hits album.

When I discovered that Glenn Frey was playing in the first annual Lexus Challenge (a celebrity-pro event hosted by PGA Tour and Senior Tour player Raymond Floyd), I knew I had to interview him. Frey is a cofounder of the Eagles, plays guitar and keyboard, and is singer and writer of some of my favorite songs. His music holds special memories for me.

The interview was easily arranged through Frey's manager, Peter Lopez, a passionate golfer himself. Glenn arrived for our sit-down interview dressed in a black T-shirt and black pants, the essence of the laid-back West Coast style. My knowledge of sports came in handy. Frey relaxed into our discussion, but as we started to talk basketball and hockey, an intensity rose in him that seemed more suitable to blue-collar New York than California cool. Frey is an avid sports fan.

The next day I walked the back nine holes with Frey during the pro-am on the Citrus Course at PGA West in La Quinta, California. It was a beautiful day, and Glenn's mood reflected the sunny skies and the great golf he was playing. Frey, a southpaw who putts with his right hand, was using a cross-handed grip on the greens that was obviously working for him. His drives were straight and down the middle. His chip shots were landing inches from the pin. He could not miss a putt. As he sunk a putt for a net eagle, he thanked Dave Pelz, whose clinic he felt had improved his short game.

An attentive gallery and our cameras brought out the performer in

J. D. CUBAN/ALLSPORT

Glenn Frey. He was having a great time. He reacted after every shot, talked with the galleries, and hugged me after sinking putts. He decided I was his lucky charm and playfully insisted that I follow him around at all the pro-ams. His wife, Cindy, a golfer herself, watched with amazement as Glenn and his club collaborated on a magical performance. I waited for the expected plunge—the golf god's would certainly balance the scales—but it never happened. He couldn't miss.

It was a memorable day for me, interviewing this musical icon amongst the mountains and palm tree backdrop of a beautiful course. You can't get much better than combining my love for golf, music, and interviewing. I was on top of the world. The crew and I were made to feel welcomed and a part of Glenn's triumph on the links.

Later that evening, Frey performed for an audience that included Arnold Palmer, Jack Nicklaus, and Raymond Floyd. "You Belong to the City," "Smuggler's Blues," "Taking it Easy," "Desperado," "Life in the Fast Lane"—a list of hits that seems endless. I watched in awe and sang the words to every song. "Plenty of room at the Hotel California. Such a lovely place, such a lovely place." Memories of those high school tennis road trips resurfaced. Almost twenty years later, those songs were back again in my life. It has been quite a ride.

LIGUORI: Every time you play golf with Glenn Frey, you see an Eagle putt.

FREY: That's right.

LIGUORI: How did you get started in golf?

FREY: Well, I didn't play much growing up. You know, a little miniature golf and things like that. I didn't go to the golf course much, but when my dad retired, which was about fifteen years ago, I decided to go on a vacation with him. And so he and I went to Hawaii, and he had played a lot of golf in his younger years and was going to take the game back up. And so I bought a set of clubs and my dad and I went to Hawaii and we played golf on Kauai, and that kindled my interest.

LIGUORI: And now you're just so passionate about it; I see you everywhere.

I see you at the VH1 *Fairway to Heaven* tournament, the Lexus Challenge, AT&T Pebble Beach.

FREY: Well, I'm going for it while I can. I've been offered to play in some of these nice tournaments before, but I always wanted to have a little better-looking golf game before I went public, so we'll see how I do. But it's something I've really been looking forward to, and having the Eagles back together has afforded me the opportunity to work for periods of time and then have big spaces of time off, so it's falling right for me that I've been able to play some golf the last year as well as playing music. It's great. I'm having the best of both worlds.

LIGUORI: Did you ever have to change your attitude about the game? Alice Cooper, for instance, golfed for years when it wasn't cool to golf. And now he's kind of ahead of the game because he's been golfing for about twenty years. Now it's the thing to do. What about you? Did you look at golfers and think, "God, that is an uncool sport; I'm not gonna do this"?

FREY: Well, yeah, I think my generation, we really played tennis in the seventies, and golf was sort of looked at as an activity. And I guess maybe if you look back at golf in the seventies, the clothes didn't help. But I think it's just sort of a natural evolution for my generation. Now guys that are getting into their forties are really getting interested in playing golf. It's a great counterbalance for rock and roll because when you make records, you're inside, in a room with no windows. It's loud some of the time. And golf is just the opposite. You're outdoors, it's quiet, you're taking a nice walk, you hear the birds chirp. It's like a minivacation. You can actually escape for four or five hours.

LIGUORI: Very therapeutic

FREY: Yeah, and be refreshed. I mean, I look at it like that.

LIGUORI: It's the rehab of the nineties, right?

FREY: It keeps me out of trouble. It's a daytime activity.

LIGUORI: Obviously, when the band broke up, you didn't think you would get back together?

FREY: Oh, no. I had no intention of coming back.

LIGUORI: At all?

FREY: I thought the Eagles should be a young band, you know, stayed in the seventies like James Dean. You know, live fast, die young.

LIGUORI: Tell the *Hell Freezes Over* story [1994].

FREY: Well, that was what Don Henley would say every time somebody asked him when the Eagles were going to get back together. And so when we finally decided to get back together, we were sitting around trying to write the press release, and Don goes, "I've got it—'Los Angeles—*Hell Freezes Over*. In a year of strange weather, the Eagles have decided to get back together.'" And so we did.

LIGUORI: You're wearing black. Do you always wear black on the course?

FREY: I do like to wear black on the golf course.

LIGUORI: It's to uphold the rock and roll image?

FREY: It's the rock and roll color.

LIGUORI: Do you like large galleries watching?

FREY: Well, I'll tell you, I'm not sure, but the few times I've played in front of large groups of people, I played better. I don't know if it's a force to concentrate. Maybe it's drawing on some stage experience, but I look forward to that. If I hit a bad shot, I'll look at all these people, at the gallery, and say, "Ever done that? Now you know how I feel."

LIGUORI: How would you describe your game?

FREY: Aw, I'm a grinder. But I'll tell you what I learned to do that's really helped my golf game a lot. It's to not beat myself up on the golf course. I think you can learn a lot about a person and I think you can learn a lot about yourself by the game of golf because there's so many ups and downs. You really have to deal with disappointment a lot, and unlike tennis where you get a second serve, you are punished for every mistake you make on the golf course usually. So you have to learn to get an even temper about it. There's a time maybe to yell if that's just to get yourself psyched up, but you really can't beat yourself up on the golf course. I think you have to go out there and have a good time.

LIGUORI: Because if not, there goes the next shot, and the next shot . . .

FREY: Mark Lye really helped me with that. He's the first PGA Tour professional who I ever met, and we were playing golf together, and it was one of my first times playing with him. And we were at Fiddlesticks in Fort Myers, Florida, and I was playing terrible, but Mark says, "You know, Glenn, you're just a couple of years away. You've got an athletic swing. You'll get it with some teachers and stuff." But he said, "You know what?" He says, "Right now you're going to have about three good holes every nine, and you should just enjoy those three holes and know you're going to have more holes like that the more you play and not worry about the bad holes." And I've really started to think like that.

LIGUORI: That's a very "real" way of looking at it.

FREY: Because I'm not playing this game for a living. I'm playing this game for enjoyment. And the nice thing about golf is when you hit the sand wedge 105 yards up in the air and it lands and rolls toward the pin, that is the equivalent of a professional shot.

LIGUORI: Sure, there's nothing better.

FREY: Now, I go skiing in Aspen, but I'm not as fast as the guys that ski. And when I play tennis with my friends, I know I'm not returning a 120-mile-per-hour serve. But when you hit a real golf shot, it's a real golf shot. It's as good as the other guys hit it.

LIGUORI: And when you think of putting three good holes together in, say, nine holes, that could be twelve good shots, which is tough to do. You put four good shots together on a tough course on one hole, that's an accomplishment.

FREY: Yeah, it certainly is. But golf is also a game that you really have to work at. Tennis, which I play, I'm kind of a "B" player. I don't really have good ground strokes. I can get my feel for tennis back in about two hours. But I can't get my timing back on the golf course. After a three-week layoff, you just can't go out and play. Another thing I like about this game is being a student. It's something I enjoyed when I did some acting jobs. I enjoyed studying the lines and analyzing the scenes, trying to figure that out. I really enjoy studying golf.

LIGUORI: Who do you go to?

FREY: Dave Pelz. I went to his short game school. Of course, he's on *The Golf Channel Academy*. And that was a terrific experience. It was down in West Palm, Florida. I've been getting some full swing instruction from some good teachers, and I've got some things to work on, and I'm learning how to practice. There are all these other things. A lot of times you're so busy when you get a moment's free time, you go to the golf course and, "Let's tee it up. I've got four hours." But that's really not what to do. You really do need to practice. I'm starting to set aside a little more time for myself to do that, and I'm starting to get a little better.
[Frey sets up for a putt.]

LIGUORI: What's your cross-handed putt all about?

FREY: Inside about eight feet, it's very much a shoulder putt, and Dave Pelz says sometimes you get a little hand-sy when you're nervous. And by going way down on the club like Bernhard Langer does, you really get a nice hinge with your shoulder and nothing breaks down and all your angles stay the same.
[Frey sinks the putt.]

LIGUORI: Those five-foot putts are the toughest ones to make because you're expected to make them.

FREY: We call it the Vomit Zone.

LIGUORI: You're a southpaw except on the greens. Yogi Berra does the same thing. He golfs lefty, putts righty, and calls himself, not "ambidextrous" but "amphibious."

FREY: That's funny. The Yogisms are hilarious. For me, I'm left-eye dominant. I'm left-handed. I always hit a baseball left-handed, so I feel very comfortable making a move from that side of the ball. But in putting, being left-eye dominant, it's good to putt right-handed because my left eye is over the ball. When I played miniature golf in high school, they only had right-handed putters, so I just putted right-handed. I tried to switch back, but I was atrocious. I couldn't get it on line or get the speed right. I got to stick with this amphibious thing I got going here.

LIGUORI: As a student of the game, do you read all kinds of books on the game and watch all kinds of videos? I mean do you really consume all of that?

FREY: I keep the Golf Channel on a lot at home. It's really great to get up in the morning and be able to watch the tournaments in Europe. You get up at 7 AM, and they're playing somewhere in France. You know, the Irish Open and stuff like that. That's great. I think too much knowledge is a dangerous thing, and so I'm not obsessive about trying to analyze everything that's in all the golf magazines, although I do look through 'em. I really like that, but I enjoy watching it more on TV and practicing.

LIGUORI: So show me your reaction when you got the invitation to play in the AT&T Pebble Beach Pro-Am.

FREY: Well, they send you an invitation and it's like *the* thing. You open the thing, and it says, "*The* Invitation." And I sort of clutched it to my throbbing chest and said, "I've got it, I've got it." Pebble Beach is my favorite golf course. I haven't been to Augusta yet. I haven't been to the great courses in Scotland. There's a few other places that I'm sure are wonderful. But Pebble Beach to me is the most beautiful golf course I've ever seen.

LIGUORI: Can't the Eagles tour in Scotland? I mean, can't you kind of arrange that?

FREY: As a matter of fact, it just so happens that we have three days off in England before Wembley Stadium and we have three days off in Ireland for a couple of outdoor dates in Dublin, so there's going to be golf time for me in the British Isles.

Anne Murray

Anne Murray's music captivates an audience; her voice is a clear beautiful instrument that penetrates the hearts of her fans. The singer can still pack an arena with loyal, enthusiastic audiences as she goes through an impressive catalogue: "You Needed Me," "Love Song," "Could I Have this Dance," "Danny's Song," "Shadows in the Moonlight"—a following who have been devoted to her since the seventies when she scored with her breakthrough hit "Snowbird." In concert, Anne's confidence in her voice and technique allows her to wrap an aw-shucks modesty around her powerful vocal expressions. She sings, sways to the music, laughs with the audience, and in her unpretentious way, captures the room. An easy sense of humor and down-to-earth humility makes Murray a big winner on and off the stage.

I knew that Anne was a golfer. I'm a fan of hers and so coordinated an interview with her around a performance she gave in Las Vegas at Bally's Hotel and Casino. She received several standing ovations throughout the show and then afterwards received the most interesting gifts. Instead of fans throwing flowers and teddy bears, some fans showed their appreciation by tossing sleeves of golf balls. I soon found out that Ann was a bona fide sports junkie.

During the interview the next day, Anne spoke of her childhood in Nova Scotia, where she developed a passion for baseball. At age ten, she could recite from memory the season and the career batting averages of the Brooklyn Dodgers. A die-hard hockey fan, she records the games when she's on the road and then unwinds by watching them at night. She treasures the autographed hockey sticks given to her by Gordie Howe and Brett Hull.

Golf is her competitive fix, and she's played much of her life. She had the same band for twenty years, and the majority of them are golf enthusiasts. Onstage, she often talks about their ongoing competition on the course. Murray has four Grammys, three American Music Awards, three Country Music Association Awards, twenty-two Juno Awards, and was inducted into the Juno Hall of Fame in 1993. Her accomplishments as a singer are complimented by her success as a business woman managing the careers of other performers. Murray's longevity in the topsy-turvy music business is proof enough of her considerable achievements. Yet during our interview she was most excited over her golf game.

ANN LIGUORI PRODUCTIONS

A golf date was arranged for Murray and her musicians. This classic songbird, who has such calm, professional control over her game onstage, carries her smooth style to the links. She has a nice swing that's hampered a bit by back problems. She can't drive it as far as she'd like, but her all-around game is consistent. She's broken 90 several times, and more importantly, she's taken her share of the band's money. The combination of golf and music has been a winning one for the band.

Anne's steady trip through popular music over the last thirty years has had its share of crowning moments, such as singing the Canadian National Anthem at the first Toronto Blue Jays game played at the Sky Dome. She's also been honored by royalty. She once covered a Beatle's tune, "You Won't See Me," and John Lennon came backstage after a performance to tell her that her rendition was the best Beatle's cover he had ever heard.

My path crossed Anne's again months later as we were teamed together at an LPGA Pro-Am with professional Kris Tschetter at the Sprint Titleholders in Daytona, Florida. I couldn't think of two people I'd rather play golf with.

▽

LIGUORI: I had the pleasure of watching you perform, and you made a couple of references to golf. When I see your fans giving you golf balls and tennis balls after the performance instead of bears and flowers, it's obvious that you're a die-hard golfer. How did you get started in golf?

MURRAY: I grew up in Nova Scotia, and every summer we'd go to the beach. And the beach in Nova Scotia where I was is sand flats, and when the tide goes out, there are red sand flats for miles. So I used to take a golf club and hit a golf ball and just chase it.

LIGUORI: I know you majored in physical education in college, and you were always athletic. In fact, if I may say so myself, I noticed when you were up on stage you have the greatest legs.

MURRAY: Well, thank you.

LIGUORI: They're very athletic legs. I can tell you still work out now.

MURRAY: That's from all the stepping I do now. When I was in high school, I had no opportunity to play any sports because there were no sports available to girls and we didn't have a gymnasium in our school. I didn't see the inside of a gymnasium until I was in my first year of university, so really I took up all of this late. I used to play baseball. I had five brothers. I played baseball, a little hockey and football, just in the field next door. I didn't learn formal sports until I went to university, so it was a quick study.

LIGUORI: Rhythm and tempo are a big part of a golf swing. Does your music help your swing?

MURRAY: I think that my music helps me, but as soon as I get a golf club in my hand, I try to hit it as hard as I can.

LIGUORI: I know you've broken 90 a couple of times.

MURRAY: Two years ago I broke 100, and now I'm breaking 90, so I feel I've made great strides over the last couple of years. I can't play on the road because I do mostly one-nighters, and you're traveling all the time. The only time you can really play is when you stay put and maybe in Las Vegas or something like that, so on the road I don't get a chance to play much. But when I'm home, I play as much as I can.

LIGUORI: When you do find time to play, who do you play with?

MURRAY: When I'm on the road, I play with the guys in my band. Three of them play. It's kind of fun, but at home, it's a bunch of old broads, ladies from the neighborhood, with whom I play, and that's great fun too because we're all about the same skill level. It's pretty funny. We're not great, but we have moments of brilliance, every one of us, now and then.

LIGUORI: That's what keeps you coming back, those moments of brilliance.

MURRAY: That's right.

LIGUORI: Does playing with your band ease the pressures and the stress of touring? One of the things that impresses me about you is you have such a loyalty amongst your musicians and the people that you work with. They've been with you a long time.

MURRAY: Well, they have been with me a long time. It took me a long time to put this group together. It's just a really good group of people. Everybody gets along really well, and it took a few years to accomplish, but they are a good group and I enjoy playing golf with them. It kind of sets up that camaraderie, and it's good on the road because you're in each other's pockets. These are great guys. We get along great.

LIGUORI: They don't seem like guys in a band.

MURRAY: No, they don't.

LIGUORI: You were teasing your drummer during the show that he better stop beating you on the golf course. He's the best golfer in the group.

MURRAY: Yeah, he's certainly the best player in our group. He hits the ball a long way. That's my problem. If I could just get to the green. I'm great around the greens because I don't hit a ball very far. I just have to hit it straight and I eventually get there.

My aim is to be able to play bogey golf. That's what I've always said. If I could play bogey golf, I could be happy, and now that I'm starting to break 90, I feel I've done more than I ever expected, so it's great.

LIGUORI: I'm sure you remember the course where you broke 90 for the first time.

MURRAY: Yeah. I was in Branson, Missouri, and I thought, well, now maybe the course is just easy, but I was playing with the guys and they were getting the same scores as they normally get and I shot an 88. So I thought maybe I was gonna be a one-hit wonder and never break 90 again. But I did it again!

LIGUORI: So that must have felt good. The second time you break it, it probably feels better than the first.

MURRAY: Well, no, I don't think anything can beat the feeling that I had the first time I broke 90. And I did it by sinking about a thirty-foot putt on the eighteenth hole, which is even nicer.

LIGUORI: Does a golf shot like that compare to anything you've done in your musical career?

MURRAY: Well, I mean it is for the moment, but I think in the career it's a little more lasting. The golf's a little more fleeting because you're on to your next game and you're trying to do better, but I liken a golf game, sort of, like doing an album because every album you do, you want it to be better than the one before. And that's your aim, so that's the way you feel about golf.

LIGUORI: How did it feel when you were inducted into the Canadian Academy of Recording Arts and Sciences Hall of Fame?

MURRAY: I was inducted after twenty-five years into the Canadian Music Industry Hall of Fame. It was quite a thrill. "Hall of Fame" means you've been around for a long time.

LIGUORI: Do you know some of the women on the LPGA Tour?

MURRAY: The first golfer I ever met was Sandra Palmer. I met her—we did a guest shot on a Perry Como special that he did in Lake Tahoe in 1975. She had just won the Dinah Shore [LPGA tournament], and Billy Jean King guested on the show. It was women in sports, and I could remember it was funny because Billy Jean got to talking and we talked about golf, and she said she played a little golf, so we went out onto the driving range in Lake Tahoe. Sandra Palmer took us there. We were trying to outdrive each other.

LIGUORI: How fun.

MURRAY: Billy Jean and I were hitting balls, and I pulled a muscle in my back, I was trying so hard. I wanted to beat Billy Jean King, and I pulled a muscle in my back and it didn't go away for about six months. That was my reintroduction to golf because I hadn't played in years. When my career was starting, I didn't have an opportunity to play at all, and then Sandra Palmer sent me golf clubs and subsequently talked to people about having me play in the Dinah Shore Pro-Am. So that first time, I played my practice round with Hollis Stacy—that was the first time I played with Hollis. Then the next time I came out to play, I was five months pregnant, and I didn't know much about the golf course and protocol and all of that. It was very hot in the desert, and they decided to put me in the shade and said they would come and get me when I teed off. Well, nobody came to get me; my group teed off without me, so I got up to the first tee all by myself, and there were about five thousand people there and I had to tee off and I hit the ball ten feet. It was one of the most embarrassing moments, and it was a horrible round of golf, too. That was in 1975, and I have not played in a pro-am since.[1] I have been asked to play in many, but I don't think I'll embarrass myself anymore because I've learned to play.

LIGUORI: That first experience sounds dreadful.

MURRAY: Oh, it was just awful.

LIGUORI: You're used to performing in front of thousands of people.

MURRAY: But I wasn't used to swinging a golf club, certainly not in front of that many people.

LIGUORI: And doing it all alone.

MURRAY: Yeah, I was all by myself.

LIGUORI: I can't think of a worse first-time experience.

MURRAY: No wonder it's taken me twenty years to be convinced to play in pro-ams.

LIGUORI: How did you take up golf? Where did you first play?

MURRAY: I had a great training ground. I started doing little clubs around the east coast of Canada. I first joined my golf club, it would probably be about twelve years ago. Women were allowed to

---

[1] I recommended Anne to play in the LPGA Sprint Titleholders in 1996, and she did just fine.

play between midnight and six in the morning. Things have changed a lot I'm happy to say, and now I can play just about whenever I want.

LIGUORI: Share some of your most memorable golf stories.

MURRAY: I can remember my first time playing Pebble Beach, and that was a thrill, but the funny part about it was that we had in the golf cart one of those disposable cameras and seagulls were everywhere and we left to take our respective shots—the seagull swooped down, dragged the camera, and took off with our camera. And there we were chasing all over this fairway after this bird because we had taken some great shots on this camera. Chasing a bird with our clubs. That was one of my most memorable times. Another was we were playing Las Vegas, my husband and I back in the early days, and he had never played golf. I don't remember the golf course, but I remember it was called "Dean's Fifth," as in Dean Martin, I guess, and I think it was a par three. There was a big pond between the tee and the green. Well, he must've put ten balls into that pond. Finally I had to hide behind a tree I was laughing so hard. He was so mad he threw his club down, he walked into the water right up to his waist, and he must've picked up twenty balls and he came back and he wouldn't play anymore.

LIGUORI: You've been successful as a performer and business woman. You obviously know how to market yourself. What does the LPGA need to do to further its growth?

MURRAY: I think that golf can use a few more personalities. I think it's very important. I realize that you have to stay focused, but I think it's not much different from performing. I think it's important to include the gallery in your golf game. It is entertaining after all, and I think the people who do that are good for the game. Nancy Lopez has always been nice to the gallery. Patty Sheehan is great.

LIGUORI: Michelle McGann enjoys interacting with the galleries.

MURRAY: I think that's great, and she's a personality. I think that's very important. I think some of the golfers should loosen up a bit and talk to the galleries. It's a sport, but it's also entertainment.

Smokey Robinson

Since the early days of Motown, when Berry Gordy discovered Smokey Robinson's lilting voice and prolific songwriting talent, the singer has been a musical legend. The sixties were an era of great songwriters, and Smokey Robinson held his place amongst Lennon and McCartney, Curtis Mayfield, and Paul Simon, as a gifted "poetic lyricist." Motown was the first wholly Black-owned crossover entertainment vehicle in American music history, and Smokey's talent helped spearhead the company's assault on popular music's mainstream. Thirty-nine years after his first major hit "Shop Around," Robinson continues to make and produce good music, when he's not indulging in one of his private passions, golf.

I met William "Smokey" Robinson in Del Mar, California, during a shoot for a Callaway Golf commercial he was making with Alice Cooper and golf commentator Johnny Miller. His bright green eyes, ready smile, and friendly disposition were all the encouragement I needed to approach him for an interview. Although he didn't know me, he immediately agreed, and during our sit-down interview, his easy, relaxed manner was refreshing. He wears his years with a peacefulness that is almost spiritual, as if he's been there and back enough times to have earned the wisdom and serenity that encircles him.

Smokey grew up in Detroit's North End, and his childhood dream was to be a baseball player. He was attracted to music at an early age, and by the time he was five years old, he was writing love poems and singing ballads. In high school, he formed a doo-wop group called The Matadors, who would later be renamed The Miracles. The group performed locally as Smokey perfected his songwriting talents under the tutelage of the visionary Berry Gordy, the founder of Motown. Smokey released his first record, "Got a Job," on his eighteenth birthday and made history at *Hitsville USA* when his single "Shop Around" sold a million copies and became the first Motown record to top the charts. A musical dynasty was off and running. Popular music would never again be the same.

Smokey found golf in Detroit during the Motown days when some of his fellow musicians persuaded him to take a break from his constant pursuit of the next hit and join them on the course. He was immediately smitten by the bug. In between writing some of the world's greatest love songs, includ-

COURTESY OF CALLAWAY GOLF COMPANY

ing Grammy Award winner "Just to See Her," "My Girl," "Quiet Storm," and "The Way You Do the Things You Do," he developed his relationship with the links. Love songs and golf—it has been a winning combination for him ever since.

Robinson's autobiography, published in 1989, was titled *Smokey: Inside My Life*. Along with his perspective of the Motown phenomena, he revealed the nightmare turn his life took when an addiction to drugs nearly killed him and a life-style of adulterous relationships brought to an end his twenty-five-year marriage. At an emotional bottom in 1986, Smokey followed the advice of a friend who urged him to contact a faith healer. One afternoon visit with the faith healer left him a changed man.

These days, his only addiction is to golf. The spiritual journey that supported his recovery and transformed his life has fostered a better perspective on the golf course. Having realized his limitations, he has less frustration and far more enjoyment from the sport. He will travel anywhere to play, and for him, a game of golf is a little "sunshine on a cloudy day."

Smokey has been inducted into the Rock 'n' Roll Hall of Fame and the Songwriter's Hall of Fame. He has received the Soul Train Award and the NARAS Living Legend Award. But perhaps most thrilling of all was his hole in one.

LIGUORI: Legendary singer, writer, producer, golfer.

ROBINSON: Ann, I was kind of believin' what you were saying at first and then you went too far. No, I love golf. I really do. I couldn't put up with it otherwise.

LIGUORI: I'll bet. How often do you play?

ROBINSON: Every chance I get. You know, there are sometimes when I might play four or five times a week. But yeah, if I'm not busy doing something, I always tell people that golf is the heroin of sports and I'm past the point where I want to play. I'm at the point where I have to play.

LIGUORI: You're another player who is addicted to the sport.

ROBINSON: I don't know anybody who isn't. You know, everybody that I know who plays golf is addicted to it. There's nothing else a guy can call me at 4:30 in the morning and say, "Hey man, let's go do this," and I say, "Okay."

LIGUORI: And you've been playing since the sixties?

ROBINSON: Yeah.

LIGUORI: That was an era in which it wasn't cool, as Alice Cooper told me, for singers and rock people, Motown people, to go out and play golf. It wasn't cool in the sixties for you guys to play golf.

ROBINSON: Well, you know what? I don't know if it was cool or not. I know that all the guys at Motown, we started around the same time on this little course in Detroit. And I don't know if it was cool or not because we didn't look at it like that. We just went out, and I got into it, and it was fun and frustrating at the same time.

LIGUORI: Did you play with the Motown guys? Is that how you first started?

ROBINSON: Yeah, I was minding my own business, and many times I want to hunt those guys down and choke them to death because I was minding my own business. I wasn't thinking about golf. And a bunch of them had started playing. [They would say to me,] "Hey, man, let's go to the golf course." [I would say,] "No, I'm not going." And finally they talked me into it.

LIGUORI: Did Berry Gordy [the founder of Motown] play?

ROBINSON: Yeah, Berry started after I did, in fact.

LIGUORI: Who exposed you to golf?

ROBINSON: He's a lifelong buddy. His name is Mickey Stevenson. He and one of the guys who was in The Miracles at the time, who just passed away recently, named Ron White, [they] started me playing golf. And Berry's brother, Robert, had started before anybody, and he started them. And then they started me.

LIGUORI: And this goes back to your Matadors days back in high school?

ROBINSON: Oh yeah, The Matadors were in junior high school in fact.

LIGUORI: And then it became The Miracles.

ROBINSON: The Miracles.

LIGUORI: And so you started playing golf while you were with The Miracles. A name that describes your game?

ROBINSON: [Laughing] Yeah, that describes it all right.

LIGUORI: I think it's great. I've been reading your history. You grew up in Detroit. Aretha Franklin was three years old when you were six. Diana Ross, Stevie Wonder, Berry Gordy, Mr. Motown—you guys were all living in the same area, right?

ROBINSON: Yeah.

LIGUORI: When you look back at those days, with all that talent in that one area, what are your fondest memories? Do you have any in particular?

ROBINSON: Oh boy. How much time do you have? There are so many of them. But I think probably one of my fondest memories will always be the very first thing that happened that was mega for me, and it was when we were playing at the Michigan State Fair. Berry interrupted the show just before we played "Shop Around" and came onstage, and he had this gold record in this frame and said, "You guys just sold a million copies." And that was just unbelievable.

LIGUORI: What a vivid memory. How did you get the inspiration for the lyrics? I'm sure many people want to know how you come up with these songs and the words. You know, people describe you as America's greatest poet.

ROBINSON: Oh boy.

LIGUORI: You've heard that.

ROBINSON: I look at it as a blessing. I look at my life as a blessing. I look at the creativity as a blessing because I don't know where it comes from. If it doesn't come from God, then—but I believe it does. I think it's just what God would allow me to do, and it's what I do. I think that anybody who's creative in anything they do, or anyone who is given any kind of talent—it doesn't have to be musical. It can be golf. It can be basketball. Whatever it is. I think those are blessings. Some people get those kind of blessings. We all get some kind. But you know, mine just happen to be music.

LIGUORI: The lyrics just come to you?

ROBINSON: Yeah.

LIGUORI: Who inspired you? Would women inspire you?

ROBINSON: They have [laughs]. Yeah, I've been inspired by some women.

LIGUORI: Listen to these lyrics from "My Girl." "I've got sunshine on a cloudy day. When it's cold outside, I've got the month of May." That just came to you?

ROBINSON: Yeah.

LIGUORI: So you can't explain it. It's just God-given talent, you think.

ROBINSON: I think so, yes.

LIGUORI: How about your golf game?

ROBINSON: Well, that's another story. I don't know where God was on that day. [He laughs.] But no, golf is one of those games where it really doesn't matter how good you get at it, see. I was here when you were interviewing Johnny Miller [PGA Tour member and golf commentator], who probably is one of the greatest. He's blessed with the game of golf. But I've seen him play, you see. Golf is one of those games that doesn't care how good you can play it. Some days you can't play golf, no matter who you are. And it took me a long time to get to that because I love golf so much and it took me a long time to learn even fundamentally how to play golf. And there was a time when I would be so frustrated, until it would keep me up at night trying to figure out why I did so-and-so that day, or why couldn't I be consistent and play golf good every day. And then I started paying close attention to what golf is. Golf doesn't care about anybody, you see. And I started paying close attention to the fact that, you know, one time I saw Jack Nicklaus shoot 80 on TV! And he's Jack Nicklaus, so who am I to cry if I play bad one day? And that helped me a great deal when I realized, when I put it into perspective and saw that golf really doesn't care how much you practice or how much you play or who you are or how great you are at it. There are going to be days when you just can't play it.

LIGUORI: Well, I'm so glad you came to your senses.

ROBINSON: Me too! [He sings.] Oh, I wish that I could play golf good everyday, but I can't.

LIGUORI: Is there any one song that is most special to you?

ROBINSON: Oh no, not at all. Because songs are like your children. I put everything into them, and it would be hard to pick one of my kids over the others and say, "Oh, I like that one the best."

LIGUORI: That's an interesting analogy.

ROBINSON: Yeah. It's true.

LIGUORI: I know a couple of years ago, you came out with an autobiography.

ROBINSON: Yes.

LIGUORI: You were very honest about some personal aspects of your life that many people had no idea about at the time.

ROBINSON: Yeah.

LIGUORI: You had a crack habit that almost killed you.

ROBINSON: Yes. Well, it wasn't actually crack. Unfortunately for me, it was pre-crack. It was cocaine. And I used to smoke it because I would mix it with weed and smoke it, you know. I never did the pipe, or whatever the stuff is that they do now. And it was pre-crack time. I really had a bout with it. The reason I wrote the book was because of that, because I felt like God had let me live through this thing to share this experience with the world, with other people who perhaps may fall into this trap. To let them see that there's no safety in your status or what you do or how happy you are with your life. Because I love my life. I love what I do. You know, if I had a choice before I was born as to what I wanted to do with my life, it would be exactly what I'm doing. And so I fell prey to that, and I wanted everyone to know you don't have to be ravaged in the ghetto or downtrodden or anything like that for that to happen to you. And that's the main reason I wrote the book.

LIGUORI: And you went to a faith healer.

ROBINSON: Yes.

LIGUORI: That must have been an amazing afternoon.

ROBINSON: It was. It was an amazing experience. But I know that I'm here to talk about it just through the grace of God.

LIGUORI: And you became a different man right after that experience?

ROBINSON: Immediately.

LIGUORI: Never looked back?

ROBINSON: No.

LIGUORI: And now do you feel as if you are as passionate and consumed with golf as you were with drugs at one time?

ROBINSON: No, because I have never lost my passion for golf. You see, golf is one of those things where you never, or I have never lost my passion for it. Ever since I first started trying to learn how to play, I just loved it. It's just one of those games that—you see, golf is a very "self" game. There's actually no competitors in golf. I would love to be able to go home some days and say, "Oh man, every time I got ready to hit my ball, they threw me down or they kicked my ball out of the way or they grabbed my club just in time or they yelled." See, golf is one of those games where, not only can no one do anything to you, they have to be quiet while you're trying to hit a ball that's just laying there. Nobody's throwing it at you. Nobody's pitching it to you. Nobody's moving it while you're trying to hit it. It's just laying there daring you to hit it where you're trying to hit it.

LIGUORI: It's just you against the ball.

ROBINSON: Exactly.

LIGUORI: More like you against yourself.

ROBINSON: That's exactly what it is. It's you against yourself. And that's why I said some days you're not going to be able to play it. You're not going to be able to beat—that's why everyone goes back, because there's no set thing. You can't say, "I know when I go out today, I'm going to shoot 68." No. You might shoot 98, or you might shoot 68. But you never know. And that's why people keep going back.

LIGUORI: What's your best round to date?

ROBINSON: My best round to date is 72.

LIGUORI: Where was it?

ROBINSON: I don't even remember where it was, because I remember the first round I shot in the seventies, which was 76. That was at a course called Los Robles, which is just outside Los Angeles. And I remember that because it was the first time I ever shot in the seventies in my life.

LIGUORI: So the 72 was just old hat after that?

ROBINSON: Well, no, because, after you've shot in the seventies so much—you see, my goal now is, I will remember when I shoot sixty-something. I will.

LIGUORI: Do you get a chance to watch a lot of golf on television?

ROBINSON: Oh yeah, sure. All the time. I watch all the Tours. I even watched the Nike Tour. I watched, of course, Tiger Woods when he won his third straight amateur title. That was a big event to me. It was something that was very, very special. And especially the way he won it. Never giving up, just drive on even though you're down. And I really watch all the golfing events that I can. I think the thing that probably helped me play golf better than any other factor watching was when I started to watch the girls play. I play in a lot of pro-ams, and I've played in a lot of the professional women's tournaments. I would watch them, because I used to have a problem with trying to hit the ball far. Trying to overpower the ball. I didn't know about timing and all this stuff. I wasn't thinking about that. And when I started to watch them, I said, "Well, gosh. They're all smaller than me, basically, and they're crushing it." So that helped me. I watch everybody play.

LIGUORI: I think most amateurs do get more from watching the women on the LPGA. They can relate more to the distance. Have you ever met Tiger?

ROBINSON: No, I haven't. But after he won the amateur title, I did send him a telegram.

LIGUORI: What would you say to him, do you think, if you met him?

ROBINSON: I would say, "Hey man, how do you hit it that far?" No, I would have to congratulate him because I'm very proud of him. I think that, first of all, he seems to be a very nice young man, and he's intelligent, and he seems to have his head on pretty straight. And I commend anybody who has control over themselves enough to play golf like he's been playing it since he was twelve. Since he was eight. He won his first tournament when he was eight. And there are a lot of guys who are like that, who just have my admiration because it's a tough game, and when you can get yourself together enough to play golf at that level, that young, hey man, that's great.

LIGUORI: Do you feel that he may change the world of golf as far as the discrimination that goes on, the private clubs discriminating against minorities and women?

ROBINSON: Yeah, I think he's going to do a great deal to change that. In fact, I saw one time, I was looking at one of the morning shows, and he was the subject of one of the segments. And this guy was on there, and I really wanted to call in, and I did call in to be truthful. I called in, but it just so happens that it had taken place in New York, and so it was done by the time I saw it in Los Angeles. And this guy was sitting there and he was criticizing the commercial spot that Nike did that features Tiger where he says, "Well, I've accomplished all these things and so on, but there are still some golf courses I can't play on." And this guys says, "Well, that's ridiculous. That's not so, and that's not true. There are no golf courses . . . ." He's never been Black. He doesn't know. Man, there are golf courses everywhere where you can't play. There's one right in Los Angeles where no Blacks, no entertainers, and no Jews can play there. So he doesn't know what he's talking about. It kind of made me angry that he would be on TV saying something like that because he doesn't know discrimination. He's never felt it, apparently. But I think he's [Tiger] going to make a great difference in discrimination as far as golf goes.

LIGUORI: A lot of celebrities tell me they have trouble becoming members of private clubs because of their race, their gender. How about for you? Have you been able to join clubs that you want to join, or have you run into that problem?

ROBINSON: Well, you know what? I belong to a club in Los Angeles called Mountain Gate, and I was one of the first fifteen members there, because I've been a member since they first built the golf course and there was nothing there but a golf course and a starter shack. And I joined then. And so I've never really tried to join another golf club because I love playing golf everywhere in the world. I don't always play at Mountain Gate. I play everywhere. My buddies and I, we go and we play all of the golf courses that we can play. We go all over the country playing. I've never really tried to join another club other than Mountain Gate.

LIGUORI: Most memorable foursome that you've ever played in—what would it be?

ROBINSON: Oh, wow. I can't say that, because I've had the privilege of playing with a lot of professional golfers and I've had a lot of memorable experiences. I don't know if I would categorize that as a more memorable experience than playing with my buddies because we have so much fun, we enjoy it so much. We're fanatical. To give you an example, there's a club not too far from where we're doing this interview called Aviara. Aviara had just opened not too long before we played it, because of the fact that it was torrential downpours in Los Angeles. And we were supposed to play in Pasadena that day, and we went to Pasadena, and it was raining and raining and raining. And we went into the clubhouse and we're in the restaurant and this guys say, "There's a new club down towards San Diego called Aviara, and Well, it may not be raining there." And we just drove towards the sun.

LIGUORI: Just to play?

ROBINSON: And we came to Aviara, and we played and had a great time.

LIGUORI: If you could put a foursome together, any foursome. If you could play with anyone in the world that you haven't played with, who would it be?

ROBINSON: It would probably be Tiger Woods, Michelle McGann, and Arnold Palmer. I love Arnold Palmer. I mean, I've been watching him for years, and I just think he's such a nice, genuine person, to be Arnold Palmer, you know. I would hope that if I ever met him that he would be who I think he is.

LIGUORI: You once filmed a Callaway commercial with shock rocker Alice Cooper. What was that like?

ROBINSON: Well, like I said, I've known Alice for many years, and so it was just like, "Hey, this is my buddy. Hey, what's happening?" That's what it was like.

LIGUORI: Doesn't it amaze you how different Alice is from his onstage persona?

ROBINSON: Like I said, when I first met him, I was surprised because that's where I met him—on the golf course. I knew who he was, of course, but I expected him to be wild and insane like his image was on stage. Totally different person. I think all performers are slightly schizoid, though. I do. I believe that because I know that when the music starts and there's thousands of people out there, I can go out there and I'm fine. Once I get started, I'm fine with it. If you ask me to sing for five people in a room somewhere, I probably couldn't do it. I'd be too bashful or something. I'd feel like, wow, are you kidding?

LIGUORI: Does that schizophrenia transfer over to the golf course?

ROBINSON: No, golf is just always haphazard, probably because you never know what you're going to do. Go out there and some days you play great, some days you don't. And I finally learned that. Some days you play great and some days you don't. And so I don't take it home with me anymore. I don't take it past the golf course. I can laugh about it now.

LIGUORI: If you were to pick a song that would describe your golf game, which one would it be? "Quiet Storm"?

ROBINSON: [Laughing] I don't think so.

LIGUORI: "The Tears of a Clown"?

ROBINSON: Yeah, that's a little better, or "Tracks of My Tears." Absolutely. It has to be something like that.

LIGUORI: "Oohh, Baby Baby"?

ROBINSON: Yeah, one of those. [laughing]

Business, Art, and Politics

Charles Schulz

Snoopy, Charlie Brown, Linus, and Lucy have been a part of the American culture since the early sixties. The characters became so popular that Snoopy went to the moon as the *Apollo 10* mascot in 1969. The phrase, "Happiness is a warm puppy," prompted hundreds of similar phrases, and the term "security blanket" has become part of our country's vernacular. This American phenomenon sprung from the mind of the legendary artist-author Charles Schulz.

It's hard to comprehend the magnitude of Charles Schulz's success. His comic strip, *Peanuts*, appears in more than two thousand newspapers every day and is read by an estimated one hundred million people. There have been one thousand books of *Peanuts* strips in more than two dozen languages, thirty television specials, four movies, a Broadway musical, and hundreds of products, from hats and sweaters to skateboards and towels. Schulz's influence is so pervasive, virtually no one compares.

As I talked golf with Charles Schulz at the Inn at Spanish Bay, overlooking the golf course on the Pacific Ocean near Pebble Beach, I realized that the bigger part of Charlie Brown sat before me in the flesh. Much of *Peanuts* is autobiographical, created in large part from Schulz's own childhood in St. Paul, Minnesota. Schulz played sand lot baseball, touch football, and ice hockey, the sports his characters favor. Influenced by the anxiety that Schulz experienced in the army, he took themes of pain and loneliness and wove them into a wonderful, childlike American tapestry, with Charlie Brown leading the charge as the lovable loser.

Schulz is one of the most complex individuals I have ever interviewed. So many of his emotions show up in his work. His profound sensitivity is the key to his greatness. During our interview, I got the impression that throughout his career, he felt underappreciated. His profession doesn't draw the attention and recognition that is afforded other authors and artists. Despite his great success, it is difficult for people to take cartoonists seriously, commercial genius aside. His hypersensitivity picks up every slight, which then finds its way into his cartoon characters.

The day after the sit-down interview, we spent the afternoon playing golf. Our mutual love for sports made it a very enjoyable experience. The golf course relaxed him; the interviewer-guest barriers were erased. It was

ANN LIGUORI PRODUCTIONS

just Charles and I on the course, stripped down to the basics of hitting a clean golf shot. He is a very good golfer, having played and studied the game most of his life. Of all the characters he has created, he most resembles Snoopy on the links.

At the end of the day, Schulz confided that there is one thing in his life that he has yet to do. He let the statement simmer as my curiosity got the best of me. He has accomplished so much in his long career. What could it possibly be? His unfulfilled desire was to play a round of golf with Arnold Palmer. His wish to play with Arnie didn't surprise me. Most die-hard golfers his age feel the same way. What did surprise me was that Schulz had never asked Palmer. His humbled posture was quite charming. Certainly a man of his influence could get to Palmer, but an innate shyness stood in his way. Taking the hint, I wrote Arnie a note and passed along the icon's request.

LIGUORI: Charles, I heard your wife call you Sparky. I guess I'll call you Sparky if that's okay?

SCHULZ: I was named Sparky after Barney Google's horse. You're too young to remember Barney, but *Barney Google* was the most famous comic strip of its day, and he bought a race horse and named him Sparkplug. I had an uncle who named me Sparky the day after I was born, so I cannot remember my parents ever calling me anything other than Sparky. In school, I was always called Charles.

LIGUORI: Where did you get the idea for Charlie Brown?

SCHULZ: You don't just get an idea. You develop things. You think about things for a long time. When I was first trying to get started, I would send cartoons to magazines such as the *Saturday Evening Post* and others. It was the drawings I made of children that seemed to please the editors the most, and that's what sold. I had no intention of ever starting to draw cartoons about little kids. It just happened. That's what sold, so I kept on drawing them. I finally sold the strip in the spring of 1950 to United Feature Syndicate, and I had to create some characters, of course, with names. I had a friend back in Minneapolis that I used to work with and his name was Charlie Brown, so I asked him one day if I could use his name. So that's how things occur. You don't really just suddenly think of something. You develop them over a long period of time.

LIGUORI: But it was named after a real person?

SCHULZ: Charlie Brown, yeah. Nice fellow.

LIGUORI: I know you play a lot of golf. You've been playing golf since you were fifteen years old, and you won't probably say this. You're too humble to say, but you're an eight or nine handicap, which is phenomenal for a man whose schedule is so demanding and for someone who still works full-time.

SCHULZ: Probably the best was right after World War II. All we caddies came back and played a lot of tournament golf. I probably got down to about a three those days.

LIGUORI: How long did you caddie? How many years?

SCHULZ: When I was young, oh, just a couple of years. I won the caddie championship. Last thing I ever won. And of course when I caddied, we never got more than a dollar. The caddie rate was seventy-five cents, and I don't recall ever getting more than a twenty-five cent tip.

LIGUORI: You've been a part of this celebrity pro-am at Pebble Beach for years. I'm sure it's so much different now than when it was known as the Crosby Clambake years ago.

SCHULZ: I can't say that because I was never that much involved in the social aspect of it. Cartoonists, we didn't even get invited anywhere. I was lucky I even got to play. I got invited through Tennessee Ernie Ford. I used to do commercials for Tennessee Ernie's radio and television programs, and we played golf one day. I was hitting the ball pretty well. He said, "You know, you should play in the Crosby." I said, "Yeah, sure, I've been wanting to do that all my life." So he talked to Bing [Crosby], and Bing invited me.

LIGUORI: You've been here for over twenty-five years, so you've seen the whole development of the tournament.

SCHULZ: From the players' standpoint, I don't notice any difference at all. The only difference I notice is that they don't put cartoons in the program any more. That's a great offense to we cartoonists.

LIGUORI: You did a couple of covers for them.

SCHULZ: Oh yeah, and we used to always draw four or five cartoons on the inside, but I guess they don't want us anymore.

LIGUORI: I'm sure a lot of your own experiences go into your comic strips, even though Charlie Brown doesn't mirror your life, because I know as an athlete growing up, you were a very, very good athlete and won a lot of baseball games. But I'm sure a lot of the experiences you've been through really do go into your comic strips.

SCHULZ: There's no other way of doing it. I think that if you don't draw upon virtually every experience you've ever had, you'll never make it because the strip comes out every day. Day in and day out. Do you realize I've drawn over sixteen thousand comic strips? Well, that means you have to think about your own life, all of the miserable things that have happened to you. Like I always say, I never forget a slight, and I've had a lot of slights, so you pour yourself into it. You become a little bit of all the characters. I am not Charlie Brown, but I'm a little bit of Charlie Brown. I'm not Linus, but I'm a little bit of Linus. I'm not Snoopy but I'm a little bit of Snoopy. That's the only way you can do it.

LIGUORI: I remember this one, and you write all these as well. You're such a great author as well as being an artist, but I remember one when Charlie Brown had lost his one hundredth baseball game, and Lucy said, "That's okay, Charlie Brown. You win some, you lose some." And Charlie Brown said . . .

SCHULZ: "Wouldn't that be nice." Well, I remember when I was a little kid, there was no Little League, so we had to make up our own teams and find some other neighborhood who'd want to play us. One day a kid in school said, "I hear we're playing you tonight after school," and I said, "Oh, I didn't hear anything about it." He said, "Yeah, we're playing you over at the playground." So we went over there after school and we played. They were all just a shade bigger than we were, and we lost 40–0. We were never in the game, and I never forgot that, so that's why Charlie Brown loses so many games 40–0. I know what it's like to get trounced. Losing is funny. Winning is great, and it would be nice if you and I could always win everything that we do. It's like happiness. It's a shame that we all can't be happy all the time. Happiness is fine, but happiness is not very funny. What is funny is losing, especially when it happens to somebody else.

LIGUORI: I read that when you were in the army, you experienced as much loneliness as you cared to experience and you kind of brought all that into some of your characters and some of your stories. You really deal with more than humor. You deal with the issues of pain and loneliness, too.

SCHULZ: A lot of unrequited love, too. Have you ever been the victim of an unrequited love affair?

LIGUORI: Of course.

SCHULZ: So we know what it's like to be turned down by somebody, or to ask somebody for a date and be turned down. It's all part of the human experience. If you can read a cartoon or see a movie or read a story where you can identify with what is happening to the hero or the heroine, this is what makes for good communication.

LIGUORI: People can really identify with your characters.

SCHULZ: I don't draw for children at all. That's too difficult. I think if somebody says to you, "I've been wanting to do some writing lately. I think I'll try to write a children's book," that's the dumbest thing you can do because writing children's books is really difficult. To know something that children will be interested in takes a lot of ability. I wouldn't even try to write a children's book.

LIGUORI: Yes, but your comics appeal to them as well as adults.

SCHULZ: Well, I write for myself. What else can you do? You cannot direct your work towards certain audiences. I think that's fatal. All you can do is draw and write what you think is funny, what you think is interesting, and hope that other people will, too.

LIGUORI: And obviously it has worked because you're in over two thousand newspapers around the world.

SCHULZ: We're in the *Guinness Book of World Records*.

LIGUORI: Amazing. And the amazing thing is, Sparky, you do it all *yourself*. You don't have an assistant helping you out. Every single character, every single episode, *you* do.

SCHULZ: Arnie [Palmer] does not have somebody hit his nine-iron for him, you see. He does it all. I do it all. He has a caddie. Of course, I don't even have a caddie.

LIGUORI: You've said that after you decide to call it quits, nobody else will carry on the *Peanuts* strip and Snoopy and your characters.

SCHULZ: That's what my wife and my children decided. I remember my daughter Amy saying, "We don't want anyone else drawing Dad's strip," and that's the way it's going to be. So once I either retire or die, then the strip ends. That's the way it should be. Nothing can go on forever. They don't have somebody else do Picasso's paintings for him. That's ridiculous. And a lot of comic strips have suffered terribly by having other people take them over. So that's what the kids wanted, so that's the way it's going to be.

LIGUORI: Is Charlie Brown a great golfer like you?

SCHULZ: Charlie Brown isn't a golfer at all. He's a caddie. He caddies for Snoopy because I think there's more money in it.

LIGUORI: You're an avid golfer. Let's start with the strongest part of your game.

SCHULZ: Probably I'm reasonably consistent. I used to be a lot longer when I was younger, but I'm reasonably consistent. I used to be a good putter. Now my hands aren't as steady as they used to be, so my putting is falling apart little by little. But I would say that would be it. Back when I was about nine years old, I used to go to the Saturday afternoon matinees with my mother, and I saw the famous Bobby Jones short films in the theaters at that time. I was totally fascinated by Bobby Jones and watching him play golf. Now for years after that, I used to tell people that I saw Bobby Jones on these shorts, and nobody ever knew what I was talking about. Now all of a sudden, they have published them, they've reprinted them, and everybody has them. I was just totally fascinated by Bobby Jones and always wanted to play golf, but I had no one to take me out and show me how to play. So when I was about fifteen years old, some of the kids in the neighborhood started chopping around with old clubs, and another friend and I rode our bicycles up to Highland Park in St. Paul, which was about a three-mile drive early in the morning. We wanted to be up there before anybody else was there, and it was about 5:30 in the morning and we were the only ones on the course. We had an old miserable set of clubs, and I shot 156. And I thought, well, next week we'll go up and we'll do it again and I'll be better. So that day I shot 165. But then, little by little, I began to buy golf clubs, so the first club I ever owned was a Brassy which I bought for $2.50. That was my only club. And little by little, I accumulated a set of clubs, buying some from Western Auto, some from the Emporium and places like that, but none that ever cost more than three dollars. So that was the set of clubs I played with when I played on the high school golf team, and I can still remember going into a department store one day and seeing a set of Sam Snead irons. That was the most beautiful thing I had ever seen in my life, but they cost $100 and there was no way in the world I could ever have that set of Sam Snead irons. To this day, I still wish I had that set of irons.

LIGUORI: Who would play in your fantasy foursome?

SCHULZ: I've always wanted to play with Sam Snead. I'll never get a chance to play with him. I followed him around in St. Paul and actually played in the St. Paul Open when Sam Snead was playing, but I think he shot 66 and I probably shot 85. But at least I was in the same tournament. I would love to play with Sam Snead. I've never had a chance to play with Arnold Palmer. It'll never happen. But wouldn't that be a thrill just to be able to play with him? But it'll never happen.

LIGUORI: How do you know? You could ask him.

SCHULZ: I wouldn't dare. I saw Nick Price playing a practice round before the Open when it was out here in Pebble Beach a few years ago, and I just admired his stance and the way his hands were and everything was so set. And I told my friends, "Come on. You've got to look at this man. I've never seen a man set up to the ball as solidly as Nick Price does."

LIGUORI: You really study these professionals when they're out on the course.

SCHULZ: You can see a lot when you're in the rough and they're out here.

LIGUORI: When you were growing up, you said you didn't have the money for lessons, so you really had to teach yourself.

SCHULZ: When the St. Paul Open was on in St. Paul at Keller Golf Course, I was the first one out on the course in the morning, and I would spend the whole day there following these people around. I remember once I was the only person following Ralph Guldahl around. He had just won the National Open twice.[1] Nobody else was following him, just me, and I remember him looking at me once wondering, "Who's this kid following me around? He's the only one here." And of course I followed Sam Snead and watched every shot that he made, and it was so inspiring. I can still remember Sam teeing off on the first hole at Keller. It was a dogleg par four, and the others kind of played safely out to the left. Sam got up there and he cut the dogleg. I can still actually hear the way that driver hit that ball, with that solid smash that none of the others hit. He hit the ball so hard.

LIGUORI: Isn't it wonderful? You don't even have to *watch* the shot. You can tell if it's a great shot or not by *hearing* it. Because you've been so

---

[1] In 1937, Guldahl won the U.S. Open Championship at Oakland Hills Country Club in Birmingham, Michigan, beating Sam Snead. Guldahl repeated in 1938, beating Dick Metz in Denver at Cherry Hills Country Club.

passionate about golf, do you find yourself doing more golf comic strips?

SCHULZ: I could do golf cartoons every day. Every time I play I'll always think of two or three ideas simply because the friends that I play with tease each other so much and we just laugh all the way around and have a good time. Golf is a perfect sport for cartoons.

LIGUORI: If you were to describe your golf game to us through one of your characters, who would reflect you?

SCHULZ: Probably Snoopy because he just gets so terribly angry and so upset. We all do. Golf is like women. Golf leads us on. You hit a perfect drive. You hit the three-wood right up there near the green, and you're thinking birdie all the way up there, and then you chunk the approach shot and you get a bogey or a double bogey. So you've been led on and then you're turned down again. I suppose that's the fascination of the game, but that's the most aggravating part of it, too.

LIGUORI: I've never heard that analogy.

SCHULZ: Don't forget it.

LIGUORI: You've had so many wonderful highlights in your career, one being Snoopy and Charlie Brown as mascots for *Apollo 10*'s landing on the moon in 1969. You were named Commander in the Order of Arts and Letters, France's highest award for excellence in the arts. The Louvre Museum honored the fortieth anniversary of *Peanuts* with an exhibit back in 1990. That must have been wonderful. Does anything you do on the golf course compare to the satisfaction that your career has given you?

SCHULZ: I think just being out there. Every now and then, I will recall what it was like those first few mornings in St. Paul [that] I was telling you about, when we were only fifteen and then maybe sixteen, to be out early in the morning. The dew was still on the grass. That wonderful feeling that a golf course has, and it comes back to me every now and then. The one thing that turned me on to golf when I was young was that you always had to try out for other sports. The baseball team, or the hockey team or whatever it was, and there was always a coach there to say that you weren't good enough. But golf, you were on your own and you didn't have to be part of another team. It was just you and that was it. And that was a great revelation.

Robert Dedman

Robert Dedman is my favorite billionaire. He combines the heart and soul of a romantic poet with the discipline and vision it takes to become one of the wealthiest men in the business of golf. Dedman taught me more about life and golf in two hours on the course than anyone I've ever met. He changed my grip, using a tip he picked up from Byron Nelson. Presto! I'm hitting the ball farther. In between lessons on how to read putts, he told of his rise from dirt poor but proud Arkansas beginnings to founder and chairman of the Board of Club Corporation International (ClubCorp), the world's largest owner and manager of private clubs and golf resorts. Some of their most well-known properties include Pinehurst in North Carolina and The Homestead in Hot Springs, Virginia.

On the plane ride to Dallas, I spent hours reading about this fascinating personality. His road to success included three degrees—in engineering, economics, and law. At the age of nineteen, he decided that he would make $50 million by the time he was fifty and donate at least $1 million to charity each year. In order to accomplish this feat, he vowed to work eighty hours a week between the ages of twenty and thirty-five, sixty hours a week from thirty-five to fifty, and forty hours a week from fifty to sixty. He held to this original construct throughout his adult life.

Dedman started ClubCorp in his spare time back in 1957, while serving as a personal legal counsel to oil billionaire H. L. Hunt. He acquired 400 acres of inexpensive land in a Dallas suburb and turned it into the fifty-four-hole Brookhaven Country Club. In 1964, Dedman quit his law practice to devote all his efforts to his fledgling company. Today ClubCorp owns or manages over 260 country clubs, resorts, and public fee golf courses around the world. His hard work and leadership have helped ClubCorp amass more than $3 billion, with annual gross revenues of approximately $1.5 billion.

I interviewed Dedman in his office at the ClubCorp headquarters in Dallas. While the camera crew set up, I perused his office, impressed by its artful simplicity. Once the crew was ready, Robert Dedman walked in. He immediately put everyone at ease with his Southern gentlemanly charm. He was very approachable. We broke the ice by talking about our mutual interest in tennis and golf, two sports that he has played all his life. Ninety minutes seemed to go by very quickly, and Dedman was more than willing to keep chatting.

PAUL LESTER
Annika Sorenstam and Robert Dedman

Dedman could tell that I was fascinated by his unusual foresight in constructing his life plan. How did an eighteen-year-old develop the kind of management skills and goals that set the groundwork for his success? His answer caught me completely by surprise. Robert Dedman credits the foundation of his success to his love and study of many of the most celebrated poets in history. Poets? A billion-dollar poet, that's a bizarre oxymoron, but his sincerity infused his assertion with credibility. He spoke of Kipling, Longfellow, Emerson, and Shakespeare, and how they were the sources of inspiration for his lofty goals.

When talking about his company, he selflessly deferred much of the credit to the people who work for him. He chose to describe his avocation as the business of "fun." Dedman's wealth of knowledge kept our conversation going long after the cameras were turned off. I'd never met anyone who could explain the wisdom of Longfellow one moment and then recite axioms to live by from his housekeeper with equal magnanimity.

The next morning I meet with Robert Dedman and his son, Bob Jr., the chief operating officer of ClubCorp, to tape the on-course portion of the interview. I quickly discovered that my delightful billionaire poet had a saltier side to him. He loves a good joke, and his delivery would impress a stand-up comedienne, although many of them had to be edited out of the show. It's amazing how the links enables one to express parts of the personality that the normal world doesn't allow. Here was a man who plans his life to provide a time and place for everything. The climb he made out of poverty in Arkansas to settle atop a pile of unfathomable goals have afforded him tremendous range.

I enjoyed our time on the golf course, particularly Dedman's reaction to the additional distance I was getting on my drives as a result of the new grip he taught me. He was delighted. My Callaway Great Big Bertha was humming as he patiently spurred me on.

I feel cheated not to have met Robert Dedman years ago. I would have seized the opportunity to tap into his willingness to share his wisdom. After our interview, his many gracious compliments hit their target. For instance, he said, "I hope your husband knows how lucky he is. You have it all. You can play tennis, golf. You're smart and beautiful. I want to adopt you."

I must admit I gave my favorite billionaire's offer more than passing consideration. Smiling from ear to ear, I wondered how does one start adoption proceedings.

LIGUORI: You're the founder and chairman of the Board for Club Corporation International, or ClubCorp, the largest owner and manager of private clubs and golf resorts. Did you play golf before you created this business of golf? Which came first?

DEDMAN: I played golf. I think I was about a five handicap or so. I played a great deal before I got into the golf business. Actually, I was a practicing attorney and had a very successful law practice, but I hadn't been practicing too long before somebody told me there were two ways to get rich as a lawyer. One was to get out of law school and marry a rich woman. The other was to get out of law school, work your tail off for fifty years as a lawyer, then marry a rich woman. And I hadn't done that. Also, the only thing better than being a high-priced lawyer is being someone who hires high-priced lawyers. So I started looking for a vehicle that would hopefully enable me to make a lot more money. I didn't actually start ClubCorp until 1957, when I was thirty-one, and I started practicing law in '48, so I had been practicing some time, and I continued to practice law for the first seven years of the life of ClubCorp, and did ClubCorp as a moonlighting, nighttime, holiday, weekend pursuit.

LIGUORI: How did you get any golf in?

DEDMAN: Well, I made it a point to because it was my business. So I always made sure that maybe I'd work on Saturday mornings, or whatever, and then play golf Saturday afternoon. And then do the same thing again on Sunday. Go to church and work a while, and then play golf.

LIGUORI: Time management has always been such a big issue for you. I remember reading how you had declared at a very early age that you wanted to make $50 million by the time you were fifty, and donate $1 million.

DEDMAN: A year.

LIGUORI: And that you wanted to work eighty hours a week between the ages of twenty and thirty-five. That's a lot of hours.

DEDMAN: That was the program. I had a life plan. I came from very poor parents economically, back in a very poor community in south central Arkansas. Actually, my parents and family were kind of the living incarnation of the term "too poor to paint, but too proud to whitewash." They were very poor. They had an attitude that the best place to find a helping hand is at the end of your own arm. So armed with poverty and pride, it gave me a natural inclination to want to do enough to extricate myself from those cotton fields of south central Arkansas.

LIGUORI: Was it your parents who instilled that work ethic in you?

DEDMAN: Sure. But I also had a tremendous desire to, you know, get rich—to get out of those fields. So naturally I was motivated to want to do that, but I started thinking, it's one thing to have a desire, it's another thing to have a program to achieve a goal, and I noticed two things. I noticed that people who did the best usually worked the hardest. Usually people who worked forty hours a week or less worked for people who worked sixty hours a week or more. So the people who worked sixty hours a week or more usually learned more, took on more responsibility, worked half as long, and made more money per hour, but they also had less time to spend their money. So they would have a propensity to accumulate their earthly resources and reinvest it and use extra resources to get a portfolio going for them in making and keeping money. And I reasoned that if you would put in eighty hours a week, you really would get, in a sense, a head start on all of these objectives. There are 168 hours in a week, and if you put 56 hours in bed doing whatever, you still have 112 waking hours out of bed. If you spend 80 hours in gainful endeavor, you still have 32 hours to play golf and tennis and make love and go to church and dance and do all of those things.

LIGUORI: And how old were you when you decided this?

DEDMAN: I was about eighteen.

LIGUORI: I don't know of any eighteen-year-old who would plan out one's life like that. What inspired you, or who inspired you, or how did you decide at eighteen that you were going to manage the rest of your life like that?

DEDMAN: I think probably poetry. Back in the olden days, we memorized a lot of poetry, and I can think back on some parts of poems that I think made a big impact on me. One was "Rabbi Ben Ezra" written by Robert Browning for his wife Elizabeth Barrett Browning. He could see that she was getting a little concerned about aging and that sort of thing, so he wrote that poem, saying, "Come and grow old along with me—the best is yet to be, the last of life for which the first was made. Our times are in his hands, who saith a whole I planned, youth shows but half, see all, and trust God, and don't be afraid." Isn't that pretty?

LIGUORI: Gorgeous. Warms my heart.

DEDMAN: Well, it does.

LIGUORI: Just hearing you recite it.

DEDMAN: Well, it should. But it also shows you that you're kind of silly if you don't plan for your whole life. I think that's what got me into thinking in terms of life planning. I think Kipling's poem, "If," got me to thinking in terms of balance, having a balanced life, and time budgeting.

LIGUORI: Recite that one for me. Do you remember it?

DEDMAN: Well, there's are a lot to it; it's a long poem, but I can recite some parts that are relevant. "If you can keep your head when all about you are losing theirs and blaming it on you. If you can trust yourself when all men doubt you, but make allowances for their doubting too. If you can dream and not make dreams your master. If you can think and not make thoughts your aim. If you can treat triumph and disaster, those two impostors just the same." So you have balance, you have equanimity, you don't get overly elated by your victories or overly dejected by your defeats. And it goes on and on.

LIGUORI: It teaches a lot of life's lessons, that poem, Kipling's poem. So instead of perhaps idolizing or emulating a business leader when you were eighteen, it was really poetry, you're saying, more than anything else that molded your future and your goals and your dreams.

DEDMAN: I would say so, I would say so. They didn't have some of the books on goal setting and life planning and positive mental attitude, and those things then that they do now. But poetry had imbedded in it those things, and the good poetry, it endures. Because poetry that endures is the accumulated wisdom of the ages, expressed beautifully and succinctly and memorably or it wouldn't endure. And most good poetry has a god, man, duty, better self theme, running through it. It works on the psyche, the culture all the time. I didn't finish the "If" poem but there's part of it, the two other parts about balance, that are so important to a lot of people you're interviewing, it's so important in life. "If you can walk with kings, yet keep the common touch. . . ." It's so important that you do that, that you don't get too self-centered, too . . .

LIGUORI: Absolutely.

DEDMAN: . . . impressed with yourself.

LIGUORI: If you have to pinpoint the secret to your success, would it be the people who work for you?

DEDMAN: If would be an attitude—it would be an attitude of setting up win-win relationships. I think everyone's relative personal and professional success in life is a direct product of their ability to set up win-win personal relationships and professional relationships. Boy-girl relationships, man-wife relationships, you know if one is winning at the expense of the other, the loser is gonna cut out. Friendship relationships, you can't have a friend without being a friend. And in business relationships, you've got to set up win-win deals, employer-employee relationships. If the employer is winning at the expense of the employee, the employee is not going to stay. It's an idiot that expects bigger loyalties than you give.

LIGUORI: How did you feel when *Golf Digest* named you the richest man in golf in 1996?

DEDMAN: Well, it's nice. It's nice. I like to think a lot more about what you can do with money than just accumulate it. Somebody said it's a lot better to spread it around like manure. Because if you pile it up like manure, it'll smell horrible. So I think it's important that I'm not just making it, but to be as intelligent in giving it away as you have been in making it.

LIGUORI: Which you have done to the tune of $25 million, which you donated to Southern Methodist University.

DEDMAN: Well, thank you. But I hope that that's just the start of mine, and there are a lot of other people who give a lot more money to a lot more things, so I still have a lot to do, you know, hopefully while I'm still on this earth.

LIGUORI: You must still have goals for yourself, you're such a goal-oriented person. What else do you see yourself doing?

DEDMAN: Well, a lot more of what I am doing now. I'm very proud of ClubCorp and our people and the institutions that we have. And it's not too often in life that you're fortunate enough to preserve and enhance institutions like we have. That kind of has a sense of eternity in it. I think it was Longfellow who said, "The lives of all great people remind us that we can make our lives sublime, and departing leave behind us footprints in the sands of time." I think, for example, you mentioned the Pinehurst area. That's an incredible footprint in the sands of time. The same thing is true of The Homestead. The Homestead is the oldest resort in this country, started in 1776, that now has superb golf. That Upper Cascades course is ranked about four in the country by *Golf Digest* magazine that you're referring to. Pinehurst is ranked number two in the country. So, to have two of the top four as ranked by the top magazine, *Golf Digest*, is something that's fun, but it also is an important stewardship role. But, to be able to acquire those properties and then enhance those properties, so that they'll get better forever, does give you a sense of nobility and belonging that are a lot more to me than just accumulating earthly resources. And we started a lot from scratch. We've just started a lot of institutions, like Brookhaven in Dallas, our very first deal 40 years ago, was an institution. The two best golfers in college in America came out of our junior golf program by winning the NCAA back-to-back: Scott VerPlank and Brian Watts. And Andy Magee, who came out of the same program, was runner-up.

LIGUORI: You must have played golf with some of the most fascinating personalities in the country. Talk about some of the people whom you've golfed with.

DEDMAN: Well, Byron Nelson is one of my all-time favorites. He was our first director of golf, at the first club we did, Brookhaven in Dallas, and he was an incredible golfer and incredible teacher and incredible human being. So he was a super guy. And I also got to play a lot in the early days with Ben Hogan, we did some consulting for Shady Oaks, where he plays in Fort Worth, so I got to play with him often, and he was a good teacher and fun to be with and that type. He was always concentrating when he was playing competitive golf. Another chap that I got to play a lot of golf with was Ralph Guldahl. He was our pro in Los Angeles at Braemar Country Club, the club that we started in Los Angeles in 1959. And he had won the U.S. Open back to back in the '30s [1937 and 1938], and then held the record at the Masters for many, many years, and he could really play tremendous golf.[1] I had a financing agreement with Braemar, that I had to spend three days a month at Braemar, so I got to play with him a couple of those days each time. And he probably taught me more about scoring than anyone. One time, they were having one of these Scotch deals with Sam Snead, and Sam always outdrove Ralph about thirty or forty yards, and Sam said to him one time when he was having to play Ralph's ball to the green, you know he was hitting a six-iron where he'd been hitting a nine-iron, and he said to Ralph—this is according to Ralph—"How do you

[1] Guldahl won the Masters in 1939, shooting a 279, a record that was matched by Claude Harmon in 1948 and beaten by Ben Hogan in 1953 with a score of 274.

short hitters ever win a golf tournament?" So I just thought that was kind of a cute observation.

LIGUORI: Any good Arnold Palmer stories?

DEDMAN: All of them were good. All of those guys were super people. They're fun to be with. Sam Snead, you could talk forever about Sam. He's fun. I played with Sam again last Labor Day up at The Homestead. His favorite course, I think, is at Homestead—the Upper Cascades course where he grew up playing. And he lives there. And he's eighty-two now, and he shot even par on that course—we played from the white tees, but he can still play. He had carpal tunnel syndrome [compression of the nerve in the hand and wrist caused by repeated flexure of the wrist] and had to have his hands fixed, but he can still play. I played with him one time when he was seventy-six, in Florida, and at that time he said, "Bob, I'll give you twelve shots and play you for $20 nassau." And I said, "Okay, and I had a 79 for a net 67, and he shot 66. He had a hole in one and a couple of eagles that day.

LIGUORI: And beat you by one stroke.

DEDMAN: Yeah. But he was six strokes under par that day, and he was seventy-six. He beat his age by ten shots—this is an incredible story. The man is an incredible athlete. And I asked Sam the last time we played together, "Sam, if you only had one bit of advice to give a golfer, what would it be?" I thought it would be something about the swing because he's always had such a long, big, fluid swing. Slammin' Sammy Snead, you remember, is a term that people called him. But he actually said, "People ought to make sure that the V's on both hands touch all the way to the thumbnail, and both of these V's point to the right shoulder." It was incredible to hear a guy who has won eighty-five tournaments,[2] or something, talking about the importance of the grip as eloquently as he did. Most of the other pros whom I've heard through the years, like Byron Nelson, say you need to make sure that the V's on both hands are touching past the first knuckle and pointing at the right shoulder. So, I just thought I'd throw that little golf lesson from Sam Snead in, gratis for everyone else.

LIGUORI: Is that the grip you use?

DEDMAN: Well, I do. I noticed that the majority of the pros at the U.S. Senior Open at Pinehurst in 1995 would check their grip. After playing as long as they have, all of them over thirty years, most

[2] Sam Snead earned 81 PGA Tour events, including three Masters ('49, '52, '54), one British Open ('46), and three PGA Championships ('42, '49, '51).

of them over forty years, and they're still checking their grip, or they wouldn't be there.

LIGUORI: Have you played with any presidents? I've seen pictures of you with George Bush.

DEDMAN: I played tennis with Bush. I don't remember playing golf with him, and I played golf with Gerald Ford. He used to play at the Inverrary Classic a lot and I got to play with him there and in the pro-am—he's a super guy. And then, as you know, all three presidents played out at Indian Wells, a club we have in Palm Springs, in 1996. I think that's the first time that three presidents have ever played together. It was Ford and Bush and Clinton in that round. But I didn't get to play with them. I visited with them in the locker room.

LIGUORI: Talk about your passion for golf. What do you like about playing golf?

DEDMAN: I like everything about it. I like the courses, you know, the green grass, the trees, the flowers, the lakes, the squirrels, the birds, just being outdoors. I think that we have a subconscious feeling in ourselves that we want to get out and play like kids and these things in the wide open spaces, which you don't get to do very much anymore, really—and golf is one of the few ways to do that. I like the challenge of it because it's you and the course, and I like the discipline of it. And keeping score, and learning to win and lose and get some good shots and some bad shots and come back. I like the concentration it requires because it gets your mind off of all of the other things that you could be thinking about—problems and other things—and I like the fun of being with the partners that you're playing with. Men and Women. It's just a ball to be outside and competing and enjoying each other, and you're mainly competing with the course and matching scores. And because of the handicapping system in golf and the different tees, you can make it an equal game where everybody can play their game and have a good time whether they're playing for money or not. I notice a lot of people seem to have the most fun when they are not playing for money.

[Out on the course, playing at Gleneagle Country Club in Plano, Texas, with Robert and Bob Jr., COO of ClubCorp.]

DEDMAN SR.: I was playing so bad that I lost two balls in the ball washer yesterday. I'm hitting the woods fine. I'm just having trouble getting out of them.

LIGUORI: [Turning to Bob Jr.] Have you heard these jokes a million times, Bob, or what?

DEDMAN JR.: No, some of those are new.

LIGUORI: You'll have to remember them.

DEDMAN JR.: Absolutely.

DEDMAN SR.: There's another cute story I always enjoy about the fellow who gets up on the first tee, like we were here today, and takes out a new sleeve of balls. There are lakes to the right and lakes to the left, and he knocks a new ball out into the lake on the right, and he takes another new ball out and knocks it into the lake on the left. And then takes a third new ball and knocks it out into the lake on the right, and the fellow playing with him says, "Hey, fella, why don't you use an old ball?" And he says, "I've never had any."

▼

DEDMAN: An awful lot of people refer to me as a jokester because I tell a lot of jokes. And some, I guess, just think of me as a big joke, but I really think it's so important that you should always take your problems seriously and your assignments seriously, but never yourself too seriously.

LIGUORI: That's wonderful advice.

DEDMAN: Because if you ever do, you can get so tense and intense that you can lose your sense of humor, and in so doing, in my own judgment, you lose your perspective to be able to see the problems in perspective. You also lose the positive mental attitude that it takes to seek and find solutions to those problems. You also want to have the persuasive skills that it takes to build the consensus necessary among the people to solve the big problems, and without humor, you won't have the leadership skills that it takes to lead the people and to implement the solutions to the problems because nobody likes to follow a sourpuss. Everybody likes to be with somebody who sees solutions and is positive and all. But there's a lot more to humor. I think it was a merciful God that invented laughter, because the more we laugh, the more we live. And there's a beautiful message in laughter itself. The more you give laughter, the more you live. The more you give laughter to someone else, obviously, the more you enjoy it yourself. So that's a little sermonette out here among the trees early in the morning.

Dave Thomas

There are few businessmen in America more recognizable than Dave Thomas of Wendy's Hamburgers. The restaurant's advertising campaign has for years brought Thomas's hard-not-to-love grin into the living rooms all over the world. Wendy's fast-food chain, named after one of his daughters, boasts more than 4,500 restaurants in twenty-nine countries.

Thomas' story is an inspirational rags-to-riches tale. He was adopted when he was six weeks old. At the age of five, his adoptive mother passed away. His stepfather and he set out on a nomadic trail that included three more stepmothers. By fifteen, Thomas had lived in a dozen homes.

The future burger mogul coped with his troubled home life by concentrating on work. He found his first job at the age of eleven as a busboy. By the tenth grade, he had dropped out of school, moved out of the family trailer and into the local YMCA. He worked full-time in a restaurant as a short-order cook. The seed was planted that would someday shake the fast-food business at its roots. He studied the cooks, the servers, the managers, and dreamt about one day opening his own restaurant.

In 1962, his dream was realized when he became part owner of four Kentucky Fried Chicken outlets. He relocated with his wife and children to Columbus, Ohio, and worked under KFC's Colonel Sanders. Six years later, he sold his share of KFC franchises for more than $1 million in cash and stock and used the money to start Wendy's—fresh, to-order hamburgers with a choice of toppings. His restaurants had two additional features, invented by Thomas, that later became a staple of the fast food industry: the pickup window and the salad bar.

I heard through the grapevine that Thomas had once traded a boat for a golf course. This prompted me to arrange for an interview with Thomas so I could ask about this and other intriguing stories. He told me that he once owned a ninety-one-foot luxury yacht worth about $2.5 million. After the initial thrill wore off, Thomas got bored with his toy and traded the yacht for the Woodlands, a country club in Spring Valley, South Carolina. Mixing pleasure with enterprise was more in keeping with his entrepreneurial energy. He renovated the club, then went on to buy other golf properties.

Thomas's life has been so driven by the work ethic that in his early career he had little regard for people who had the time to play a lot of golf.

ERIN O'BOYLE PHOTOGRAPHICS

Today Thomas is a twenty-four handicap, and in recent years, he has found more time to squeeze golf into his intense work schedule. He is funny and relaxed on the golf course and does not take himself too seriously. He views golf as an occasion to socialize and research human nature, the perfect opportunity to get to know what people are really like. We decided there was no better test for prospective employees than to observe them in a round of golf. Dave has as much fun on the course as he does in his famous Wendy's commercials.

Dave and I walked several holes at one of my favorite golf courses, the Mountain Course at La Quinta. As we approached the sixteenth hole—160-yard, par three with nothing but rocks between the elevated tee and the small green—Dave handed me one of his special "Big Dave seven-woods" and issued a challenge: Give it a shot. I saw there was no margin for error on the hole, as the mountain would eat up anything that did not land on the green. It was obvious that Dave was conducting a bit of research on me. With Wendy's marketing and advertising staff looking on, I took a few practice swings with the new seven-wood. Ready or not—I connected! The ball landed about ten feet from the pin.

Dave flashed that adorable Wendy's grin. The unassuming entrepreneur graciously lauded my successful shot. You've got to love a guy who sells hamburgers dressed in short-sleeved shirts and ties.

LIGUORI: Dave, hamburgers are your specialty, and you've done so well with it. But I want to talk about your golf game because I understand that you traded in a yacht for a golf course. Why?

THOMAS: It cost me a lot of money, the boat, and I made a big turnaround. Now I make money, so that was the reason I did it. I can tell you this. I think with the golf course, you have more fun. The boat, there's always something wrong.

LIGUORI: Taking care of a country club, that's a big deal. You can just go and play; you don't have to worry about running the place?

THOMAS: Well, I took my captain who was on the boat and I made him the general manager of the golf course. And my captain, when he was running the boat, I used to give him two shots a hole and still beat him. Now he says he's a ten handicap, but I think he's about a five handicap.

LIGUORI: What's your handicap?

THOMAS: As much as I can get. The problem is, I have so many golf clubs that I don't know which ones to really use, so once in a while I have to have a meeting with all my golf clubs.

LIGUORI: I read a quote where you said, "Years ago, I was a caddie and I hated it." And then you said that anybody who had enough time to hit a golf ball must have something wrong with them.

THOMAS: That's true. In fact, Ron Musick is one of our executive vice presidents, and he's been with me about thirty years, when I was at Kentucky Fried Chicken. And he says that I said that anyone that played golf—and this was like thirty years ago—there's gotta be something wrong with them. And he said he automatically got rid of his clubs.

LIGUORI: So what's wrong with you? You now like the sport.

THOMAS: I must've changed because I really like golf. I think golf is good relaxation. It's good exercise, and you meet so many nice people playing golf. I've met so many people. When you spend three or four hours on a golf course with somebody, you really can find out what kind of character they are. Are they nice?

LIGUORI: I was just going to say you should use that perhaps as a prerequisite before you hire any key people. Do you take them out on the golf course?

THOMAS: We've done that. I don't think that's a mandatory thing, but we do that because I think you can find out about a person's personality.

LIGUORI: You know so many people, and you wrote about a lot of these people in your book *Well Done! The Common Guy's Guide to Everyday Success* [1994]. You travel half the year, and you meet so many people. Who are some of the more interesting people that you've golfed with?

THOMAS: Well, Arnold Palmer, and the last time we played, he beat me.

LIGUORI: You have some interesting advice throughout your books and some of these "toppings," as you call them, could apply to golf instruction.

THOMAS: Yeah, it should.

LIGUORI: "Pay attention to basics." "Focus on only one thing at a time." "Have a sense of urgency." Secrets of success you can apply to everything from business to golf.

THOMAS: You know the thing with golf is honesty. It's an honor game. I just like to see young people go out and play golf because I think it means so much to their character and honesty and integrity. I think golf's a great sport, not that I'd want to be a professional because I don't want to go practice. I was playing with President Ford and Jim McDonald, who was president of General Motors, and Jim McDonald told President Ford, "You know, I never thought I'd be playing with a Ford." And I said, "Hey, Jim, I'd never thought I'd be playing with a McDonald."

LIGUORI: I love the story going back to your adoptive grandmother, Minnie, who advised you to never cut corners.

THOMAS: That's right.

LIGUORI: Years later somebody asked you, "Why are Wendy's hamburgers square?"

THOMAS: We don't cut corners. But it's really operational. She was a fantastic lady, and I did learn a lot from her. I learned when I was growing up—I always felt that if you didn't work, you didn't eat, and I literally would like to see us go back to that same kind of philosophy because I think there's a lot of people today that don't work and need to work. If you're able to work, you should work. There's no reason not to. I'm really proud of our whole industry because we do employ so many first jobbers, and they learn and earn at the same time. Fifty percent of the CEOs and Fortune 500s started in some kind of food operation. And our whole industry's grown up a lot because when I was going to school, teachers used to tell me if I didn't study, I might end up in a restaurant.

LIGUORI: And that's what you wanted to do. You wound up in a restaurant, founding one of the most popular food chains in the world.

THOMAS: Today, it's a sophisticated business, and it's large. We encounter more people than any industry in the world.

LIGUORI: Were there any hopes of becoming a proficient golfer?

THOMAS: I've never been accused of being a golfer, I can say that.

LIGUORI: But you have fun with it, and that's what's most important. Golf can be the most frustrating sport in the world, but it doesn't seem as if you let your bad shots bother you.

THOMAS: One thing about it, I'm not that good. I mean, I can't complain.

LIGUORI: And that's an honest man for you.

Mark McCormack

Mark McCormack is strung as tightly as a golf ball, but beyond his intensity and overstuffed appointment book, scheduled to the precise minute, he has a great sense of humor and a soft side that would surprise many of the same intensity-driven people who work in the business he created. His wife, Betsy Nagelsen, a tennis professional who competed in twenty-four straight Wimbledons, provides a balance to his life. She is very low-key and spiritually centered. These are qualities I'm sure work well for Mark, as he commands his massive sports empire. On the strength of his vision, hustle, ripe historical timing, and one very important handshake, Mark has taken the business of representing athletes to places one could have only dreamed of before the athletes' revolt of the sixties.

Mark grew up playing golf and, by the time he reached his college years, was good enough to play on the College of William and Mary's varsity team. Mark attended Yale Law School and later practiced law at a high profile firm in Cleveland. He kept a casual hand in the world of golf, advising players he'd known when he competed. He would arrange exhibitions and offer legal advice to professional golfers, which in those days were relatively simple matters. Mark's transformative moment came when he sealed a deal with a handshake to represent Arnold Palmer's business interests. Palmer was on his way to defining America's golf character, and Mark parlayed his relationship with this budding sports legend into IMG (International Management Group), the first firm in history devoted to the management and marketing of athletes. Mark's company grew so fast that it reached into uncharted territory: television production, a literary agency, lecture bureau, licensing agency, and financial planning firm. His powerful client list now ranges from Monica Seles and John Madden to Itzak Perlman and the Nobel Foundation.

Mark is an accomplished writer whose big-splash effort was the book, *What They Don't Teach You at Harvard Business School.* He devoted a chapter on how observing someone on the golf course reveals a lot about them. His formidable sense of humor is present in his writing as well as during his relaxed moments, which are few. When does this workaholic have time to play golf? Hardly ever. Mark has pretty much given up playing his goose that laid so many golden eggs. The game now frustrates him. He's such a perfectionist and expects to excel at whatever he does. Golf rarely stands for that attitude, so there's been a parting of the ways. Unless a client wants to meet at the golf course, he doesn't have the time to do the game justice.

PHOTO COURTESY OF MARK McCORMACK

Instead, his busy schedule has driven him to the tennis courts, where his wife, Betsy, has distinguished herself. She owns twenty-five doubles titles, including two Australian Open doubles victories. You would think Mark would be in good hands, but that would be too simple. Betsy feels that Mark is too serious on the court, and he counters that she plays too much "social" tennis, so they try not to pair up at charity events.

The team of Mark McCormack–Arnold Palmer has had as big an impact on the sport of golf as any in the last half century. And now with Tiger Woods as a client, McCormack's empire will continue to shine well into the twenty-first century.

LIGUORI: Mark, you are the founder and CEO of International Management Group and really the founding father of sports agents.

MCCORMACK: As long as you don't say founding *grand*father, it's okay.

LIGUORI: I mean, it really is amazing to look at the entire empire. What comes to mind when you think about what you have accomplished through the years?

MCCORMACK: Everyone always says I figured this all out ahead of time and had this grand plan. The answer is no, I sort of went step by step. It was literally a domino kind of effect, not any great grand plan. I was very lucky. The timing I had was extremely fortuitous. I got the three best golf players in the world [Jack Nicklaus, Arnold Palmer, and Gary Player] before any of them had really done a lot. Nicklaus was still an amateur; Palmer had won one major championship before I represented him. Player never played in America except for one time before. Then the three of them won everything in sight, and television hit about the same time, so I had everything. If anybody wanted a top golfer, they had to come to me. Golf has become more popular, and I had some thoughts about how to tie corporations into golf. That worked really well, and then I started getting approached by, initially, a lot of other sports personalities from other sports. They said, "Look, you've done some great things in golf. Can you do this for our sport?" And again, we got the top people and we had great timing. I'd like to think we had some good talent at the same time and good vision in terms of globalization and internationalization of what we were doing.

LIGUORI: Well, obviously it was more than luck and timing. There were a lot of mental strategies. . . .

MCCORMACK: Well, as Gary Player once said, "The harder I practice, the luckier I get," so I'd like to think there's a little bit of that there, but you know, without the good luck and without a divine blessing somewhere or other, none of it would have happened, I'm sure.

LIGUORI: Is there anything about the direction of the sports marketing business you dislike?

MCCORMACK: I think you can never keep it perfect, and I think that the moneys have gotten a little bit out of hand. I think the individual sports personalities are being paid too much for indifferent performance. I think the whole "union" approach—and this doesn't just mean players unions in the team sports—but in golf you get paid for mediocrity. You get paid for getting into a tournament, not for performing, and that's because of in effect the union syndrome. Prize money structures are determined by a vote of the policy board which are elected by vote of the players. And only 4 percent of the players are top players. Most of them are middle players and many of them are people that ought to get jobs somewhere and not try to be golf champions. The result of that is you have too much prize money spread down too far and too much equality of prize money. Whereas I think the public would be fascinated to see a tournament where the winner got a million dollars and second place got nothing. I mean, now you've got a man on the eighteenth green putting for a million dollars and I think that kind of stuff is appealing, but that doesn't happen. So I think the spreading out of things and the parity approach in sports is bad.

LIGUORI: You are quite an accomplished golfer yourself, as a participant in many amateur events.

MCCORMACK: I *was* a fairly accomplished golfer. I played in the U.S. Open, so I was good enough to get into it. I played in four U.S. Amateurs and four British Amateurs. But although I was good enough to get into those events, I wasn't good enough to do very well in them, and I knew that. So the last twenty years or so, I've played very little golf. I've tried to become a tennis player only because tennis, I think, is better exercise than golf. You can play it in a shorter span of time, and I don't expect anything of myself. Golf, I once did it to a certain level and I get out now and I see a tree and I want to fade the ball around the tree and I used to do that eight out of ten times. And now I don't do it and I get mad. Golf is supposed to be fun and relaxing, and for me, it's frustrating.

LIGUORI: Talk about your relationship with Arnold Palmer now, because that really is what started this whole thing.

MCCORMACK: Well, I don't see Arnold as much now as I did. We both have homes in Orlando, and we see each other when we're there. We still operate his businesses for him. He's got a big staff of people, golf course architects and design. He's got an automotive business, an aviation business, and a great worldwide licensing business, which we oversee. Arnold and I have never had a contract. We have had a handshake. We've resolved everything between us as reasonable human beings who trust each other, and that's been a great relationship.

LIGUORI: And you were college buddies, right?

MCCORMACK: Well, we went to college at the same time. He was at Wake Forest and I was at William and Mary and our teams played against each other. I knew him then. I was not a buddy of his.

LIGUORI: There's a great quote that Chi Chi Rodriguez said. "When I started on the Tour, we were playing so that maybe we could be the head pro at a club. Now thanks to Arnie and Mark McCormack, the guys on the Tour are playing to buy the club."

MCCORMACK: Well, that's flattering of him to say that, and Lee Trevino has said some similar things. Neither of them are clients, and that made it even more important for them to say it. But I certainly think that Arnold has had a charismatic effect on the sport that very few people have ever had. Michael Jordan has it. Tiger Woods may have it. He has certainly burst on to the scene in a way that nobody in the history of golf has ever burst onto the scene. But then again, golf is more mature than it was when Palmer came on into it, and Palmer came into it at a time when it was a lot more mature than Bobby Jones. So it's hard to really compare the impact of a Tiger Woods to an Arnold Palmer to a Bobby Jones. But Woods has certainly been a phenomenal addition to the golf scene.

LIGUORI: And I know IMG went after him very aggressively, after his father, prior to when Tiger turned pro.

McCormack: Well, that's slightly overstated. There was no secret how good Tiger Woods was going to be. I don't think anybody knew he would do what he did, but he was certainly a very highly desired young golfer. And we, many years ago, had an arrangement with his father, who was going to all the junior golf tournaments, and we didn't have the staff to go to all the junior golf tournaments. And we hired him because we knew he'd be there to file reports on all the junior golfers that he was seeing. This is when Tiger was quite young. When Tiger went to Stanford, of course, we had no arrangement with his father because that would have violated the NCAA regulations. But we did establish a relationship with his father. He knew us. And we are after all, the biggest and best in the business, and Tiger wants to be with the biggest and best.

Liguori: Obviously a smart thing to do, to develop that relationship with Mr. Woods, wanting to represent his son, eventually.

McCormack: You have to in sports today. You have to start very young. I mean, Martina Hingas is sixteen years old, and we've represented her three years.

Liguori: Getting back to Arnold Palmer, the image that will always come to my mind when I think of Arnold is him walking over that bridge on the eighteenth at the British Open. He turns around, smiles, and waves. The man has the most charismatic smile in sports, don't you think?

McCormack: Yeah. He wears his emotions on his sleeve and everyone knows exactly how he feels, whether it's sentimental, mad, happy, or whatever. And that's what is so appealing about him. He would play golf like all of us hope to play golf. He'd go for it, and if he missed it, you knew he missed it and he was mad, but you admired him for trying.

Liguori: Yet when he first started out, Palmer had to *play* for the big money. Tiger Woods already had the $40 million Nike contract before he even played in one professional tournament. Do you feel that that's going to make a difference with the stars of tomorrow?

McCormack: Well, it didn't seem to make a lot of difference to [Tiger's] first five weeks. I mean, he won twice and had four top-five finishes in a row. So I think he demonstrated what I said to you earlier, that he wants to win. He wants to be the best golfer that ever played. And whether he has $40 million from Nike or $5 million from Nike, or a $100 million from Nike, it doesn't make any difference.

LIGUORI: Do you think the golf industry will continue to grow?

MCCORMACK: I don't think any sports will grow as expeditiously in the next decade as they have in the past. I mean, I can't see NBA basketball, I can't see Michael Jordan getting the same multiple of salary next time around that he got in the last ten years. I can't see the tickets going up by the same amount, and I can't see the television rights escalating at the same rate. So I think it's going to stabilize a little bit.

LIGUORI: How do you feel about the ever-changing television environment, with the many new sports channels that have emerged as well as direct satellite systems? There are more viewing options, but audiences and ratings are affected.

MCCORMACK: Well, when you have three hundred channels to look at, obviously the ratings will be a lot different, but I think you're getting more and more bouquets of channels, more and more tunnel vision or narrowcasting. The Golf Channel, which we were very instrumental in the creation of and do a lot of work for, in terms of programming and other things, is an example of that. It may be a small niche, but that niche is an affluent niche, really, to advertisers and people who like golf will watch it all day. And the same is true in other sports. There's talk of tennis channels or speed channels, classic channels, automobile channels, food channels, and war channels.

LIGUORI: Getting back to your golf game, when you *used* to play—what did you like about it? Why were you so passionate about it?

MCCORMACK: I like excelling at things, and as a youth, it was something I excelled at, and I could look around at somebody who was a better football player or a better scholar or a better this or that, and I could gain self confidence by thinking I can beat that person in golf. [To say,] I'm the best golfer in my high school or my college or my city or my state.

LIGUORI: Wendy's Hamburger founder Dave Thomas once told me he plays golf with a perspective employee just to learn about him. Eighteen holes of golf is a window to their soul, so to speak.

MCCORMACK: Well, I wrote a whole section when I wrote *What They Don't Teach You at the Harvard Business School* on learning about people on golf courses because I think you can tell more about somebody from a competitive round of golf or just a social round of golf than you can from an awful lot of business meetings.

Dan Quayle

When I began my research for the Dan Quayle interview, I went to the Internet, and the first quote to jump out at me went like this: "I was recently on a tour of Latin America, and the only regret I have was that I didn't study Latin harder in school so I could converse with those people." What? I wondered if these "Quaylisms" were made up by those who have nothing better to do than to criticize the former vice president. Then again, the "potato debacle" was there for all to see. When George Bush selected the forty-one-year-old Indiana senator to be his running mate, the relatively obscure politician hit the national spotlight with such force it seemed as though he were fired from a cannon, landing into a net of political jokes, answering the prayers of late-night television comedians.

I always try to go into an interview with an open mind. But with all the publicity surrounding Quayle's vice presidency, from his public fumblings to his battles with fictitious television characters, I figured this one was going to be difficult. I also felt a degree of sympathy for someone who has been the victim of a political drive-by shooting.

Quayle, once a scratch golfer, plays several tournaments a year, including events on the Celebrity Golf Association circuit. It was at the White Eagle Golf Club in Naperville, Illinois, during the summer of 1996 at a CGA event, that we caught up with the former vice president.

Under the direction of Anne Hathaway, Quayle's press secretary, the logistics for the interview were arranged with a sturdy, comforting professionalism rarely seen in the world of athletes and rock stars, whose schedules often change with their moods. It was a pleasure not to worry if Quayle would show up or not. We did our sit-down interview in the club's trophy room. Its fine tapestries and mahogany added a Pennsylvania Avenue feel to the atmosphere. Quayle arrived on time. His press people made certain that my makeup person powdered him properly, then carefully described the camera angles we should use during the taping. I've only experienced such scrutiny from press secretaries of politicians. New York Mayor Rudy Giuliani's people were just as careful when I interviewed Rudy for my other show, *Sports Innerview*. But I don't have a problem with that. Politicians can never be too careful.

REUTERS/MARK BAKER/ARCHIVE PHOTOS

I was quickly impressed by Dan Quayle's charm. He was congenial and polished, sexy in a decidedly Republican way. We began the interview talking politics. This unleashed a partisan flow of consciousness. It bugs him to no end that the Democratic establishment scalded his image when he took on the family values issue. Doing battle with Murphy Brown would leave scars on anyone. The wounds he suffered over the issue of the family are deep and sensitive, leaving him trapped in political limbo, too young to retire, yet too exposed to reinvent himself. President Clinton's adoption of his family values platform offers some vindication, but Quayle's awkward political timing leaves him outside of the nation's window looking in.

Dan Quayle the politician and Dan Quayle the avid golfer, are two very different people. We had a great time on the range. His extensive knowledge of the game was culled from a passion he developed as a child. He swings easily and with much confidence, smacking one ball after another 260 yards, while casually talking with me. His unassuming nature and easy confidence uncovers a sly, inviting sense of humor. The golf course offers the opportunity for Quayle to be himself. He has the perfect temperament for a golfer—confident and focused. Had he chosen this line of work and been good enough, he would probably be one of the most popular players on the Tour.

If the voters had been able to see Dan Quayle on a golf course enjoying himself, while entertaining us all with his wit and charm, the 1992 election might have gone in his favor. At the very least, he would have shot a better score. Golf often brings out the best and worst in us. On that beautiful summer afternoon, in a game that humbles so many, Dan Quayle was at his best.

LIGUORI: You're a four handicap, which is very good considering your schedule.

QUAYLE: Well, I was fortunate.

LIGUORI: How do you have time to play?

QUAYLE: I *don't* have time to play. I was very fortunate to take this game up when I was eight years old. I grew up in Phoenix, Arizona, and played a lot of golf from age eight to about age twenty-two, all through college, and then I sort of slacked off, but it's a lot like riding a horse—once you learn how to do it, you can always do it.

LIGUORI: Sounds too easy.

QUAYLE: Golf is easy if you relax and enjoy it. Don't push yourself. Try to have good thoughts and just go out there. It's just a ball and put it in a hole—that's what my wife Marilyn always tells me. "It's just a game, Dan, just a game."

LIGUORI: I'll remember that advice. Just keep it simple.

QUAYLE: That's right, that's what you want to do. Keep it simple, be relaxed.

LIGUORI: I know you were captain of your collegiate team.

QUAYLE: Yes, down at DePauw University. You've never heard of DePauw University? In my college days, we weren't knocking at the number-one slot of the NCAA golf championship, I have to confess.

LIGUORI: You missed out, darn it.

QUAYLE: But we did reasonably well. We had this golf course down in Greencastle [Indiana] called Windy Hills. It was nine holes and they had different tees, and it was *some* track. It was very much of a public golf course, and if you didn't live there and if you didn't play the golf course day in and day out, you had not a clue how to play it, because there are a lot of trick holes and trick shots you had to have in order to compete. And therefore our team, when I was there, I don't think we ever lost a match at the home course. And we beat some fairly good teams. Some of the good teams quit coming because they didn't like the golf course. But it was fun, and I enjoyed playing golf all through college. Took it very seriously. And then went on to other things, like politics.

LIGUORI: A lot of other things to say the least. You know you always beat the political odds with elections. You unseated a sixteen-year incumbent when you first ran for Congress, then you beat out a three-term incumbent to become a U.S. senator. How about on the golf course, beating the odds?

QUAYLE: Well, I always try to beat the odds by beating par, but that doesn't happen very often. Golf is a little bit more brutal to me than politics has been, if you can believe that. Because if you go out and try to break par or shoot par, then that's pretty tough to do. I can do it every once in a while, but not very often. And that's always the goal. In politics, what you do is you go out and take your opponent on, and you tackle the issues, you take your case to the American people, and they decide. In golf, you're the judge because it's you and the golf course. Nobody else has a say in it.

LIGUORI: You against yourself.

QUAYLE: You post a number, and that's it.

LIGUORI: That's right. Very tough. A lot of people find it one of the most exasperating sports. You have to have the right temperament to excel in golf.

QUAYLE: Temperament's very important. You've got to be patient. You can't get frustrated. Everybody's going to have a bad day, and you just have to whistle about it, sing a song, and move on, because if you really let it get to you, then you won't be having any fun. And I think we all fight that. When we hit a few bad shots we go, "Well, I'm not going to be able to score well today." That's why I'm out here, to try to shoot a good score. I probably won't play for another week, so you can let it get to you, and you just sort of have to think good thoughts and try to put it behind you and have fun. But golf is a humbling game because it does appear to be easy. After all, it's just putting a club in your hand and a little ball and you knock it in a hole several hundred yards down the way. That shouldn't be too difficult, and there doesn't seem to be a lot of athletic ability—certainly brute force isn't required, and the bigger you are doesn't necessarily mean that you're going to be that much better. So everyone says, "I can play golf," until they get out there and find out that there is a lot of small muscles that come into play when you really don't want them, that there is a lot of coordination involved, and it's a wonderful game, though. More and more people are enjoying it. America's going golf crazy. There are more public golf courses being built in America then ever before.

LIGUORI: Who exposed you to golf, your father?

QUAYLE: My mother. My mother was the golfer in the family, and my dad was not.

LIGUORI: Really?

QUAYLE: She is the one who played, but not a lot. Her brother, my uncle, was a very good golfer. He was a scratch handicap at one time. But we all were at one time. But I played my first golf tournament when I was eight years old. I won the Arizona twelve-and-under when I was twelve. I was third in the state high school tournament when I was a freshman in high school in Arizona. I was tenth in Indiana my junior year. And so I started early. As a matter of fact, I was probably a better player on a peer group basis when I was younger than I am now.

LIGUORI: Were you competitive in other sports as well, or did golf consume you?

QUAYLE: In basketball I was a little bit competitive, but I just wasn't very good. I was a fairly good shot, but I was not quick. You have to be very quick in basketball, and I was always the sixth man on my team in Arizona where I grew up. And then when I moved back to Huntington, Indiana—they take basketball very seriously in Indiana compared to Arizona—and I thought coming from Phoenix, Arizona, actually Scottsdale, coming back to Huntington, Indiana, I would be the star of the team. Well, that year Huntington and Indiana came in second in the state, and we had every basketball team in those days participating in the state tournament. I didn't make the team when I transferred back my junior year. It was a great disappointment. So I said so long to basketball. I played football in my freshman year, but golf was the only sport that I really excelled at.

LIGUORI: So it was good training in a sense, playing golf in Arizona. I'm sure there are a lot of fine golfers in Phoenix.

QUAYLE: I grew up in Phoenix in the fifties, late fifties and early sixties. There weren't very many people in Arizona at that time. Arizona was just taking off. At that time, I think we had one or two congressional seats. Now they have five or six, I believe. So it has just grown by leaps and bounds out there. When I was there, it was a very small state.

LIGUORI: Does your wife Marilyn play at all?

QUAYLE: She will tell you that she knows how to play. She plays in scrambles. She does it for business reasons rather than for the love of golf, and I say, "Marilyn, fine, whatever, I think it's great that you're playing golf." She likes to hit drives. She likes to play scrambles because they can take her drive. She hits the ball quite far.

LIGUORI: Does she play from the reds?

QUAYLE: She tees off from the reds, so she's somebody you want on your team, because she drives the ball so far and you can usually take her drives.

LIGUORI: There's no competition amongst the two of you on the golf course?

QUAYLE: No, she doesn't like to play with me because she thinks I'm too serious on the golf course. And I probably am from her perspective. Because from her perspective, it's just a walk in the afternoon, and I have a walk in the afternoon, but I want to shoot a score. I want to put a number up there. I want to make a birdie. I want to think about the next shot. She's really not into it that much.

LIGUORI: So it's not social golf when you go out with Dan Quayle?

QUAYLE: I prefer not to play social golf, although I enjoy it and I do play quite a bit of social golf. Just because I'm an amateur I don't play that much, so you have to play social golf, but I enjoy playing competitive golf. I'll probably play in three or four tournaments this year. We'll have to wait and see how I do.

LIGUORI: The Celebrity Golf Association events?

QUAYLE: The CGA. I'll play in two CGA events. And then I have a couple of good golfing partners that I play in some four-balls and amateur tournaments.

LIGUORI: Do you like the CGA environment? Do you like the fact that you play golf with Michael Jordan and Mario Lemieux and these amazing athletes mixed in with former legends and people like yourself? I mean, it's an interesting environment.

QUAYLE: It's an interesting mix. And every one of us who tees it up wants to win this golf tournament. And every one of us is exceedingly competitive. We've all excelled in something other than golf, although the competition here is very stiff. There's some very good golfers here. As a matter of fact, a couple of them have played, I believe, on the Nike Tour and some have played on the Senior Tour, so this is not what you call a weekend golf tournament. I mean this is serious business. I've participated in amateur events, but they play as professionals. They make money. Some of the golfers here really put it in their family budgets to make a certain amount of money out here on the CGA Tour. Fortunately, I have a daytime job. I don't have to worry about making money here, and I don't take any. But these celebrity golfers—that's what they call us—are very competitive, and it's interesting to watch these golfers compete when they had some other profession that they were very good in, whether it was singing or football or basketball or whatever.

LIGUORI: And you thrive on the competition.

QUAYLE: Every competitive instinct I have will be put into trying to shoot a good score. Now I may push it too hard. I may reach a level of frustration. I may not relax and think positive thoughts like I tell myself that I should do and, therefore, not do as well as I would like to do. You never know until you go and tee it up. But, no, we're all very competitive. I'm competitive, and when I'm out there and when I tee it up, I'm thinking only golf. If my mind drifts off to something else, I know that I'm not going to do very well, and I just make myself focus right back onto the golf course.

LIGUORI: You've been called the "founding father of family values."

QUAYLE: I *have* been called that before.

LIGUORI: And six months after the 1992 elections, the *Atlantic Monthly* headlined, "Dan Quayle Was Right."

QUAYLE: And you said, "Six months after the elections." Now, where in the heck were they when I needed them?

LIGUORI: Timing is everything.

QUAYLE: I know it. After the election, they finally come out and say, "Okay, all this ridicule and controversy and nonsense, time out, he was right." What we were trying to do is to have the discussion of the family and family values at the forefront of our political debate. It is certainly there today. We initiated it several years ago. Bill Clinton in 1992 was very critical of me and my speech on the family and family values. In 1996, he doesn't criticize my speech; he *gives* my speech. So it shows how much we've made in terms of progress toward discussing this issue in nonpolitical terms. Everyone's talking about it.

LIGUORI: Why was it so controversial back then, in '92?

QUAYLE: That's a good question. They weren't ready for a serious values-oriented speech. I chose the topic which was the poverty of values. It had absolutely nothing to do with this particular TV sitcom [*Murphy Brown*]. That was one line in a very comprehensive speech, about a forty-minute speech. The poverty of values, the challenge that we have as mothers, as fathers, as parents, as families in raising our children. And I talked about the importance of personal responsibility, and I also lamented the fact of the increased number of children born out of wedlock and the fatherless homes that we were seeing. When you take a father away from a child, or the child never knows who the father is, that's one half of the family gone. It's not a divorce situation. It's not a situation where you have a premature death. It's a situation where this child will never know who his father is. Not only will he not know who his father is, he won't know his father's sisters, brothers, aunts, uncles, parents, someone that might be able to help that child along the way. When you take one half of the family support system away from any child, they just don't have the same chance as the child who knows who his mother *and* father were.

LIGUORI: Someone came up to me when they found out I was going to sit down with you today, and he said that last year he came up to you with a golf ball that had "Clinton" on it and on the back it read "guaranteed good lie." And you signed it.

QUAYLE: And I signed it. But they come up to me all the time and give me this ball that has Clinton's picture on there, and it says something like a guaranteed good lie, so the good-natured person that I am, I always sign it. I say, "Here, go put that in your trophy case and don't vote for him."

LIGUORI: Some people say you were one of the most misjudged figures in political history. Do you agree with that?

QUAYLE: That's probably fair in the area, let's say. People that get into politics and get into public life, you never know what to expect. You never know what's going to happen. That's part of the excitement of it. And things that come your way, you have to deal with it. And I would say my entrance into national politics was one that happened very rapidly, one that the media was not really prepared for, a conservative junior senator from Indiana at the age of forty-one to be George Bush's running mate. They were ready for someone else. It was a surprise to them. I found out that they don't like surprises, and they came at me very hard and very unfairly, but this is part of the program. This is part of the territory, if you will. This is what goes on. The question is, how do you sustain it? How do you endure it? Do you wither up and just leave, or do you hang in there. Do you stand for your convictions, stand up for principle, stand firm for your ideals, and make a difference? And that's the course that I chose. I didn't complain. I didn't like it—it was painful. I thought it was terribly unfair, but you go on and you don't let your critics get you down and you don't pay attention to the nonsense that's out there. You have a job to do, you do the job, and let the people be the judge.

LIGUORI: And you still say that the golf arena is *tougher* than the political arena?

QUAYLE: Well, let me say that the pressure is different trying to make a three-foot putt on the eighteenth hole compared to giving an important speech to the Chicago Civic Club where you know that it's going to be well reported in the papers the next day.

LIGUORI: If you could play with any world leaders in a foursome, who would you chose?

QUAYLE: In a foursome, world leaders in a foursome . . . Well, I'd like to play with British Prime Minister John Major—he was a cricket player; he'd be fun to play with. German Chancellor Cole, he would be entertaining to play with, and I think Russian President Boris Yeltsin. Boris Yeltsin on a golf course would be interesting. He doesn't play much golf. He does play tennis; he's a tennis player. I don't think he plays any golf; they don't have any golf courses in Russia. I think they're building one of the first ones now. But to see Boris Yeltsin trying to kill that ball would be rather interesting. He'd be a crowd pleaser.

LIGUORI: Of all the courses you've played, which is your favorite?

QUAYLE: It's hard to answer that question because there's a bunch of them. I'll put them in a group. You've got Pine Valley [New Jersey], you have Cypress [California], you have Augusta [Georgia], you have Ballybunion [Ireland], you have Pebble Beach [California]. That pretty well covers the waterfront.

LIGUORI: I heard it was tough to get into Crooked Stick even as vice president of the United States. [Crooked Stick, located in Carmel, Indiana, hosted the PGA Championship in 1991.]

QUAYLE: Well, Crooked Stick is a very good golf club. No swimming, no tennis, no paddle tennis. Only golf. And a very reasonable and appropriate clubhouse. They have 225 members, and I was made an honorary resident member. But that did not entitle me to forego paying of the dues. I was an honorary resident member, but I still have to pay the entire dues.

LIGUORI: No discount for the vice president?

QUAYLE: No discount at all.

LIGUORI: Even with a swing like yours?

QUAYLE: No discount.

LIGUORI: Can you describe the most challenging part of political life and how it compares to perhaps the most challenging shot here on the golf course?

QUAYLE: Well, politics is a couple of things. One, you have to make tough decisions, and then you have to have the courage to stay with that decision. Because the day you make your decision, you know that half the people are going to be offended and are going to reverse their decision. You just have to have the guts and the determination to say, "I made a decision and I'm gonna stick with it." The other thing in politics that you have to put up with—not anything against you—is the media. I mean those folks . . .

LIGUORI: You're complaining about me already?

QUAYLE: It is a good interview. We got to see what the taping's going to be like, though. You have a lot of editing to do. In golf, I think the biggest challenge is to be yourself and to live within yourself. Accept the stakes out on the golf course and move on. And it's tough to do sometimes. It's an emotional game. You've got to be focused. And when you take somebody like me that has a very busy schedule and wraps fifteen different things around a golf game, before and after, it's sometimes difficult to focus just on golf, and when you don't focus on golf, you're not going to play well. I don't care who you are.

LIGUORI: There are similarities in golf and in politics, as far as what it takes to succeed.

QUAYLE: There are a number of things where you can compare it. One, you have to be focused. Two, you've gotta trust yourself. You've got to trust yourself in politics; you've got to trust yourself on the golf course. And three, hey, its competition, open competition. This is a free society. Come out here and play this golf course. Golf and politics, best person wins usually.

LIGUORI: I know you remember the best score you've ever shot.

QUAYLE: Sixty-seven.

LIGUORI: Where was it?

QUAYLE: La Fontaine Country Club in Huntington, Indiana.

LIGUORI: See, everybody remembers their best score. No hesitation.

QUAYLE: No hesitation.

LIGUORI: The course was in your home state.

QUAYLE: Home state, home golf course, Saturday afternoon, no breeze, soft greens, made lots of putts. Should have had 65, but I had 67. It was the best I've ever done, so I was happy.

LIGUORI: You were in "the zone" obviously.

QUAYLE: You get in the zone. I was only a junior in high school.

LIGUORI: Is that right? Have you come close to that score since?

QUAYLE: Yeah. I've had 69 a number of times. I haven't had 68 or 67, but I had 69 a couple of times.

LIGUORI: Do you watch a lot of golf on TV?

QUAYLE: As much as I can. Just for example, the U.S. Open, I got to see about forty-five minutes of it. I travel and I'm doing other things, so I don't get that much time.

LIGUORI: Did you feel for Greg Norman when he blew that six-stroke lead at the 1996 Masters?

QUAYLE: I was watching the Masters. I turned it on at the ninth hole when he hit that pitching wedge—it was either a pitching wedge or a sand wedge. And you know you've got to get it above the hole. And he didn't get it above the hole. I said he could make six from there. I've been there before. He makes a great five, but then he just bogeyed ten, bogeyed eleven, and just missed a really little putt on eleven, hits it in the water on twelve, and is two shots behind. And I'm sitting there thinking, well, I suppose he can come back. And he almost did it on fifteen. If that chip had gone in on fifteen, it could have been a big turnaround, but it didn't. Faldo made his, so they go on to the sixteenth hole. He's still two down. He hits in the water on sixteen. It's Sunday afternoon. I just basically shut it off. I couldn't watch anymore. It was too painful.

LIGUORI: It was so painful. I really felt bad for him.

QUAYLE: Yeah.

LIGUORI: But that's golf, right?

QUAYLE: That's golf.

LIGUORI: Did you play a lot, Dan, when you were in office?

QUAYLE: I didn't get to play very much. The person that does play a lot is Bill Clinton, and I think it's great. The press basically stays off his case. It's great relaxation for him. I think he deserves it. He works hard. I don't agree with anything he does, but he works hard. He deserves to have a little time off. Now, when I went out and played golf, they were all over me. For some reason, Republicans can't play golf. It's okay if Democrats do. So I did not play very much. But Clinton has set a very good standard. He plays at least once a week, and I think that's a minimal standard for all presidents.

LIGUORI: If you were playing President Clinton, who would win?

QUAYLE: Who do *you* think?

LIGUORI: It's not even a contest? Who would win? I've never seen him play.

QUAYLE: You've never seen him play?

LIGUORI: No. What's his handicap?

QUAYLE: Who knows? What's his handicap? I don't know, you'd have to ask him.

LIGUORI: We're talking about golf now.

QUAYLE: We're talking about golf, and I'm going to be respectful of the game and not talk about Clinton's golf game and the way he plays.

LIGUORI: I get the feeling that there's no contest between you and him on the golf course.

QUAYLE: I don't think that would be much of a problem.

LIGUORI: Dan, what was the toughest match you ever played while you were vice president?

QUAYLE: Well, I didn't play many matches. Most of it was, well, a matter of fact, all of it was just social golf, and when you're vice president, you'd be surprised on how many three-foot putts are given to you. So I didn't have very many tough matches at all.

LIGUORI: You miss that now, right? No more "gimme" putts?

QUAYLE: I putt 'em all now.

LIGUORI: What did you think, Dan, when, at the Bob Hope Classic in Rancho Mirage, California, Gerald Ford and George Bush played with Bill Clinton, and Ford hit someone in the gallery.

QUAYLE: Gerry Ford started that precedent. And I think future presidents have lived up to that. But you get out here and you get a big gallery, and if you're an eighteen, nineteen handicap, you're probably gonna hit somebody. Especially if you have big crowds.

LIGUORI: Can you believe the galleries stand so close? Even when the pros play, because anybody could have a really bad day.

QUAYLE: They want that bird's eye view. They want to be in there close; they want to get close to them. They want to feel the swing. Sometimes they do.

LIGUORI: But if I were President Ford, I'd say, "Get back, get back a little. Give me some room."

QUAYLE: He loves people. He warns people. As a matter of fact, they have a warning sign up when President Ford is playing these days that says, "Beware of flying golf balls."

LIGUORI: Get out of here, they do?

QUAYLE: I'm just kidding.

LIGUORI: They should.

QUAYLE: He tells that joke himself, I'm sure.

Ely Callaway

Within moments of initially visiting with Ely Callaway in his office, I was given the gracious Callaway treatment. Country music star Mac Davis and I were in his office less than five minutes before Callaway handed us a brilliantly colored children's book published by his son's company, as well as a documentary on Bobby Jones's life that Callaway put together, which aired on CBS. Ely Callaway, founder and chairman of Callaway Golf, is an entrepreneurial and marketing genius. Everything he touches turns to gold.

Success has paved Ely's path throughout life. He was a top executive in the textile industry and later became the owner of a major winery, Callaway Vineyards, which he subsequently sold to Hiram Walker and Sons. A year after the sale, Callaway turned his attention to golf. He came across a wedge with a steel-cored shaft covered by a wooden veneer. The club was designed to look like an old hickory shaft but performed like a steel one. It was called the Hickory Stick. Ely liked it so much he bought the fledgling company and renamed it after himself. Two years later, Callaway introduced a line of cast, perimeter-weighted irons, called S2H2, featuring the design that lacks a hosel and redistributes the weight to the clubhead, which creates a lower center of gravity. They were so well received that Callaway Golf enjoyed revenues of $4.8 million. A year later, S2H2 metal woods were on the market and sales grew to $10.4 million and doubled the year after.

With the enterprise up and running, Callaway was poised to outdrive his competitors with the invention of the Big Bertha line of metal woods. The line quickly became famous for the huge, hosel-less clubheads (25 percent larger than normal clubheads). Ely named the club after a giant cannon used in World War I called Big Bertha. He started in 1983 with an initial investment of $400,000 and four employees in a 1200 square foot office. Thirteen years later in 1996, with 2000 employees, the company grossed $650 million.

When I interviewed this master of success, I wanted to get inside his head and learn what qualities enabled him to produce so consistently throughout his career. I was intrigued by this because I've learned that successful individuals in the business world usually apply rather simple philosophies—a powerful, efficient work ethic that is comprised of honesty, generosity, timing, great instincts, and the need for constant challenge. Ely fit the bill on all counts. His very presence, with his seventy-seven-year-old wrinkled face, silver hair, and reassuring eyes, seemed omnipotent.

PHOTO COURTESY OF ELY CALLAWAY

Ely has developed the difficult posture of the laid-back workaholic. He does not display the high intensity and stress level one would think a man in his position would have. Ironically, he's not an avid golfer. Instead, he spends a lot of time at the Callaway testing center, evaluating product. He was quite an accomplished player at one time, enough to win his club championship back in 1967 at Wee Burn Country Club in Darien, Connecticut, with a handicap of three.

His destiny to excel in the golf business was almost preordained, although he did not get into the business until the age of sixty-four. The legendary golfer, Bobby Jones, winner of the Grand Slam of golf in 1930, was his mother's first cousin once removed. He got to know Jones and later obtained the marketing rights to Jones's name and image.

Utilizing a lot of drive, smarts, and even genetic ties to one of the greatest champions of all time has enabled Ely Callaway to become the undisputed king of clubs.

LIGUORI: Ely, you're the founder and chairman of Callaway Golf. This is your empire.

CALLAWAY: Well, it's my office.

LIGUORI: It's so fascinating to read about your success story and see how well the clubs have done. Everything you do is successful. Why do you think that is the case?

CALLAWAY: Well, it isn't. It's just that you hear about the successes and you don't hear about the effort, trial and error, and failures. But on balance, we've been pretty lucky.

LIGUORI: Well, come on. It's more than luck!

CALLAWAY: Well, it's more than luck, but it's also absence of bad luck. Just as much as it is good luck and hard work and being able to relate to people.

LIGUORI: Timing as well, I'm sure.

CALLAWAY: Timing is tremendously important, sure.

LIGUORI: Instincts are very important as well.

CALLAWAY: A lot of instinct. A lot of everything that goes on at the very top level in business, in my opinion, is instinctive. Gut feeling.

LIGUORI: So trusting your own instincts, obviously, is a key to your success. Talk a little about how you made that transition from wine to golf.

CALLAWAY: Well, I had sold the winery because when I created the vineyard and the winery, my preference was to sell it, not to keep it for my family. And so I did sell it, after thirteen years. And I had some money and some time, and at that point, let's see, I was about—when I sold the winery, how old was I? I can't remember.

LIGUORI: You're seventy-seven now.

CALLAWAY: So I was sixty-three when I sold the winery. And so I had a little money and I had some time, and I like to stay busy, so I just—you say how do you make the change? You just do it. I found a little tiny company that seemed to have a real interesting potential in a small niche of the market of golf clubs and bought the company. That's how you do it. You make decisions, and you act and do it.

LIGUORI: But you had to feel good about this, obviously. What made you buy the company? What about it?

CALLAWAY: Well, the product was unique, and the product was good in my opinion. It filled a little niche in the golf club market that nobody else ever had, and that was a highly specialized club with a very unusual shaft—hickory with a steel shaft running right down the center of the wood. It was beautiful. It worked beautifully. It felt good. And the company had been in business four months only, so it wasn't a big investment to make.

LIGUORI: So then you just dove right in.

CALLAWAY: Yes, the next thing I know, I'm in the golf club business.

LIGUORI: A lot of people say it's not only good instincts and hard work but obviously you also have to have a knack for picking the right team of people to work for you. As the president of my own production company, I can attest to the challenge of selecting the right players to make up a winning team. How do you select *your* team?

CALLAWAY: A lot of that is instinctive. It has to be because you don't know the people. Really, you never know them until you hire them. It's like getting married. You don't know your partner until you marry them and live with them a while. So a lot of the judgment in selecting the people is instinctive. I had had a lot of experience at picking people who turned out to be effective in their jobs. Selecting them, motivating them, and then rewarding them. I've had quite a bit of experience. At Burlington Industries, when I left there, we had 86,000 employees. It was the biggest textile company in the world by double. And so I had been there seventeen years, so you learn a little bit as you go along.

LIGUORI: Did you play golf back then?

CALLAWAY: Yes.

LIGUORI: You probably played more golf back then than you do now.

CALLAWAY: I did, yes.

LIGUORI: And that was in Darien, Connecticut?

CALLAWAY: We played at Wee Burn Country Club in Darien and Pine Valley in New Jersey.

LIGUORI: When did you start playing golf?

CALLAWAY: When I was ten or eleven.

LIGUORI: How did you get exposed to the sport?

CALLAWAY: My father, who played, who was an average hacker, but he encouraged me to play because he felt—and he was correct—that it was one of the few things a kid can do, if he's good enough, to compete effectively with adults. It's one of the few things a young person can do, and he recognized that, encouraged me to do it, and by good luck, I did spend a little time at it. I began to get some self-confidence and self-esteem when I used to compete against adults and win.

LIGUORI: As a ten-year-old?

CALLAWAY: No, I didn't start winning until I was sixteen.

LIGUORI: Okay. But you were in that environment at a very early age. Playing, competing with adults, socializing with adults.

CALLAWAY: Yes, more than I would if I hadn't taken up golf. I also played with a lot of kids.

LIGUORI: Were you athletic in other areas?

CALLAWAY: Not particularly. I was pretty good at tennis and swimming.

LIGUORI: And what about the sport made you feel so passionate about it?

CALLAWAY: Well, like everybody, I was intrigued by the fact that it's an impossible game. You cannot master it. Even at a young age, I thought that it was a very unusual challenge. Also a lot of fun, because it's rewarding to hit a golf ball reasonably well. And the fact that I could, as a child almost, compete against adults. It made my father very proud, and I was delighted.

LIGUORI: And now you play once a month, if that?

CALLAWAY: Generally now I just help to test the new products we create.

And in doing so, since we're involved mainly with drivers, fairway woods, and irons, I don't have to worry about too much getting the ball in the cup.

LIGUORI: When you look at what you did with the company since its inception in 1983, it's quite remarkable. You made a $400,000 initial investment.

CALLAWAY: And the smallest golf club company in the world, that employed four people in 1200 square feet, that had been in business four months. And in thirteen years, by 1996, Wall Street is predicting that we'll do about $650 million, and we have 2,000 employees. We are by, let's say triple, the biggest golf club company in the world.

LIGUORI: And still growing?

CALLAWAY: And still growing, yes.

LIGUORI: In a marketplace that seems to be slumping.

CALLAWAY: Well, it's been flat since 1990. The golf club market, worldwide, has been flat on sales since the middle of 1990.

LIGUORI: Why do you think that is?

CALLAWAY: Well, because for the ten years prior to that, the golf club business was growing at a very rapid rate. So it slowed down. It's not bad, but it's been essentially flat during the time in which we grew the most.

LIGUORI: So how has Callaway been able to increase sales in a flat marketplace?

CALLAWAY: We've increased sales, and we've also been very profitable. That combination is unique for a new, fast-growing company. And we've done it because the core philosophy of the company is to be sure that we work hard enough to create a product that is demonstrably superior to our competition and pleasingly different from. Sounds simple, but it's very, very difficult to do. But that's one of the main reasons why we have grown as we have.

LIGUORI: And you were saying earlier, before you even went into the business, you checked out all your competition.

CALLAWAY: Yes. We analyzed the strengths and the weaknesses of the major players in the golf club business before we went into it.

LIGUORI: At that point, what did you discover?

CALLAWAY: Well, we thought there was a lot of room for improvement in the way golf companies created their products and in the way they serviced their customers.

LIGUORI: So why did you concentrate mostly on the driver, initially?

CALLAWAY: Because it was the most unpopular club in the bag, and we figured if we could change that, and change people's attitude from fear to affection about the driver, we would have something very, very unique. And that's why we concentrated on it.

LIGUORI: Ping, at one time, was known as *the* irons. Callaway, *the* drivers, the woods. Is that still how you wish to be perceived in the business?

CALLAWAY: It's not true any longer because we are the largest manufacturer of irons, as well as metal woods, in the industry.

LIGUORI: So the irons have caught up.

CALLAWAY: Absolutely. This year [1996], we will sell more dollars worth of irons than anybody else in the industry and anywhere in the world, as well as the metal woods.

LIGUORI: And even people who can't afford a $500 Great Big Bertha titanium driver will buy it if they think it's going to help their game.

CALLAWAY: And they think that because they hear it generally from their friends and neighbors. So you're right. An awful lot of people who buy the Big Bertha irons and woods you would think can't afford them. But they do buy them. They buy them enough for us to this year sell more than $600 million worth at wholesale. So in my opinion, that applies to any product, any consumer product in the world, and that is if you make it truly superior to your competition and pleasingly different from and more rewarding to the user in some significant way, you will sell them.

LIGUORI: To what point, Ely, does the product, though, infringe on the purity of the game, with all the new technology?

CALLAWAY: It hasn't done anything even remotely like that. You mean making the game too easy?

LIGUORI: Well, with all the new technology, golfers are able to drive the ball so much farther, making the courses shorter.

CALLAWAY: It's not that much different. Two-thirds of the problem is putting. You still have to get the ball in the cup, no matter how close you drive that ball to the green; you've still got to get it into the cup. You've got to pitch it close and then sink it. So equipment has done very, very little to improve the average golfer's scores, and they usually come up short with their short game.

LIGUORI: One still must get the ball in the cup.

CALLAWAY: So the new technology has done only one thing in my opinion. It has made the game more enjoyable for more people. It has not made the game such that it's a whole lot easier in scoring. If you look at the scores, you see even among the professionals the improvement over the last twenty years has been minuscule.

Anyway, most professionals are better and stronger—in better condition—than they were fifteen years ago.

LIGUORI: So when are you going to develop a putter that guarantees the ball goes in the cup every time?

CALLAWAY: Never. Never. In heaven only. And we'll call that the Heaven Putt.

LIGUORI: You have the Heaven Wood?

CALLAWAY: And a Divine Nine.

LIGUORI: How do you come up with the name of your clubs?

CALLAWAY: You think. You think about it and you try to come up with an identification that will be pleasant and will have some significance one way or the other. Everybody in the company thinks about names for our clubs—all the top executives anyway. And every now and then we come up with a winner. Again, again, this is a big part of intuition.

LIGUORI: How did you come up with Bertha?

CALLAWAY: Big Bertha came into being because I was old enough—it's one of the few instances where age has been a real benefit. I was old enough to remember reference books in high school showing this giant canon on a railroad car. It was so big. It had to move on a railroad car, and it was a German canon in World War I, and it was named Big Bertha after the daughter of the owner of the foundry. It was named Big Bertha.

LIGUORI: So *you* named it first.

CALLAWAY: Well, yes, I was the only one around that ever remembered anything about it. People name golf clubs very often after weapons.

LIGUORI: We were talking earlier about Tiger Woods, and I saw you doing an interview in which somebody asked you if you think he should have turned pro or stay in school. And I was very impressed with your answer, but he didn't listen to you.

CALLAWAY: He didn't listen. Right.

LIGUORI: You said he should have finished his education.

CALLAWAY: That's my personal opinion. I think he would be—in the long run over his whole life—he would be a broader man, a happier person, a more constructive one if he had allowed himself to finish that great university Stanford, instead of turning pro so quickly. But that's a personal opinion. He's going to do fine anyway. He's going to make all the money on earth that he can possibly count, but I just think he would be a more fulfilled man if he had gotten that education.

LIGUORI: I understand that Tiger Woods has not tried Callaway clubs.

CALLAWAY: As far as we know, he has never given any of the Callaway clubs, irons or woods, any serious attention.

LIGUORI: Why do you think that's the case?

CALLAWAY: I really don't know.

LIGUORI: You tried to go after him?

CALLAWAY: Yes, after he announced that he was turning pro.

LIGUORI: I'm sure everybody did.

CALLAWAY: Everybody did. We apparently made the mistake of not getting to know him and getting close to him sooner than we did. We waited until he turned professional, and some other people apparently got to him a little bit sooner.

LIGUORI: Does it upset you that he's not one of your guys?

CALLAWAY: No, no. We're disappointed. But we do believe that our big Bertha woods and irons would help his game. By the way, for instance, the Great Big Bertha driver, or one version of the Big Bertha driver, is used this year by an average of about 60 percent of all the professionals playing on five tours in Europe and the United States, and 80 percent of them are not paid endorsement fees by Callaway. They just use the club because they think it's going to help them win.

LIGUORI: Is there any one issue, Ely, in the game that irks you? Anything about where golf has come that doesn't sit right with you?

CALLAWAY: No, I think that golf is a game that is very popular and becoming more popular. It's a very rewarding game for millions of people. And the USGA regulations on equipment don't bother us. If I had my preference, I would say the only thing that could be improved is the fourteen club rule. I don't think that it does anything constructive to limit the number of clubs that a person should play with, whether it be a professional or not. If everybody has an opportunity to have any clubs they want, I think that would be best, because it would add to the enjoyment of the game. It wouldn't reduce scores much, but it would simply be more fun. That's my only major complaint about the regulations governing the industry.

LIGUORI: What is out there that you yet have to do? Anything? Is there anything out there that you have dreams about as far as—you're seventy-seven, you've had this amazing career in so many different businesses, which keeps you working everyday. What out there do you still want or need?

CALLAWAY: Well, the best thing that could happen to me personally is to continue to be healthy and interested enough to be active.

That's all I need. I'll really be highly rewarded if those two things happen.

LIGUORI: I've got to get you out on the golf course. You've got to play a little bit more.

CALLAWAY: Well, I'm playing at work. I'm not working at play.

LIGUORI: You were related to Bobby Jones. Your mother's first cousin.

CALLAWAY: Yes, he's my mother's first cousin once removed. So that influenced me as a kid to be a little more interested in the game than I otherwise would have been, because Bobby Jones, when I was eleven years old, was the most famous man in the world I think. Certainly one of the two or three most highly respected and famous, and if you've got a cousin who occupies that position, you're interested in what he's doing. Can I do it? So it was easy for my father and mother to say, "Why don't you try golf?"

LIGUORI: But back then, you never dreamed you'd be in the golf club business.

CALLAWAY: Oh no.

LIGUORI: Isn't it ironic how things come full circle?

CALLAWAY: But the one thing I think people can learn from, based on my experience, that is when I bought the Hickory Stick company, the little golf club company that had four people, been in business four months, had 1200 square feet, I had no conception at all that we would end up being a large golf club manufacturer. There was no great vision or plan to achieve that goal, and I think that we did it one step at a time, always trying to make the best product we could and not trying to have a goal that was so far out and so ambitious that you get discouraged. So my philosophy in business is there is a danger in too much planning too far ahead. Make a product that is better than your competition, do it as well as you can, hire the best people in the world to help you do [it], and be patient. And also take one step at a time.

LIGUORI: What's the best round of golf you ever shot?

CALLAWAY: I can't remember, but the best handicap I ever had was three, in 1967, and I won the club championship at the Wee Burn Country Club in Darien, Connecticut.

LIGUORI: Did you ever shoot a hole in one?

CALLAWAY: Yes! I've had two, only.

LIGUORI: And the best part of your game, would you say?

CALLAWAY: The best part of my game when I was playing well was driving the ball straight and putting.

LIGUORI: What clubs did you use?